BLADES
BUSINESS
CREW 2

BLADES BUSINESS CREW 2

More tales from one of Britain's most notorious football gangs

STEVE COWENS

JOHN BLAKE

Published by John Blake Publishing Ltd,
3 Bramber Court, 2 Bramber Road,
London W14 9PB, England

www.johnblakepublishing.co.uk

First published in paperback in 2009

ISBN: 978-1-84454-799-9

British Library Cataloguing-in-Publication Data:

A catalogue record for this book is available from the British Library.

Design by www.envydesign.co.uk

Printed in Great Britain by CPI Bookmarque, Croydon, CR0 4TD

3 5 7 9 10 8 6 4 2

Papers used by John Blake Publishing are natural, recyclable products
made from wood grown in sustainable forests. The manufacturing processes
conform to the environmental regulations of the country of origin.

Every attempt has been made to contact the relevant copyright-holders,
but some were unobtainable. We would be grateful if the appropriate
people could contact us.

To the lads no longer with us, gone but not forgotten:
Shaun Hessian, Lester, Bunny, Slater, Steve Chapman,
Maz, Nicky, Dave Webb, Roy Zide, Drip, Pye-Eye,
Big Herman, Chris Shaw and Scott. United for ever.
RIP

This book is dedicated to my son, Jack.
You are my hero, my best mate and I love you, brother.

ACKNOWLEDGEMENTS

Thanks to all the boys for their contributions to this book, especially Bob, Ron and Penners.

Thanks to Gary for his advice and time.

Thanks also to all my TRUE mates over the years, too many to mention. You know who you are.

And to all the football lads I've met through the years – regards and respect.

CONTENTS

1
KICK-OFF

When I wrote *Blades Business Crew*, I didn't really know what I was letting myself in for. I expected and accept that lads from Leeds, Chelsea and Wednesday etc. are going to have a dig at you. According to some of them, you're a bullshit merchant. 'This didn't happen...' 'That's a load of shit...' etc. I didn't, however, expect a minority of individuals from my own firm to be jealous of the fact that I've written a very successful book. The way I see it is that I was one of many United lads who grew up together at football when violence was in its prime; any one of them could have penned their memoirs but it was me who wrote a book in 2001 and left the scene.

During the long period of time I was involved with the BBC (Blades Business Crew), my only real aim was to try to be first into battle and be *game as fuck*. No one can say otherwise. In my view, I have done as much for Sheffield United's firm as anyone. Bigheaded? No, just truthful. I've never made out I am or was *the* top boy among United's firm. We had and still have loads of top boys, lads who have stood side by side in battle. In all my time with the Blades, only one person could ever be considered as 'top boy' and he's no longer with us.

Everyone who knows me knows what I'm all about. I've always carried with me a code of conduct that even my blue-and-white Sheffield Wednesday enemies from across our great city can't deny.

The changing face of football hooliganism over the past four decades has been a rollercoaster ride of highs and lows. The lows include: the deaths at Heysel in 1985 and any death surrounding the scene; the growing use of weapons within the hooligan gangs; the times when beating the shit out of one lad from the opposition was commonplace; the police stitch-ups from so-called 'undercover operations' that went tits up in the Eighties when the courts threw out the evidence. Tied in with this is the frequently weak evidence that nearly all football lads have had to face in court following arrest. The view of judges, the police and courts that if you fight at football you're worse than rapists, drink-drivers who kill and paedophiles, is backed up by the sentences that have been handed down.

The highs include: the camaraderie and togetherness that football lads create which forge friendships so strong that lads risk their lives for each other; the unwritten codes of conduct that many lads from firms took on board; the continual battle to outwit the police in pursuit of rival mobs; the toe-to-toe battles when both sides refuse to back off and the high of seeing a rival firm in retreat; and the casual terrace fashion that the football lads have created that has spanned into three decades.

Football hooligan trends consistently changed and the police shifted tactics accordingly. In the Seventies, hundreds of angry young male football fans ran amok in big numbers, invading opponents' Kops in the ground. Everyone in opposition to your team was considered fair game for a kicking and the scarf collectors were bang at it.

The Eighties came along and so did a new breed of hooligans who gave themselves a name of identity in the 'casuals' or 'trendies' as we called ourselves then; that youth included myself. That era also saw the Stanley knife appear in a lot of pockets, a weapon that makes me cringe at the thought of its use. As the Eighties' thugs matured during the height of the fighting –1985–95 – a code of conduct thankfully emerged among most of the firms.

The late Eighties saw the happy, trippy days of 'E' culture and the rave days 'love-in' had the hooligan thinking differently and forging friendships that lads wouldn't have dreamed of a few years earlier. Lads then started to plan lives away from football and a lot of them moved into business – some legal, some illegal. This era saw the emergence of wide boys with an eye for making money.

Amidst of all this, the police, in attempting to stop hooliganism, tried and failed with a new tactic – undercover infiltration of the mobs. Trials against high-profile firms like the Chelsea Head-Hunters and West Ham's ICF collapsed because of weak evidence. The court cases cost the taxpayer hundreds of thousands and the arrested lads were able to sue the police force for tens of thousands; again, the taxpayer stumped up.

The late Nineties saw a lull in violence as the police got

to grips with the scene and the seasoned thugs were now in their mid-thirties and recognised on sight by the police. Youngsters coming through the ranks were arrested at will by the officers who wanted to send a message to this new breed. However, the millennium brought an upsurge in football-related violence. The youth started coming through again and a lot of seasoned, retired boys came back for a last bit of excitement before sticking on the carpet slippers and leaving the scene for good.

It was the Seventies that really kicked the hooligan scene off. Yes, at that time it was mindless violence at its worst and the later that decade wore on the more rival football firms started to carry weapons. This was the era I thankfully missed out on – the Doc Martin, Fred Perry, Harrington jacket era that really started organised football violence. It's an era that I couldn't really write about in my first book simply because I wasn't around to tell the tale; I was too busy being a rascal hedge-hopping, apple scrumping, trout poaching and doing things that the teenagers of today would think boring and not outrageous enough to contemplate.

I've heard many stories from the lads of that era. These blokes are proper characters and if the brains of most of them weren't so scrambled for one reason or another then they could have written a book themselves on their exploits.

This book is entirely different from *Blades Business Crew* as it takes a look at times at the lighter side of life and is intended to help people understand that just because you have fought at football doesn't mean you are a complete lunatic. Lunatic, yes... But complete? No!

4

KICK-OFF

Football violence is not big and it's not clever and it's a game that is not worth getting into nowadays but you can bet your fire-cracking arse I loved every minute of it and, if I could live it all again, I would with bells on.

2
ME, MYSELF AND I

Those of you who have read *Blades Business Crew* will probably think I've spent most of my life at the sharp end of football violence. People who don't know me have asked others what I'm like as a person. Well, although I was heavily involved in football violence and, in truth, it did take up a large portion of my younger days, the following should throw a bit of light on my past away from the hooligan front and also take a look at some of the characters I've met and some of the things we got up to.

Blades Business Crew was written by a football hooligan for football hooligans. I make no bones about it – it was written for that market, but I have often been asked by readers why I didn't write more about myself away from that scene so people could get an insight into the person who had spent a good chunk of his life in combat.

Football hooligans – or 'boys' as I prefer to call them – come in all shapes, sizes, colours and backgrounds. You cannot categorise or stereotype one lad in relation to another; all are different. Some can't actually fight but they have loads of bottle, which, to a hooligan, is the essential part of their make-up.

I'm going to lay my soul bare here. In truth, I'm like one of those sweet sensations, tough on the outside but soft in the centre. I value my family and friendships, and I'll protect those people with my life if need be. I can be emotional at times and care dearly for the people around me. Almost everyone who meets me for the first time can't believe that I have been involved in so many fights. They see me as a big, cuddly teddy bear – Bungle, that's me.

Recently, I attended the funeral of a retired United lad's ten-year-old son. I'd never had the chance to meet the young lad before but, when I saw the effect his death had on the family, suddenly the faces of my own son and daughter flashed into my head and I lost it, and I don't give a fuck if people think that's soft. I have a soft underbelly and I like myself better for having it. I'm no hard-faced cunt who doesn't give a fuck. I give a fuck about most things and I feel a better man for being that way.

So here goes.

Anyone wanting just to read about football violence should skip a few chapters although, as you'll see, violence has never been far away in my life.

I suppose when someone like me gets involved in the things I have at football then there's always an expert in a certain field furiously trying to put his finger on a point in the person's life that has made him choose that path to travel or has made him do the things he has. Well, I'd be lying if I said growing up in our household was all sweetness and light. I'd also be lying if I said I was dragged up. My mum and dad no doubt loved me, but they spent too much time falling out over one thing or another, usually money.

My mum suffered from severe depression and thus had problems with her nerves. She spent quite a bit of time in hospital and the ward she was in was no place for a youngster like me to visit. I went a couple of times and felt that all it needed was Jack Nicholson running around the room with a carving knife; it was a frightening place for a small boy.

Dad's vice was gambling. He could never get his nut around what his addiction was doing to our family and we actually lost our house on a couple of occasions, only to be bailed out by the rest of our relatives. The one thing it's taught me in life is that gambling is a mug's game; you never see a skint bookmaker.

Like all gamblers, my dad thought he won more than he lost, which is complete bollocks. Over the years, he has slowly learnt how to control his gambling and seems to have it under control. Gambling is definitely an addiction and I always find the people stood looking up at the TV screens in the bookies a bit sad. They're living a dream that's never to be realised. (By the way, I love you, Mum and Dad.)

My dad loved a beer as well but not to the extent to which he was a rolling drunk. The worst memory of my youth was when my mum overdosed and was taken to hospital. I thought she was going to die and that day will live with me forever.

Things seemed to change a little for the better when my sister Vikki was born, all cheeky smiles and blond pigtails.

I spent a lot of time away from home at my nan's and auntie's. My four cousins were like brothers to me.

I upset a few of my family by using incorrect terminology in my first book – 'black sheep of the family' was wrong. What I meant to get across was that I was different to my cousins, that's all. In truth, I am grateful for their love and care during a difficult time for me.

It was not all doom and gloom in our household as I also have a lot of happy memories like going fishing with my dad, and my mum fighting off fellow jumble-sale enthusiasts who dared to try and get in front of her bargain hunt. I wasn't the best dressed kid around; me and Mum still laugh at a note I left her when I was around 12 years old. It reads that I was fed up that my little sister got everything and the fact that I could fit all my clothes in the bread bin. That's probably why I've spent so much money on clothes over the years; I wouldn't like to put a figure on what I've spent on designer clobber, but, as exaggerated as it may sound, it's well over a hundred grand, probably a lot higher than that in reality.

I'm lucky in the fact that both of my parents are alive today and neither live far from me so I see them regularly and I'll always love them both. The thing with my mum and dad is they can't live together, nor can they live apart, so what do they do? They live next door to each other! Maybe now people might start to understand why I'm daft.

WORK AND PLAY

On leaving school, I applied and got a placement at college to study art. My plan was to do courses which would set me up in the sign-writing business. I aimed eventually to own my own business, something I've always wanted to do. While I'd been trying to get on at art college, I'd been writing around for jobs unrelated to my course, and got a couple of interviews.

I talked to my family about it and was given advice which, looking back, wasn't what I wanted long-term. I wanted a career but was advised to go to the interviews and get a job if I could. It's a decision I've regretted ever since. My first interview was at Arnold Laver, a local timber merchant, and, when I met David Laver, he was immediately impressed by my United pin badge. The Laver family has been involved in United to various degrees since the Forties. The interview went well and I was offered a job for a piss-poor £26 a week.

It took me around three weeks to suss out that most of the sales team were topping up their wage illegally. To be fair, I couldn't blame them because if you pay people a pittance then it doesn't take Einstein to work out that if the chance arises they'll make some bucks another way. I was taken under the wing of a bloke called Dick; he was Fagin and I was the Artful Dodger. So I'd end up serving most of the 'straight' customers as he was always busy with the 'fiddle' men.

If Dick was serving a bent customer and another came in, then I'd serve the iffy bloke and leave Dick to book him out. This suited me; I wasn't actually fiddling myself but got paid by Dick for helping him out. The money was good for a 16-year-old and I soon amassed a decent amount of cash. Everyone at Laver's was up to the same thing, and the only problem I had was with the supervisor who, despite the fact he was bang at it himself, didn't take kindly to me earning a bit of top-up. After all, I'd only been on the firm's books a couple of months.

After asking Dick for his advice, he told me to ignore him as he was like that with all the new starters. True to form, I ignored Dick's advice and told Pete (the supervisor) to fuck off or I'd plant one on him, the fuckin' hypocrite.

The extra money gave me the chance to follow United all over the country. At that time, I was in the middle of a brief 12-month period during which I was a long-fringed New Romantic, spending weekends dancing in clubs like the Crazy Daizy and the Limit to tunes like Visage's *Fade to Grey*, Spandau Ballet's *To Cut a Long Story Short*, Kraftwerk's timeless classic *The Model* and an up-and-coming Sheffield band called the Human League, whose early pre-commercialised stuff like *Being Boiled* and *A Crow and a Baby* were a far cry from the later material they produced when the two girls (who were actually in the same year as me at Frecheville school) joined the band.

As a New Romantic, you had to dance like someone was trying to interfere with your ring-piece, wriggling your hips and flicking a stupidly overgrown fringe from your face. Punk rock was on its last legs and a new evolution in music was starting. The old mod/ska/two-tone/skinheads still had The Jam, Clash, Madness and The Specials going strong and differed entirely from this new electric sound that the piss-poorly named New Romantic scene offered. I stopped well fuckin' short of putting make-up on like some, but the scene (as effeminate as it was) still holds great memories and the music is still played on vinyl in the Cowens' household when the mood takes me.

As the extra money kept rolling in, it enabled me to go

headlong into the casual movement. I swapped Bowie trousers for Farah slacks, side-buttoning shirts for Slazenger or Pringle jumpers and strange shoes for Adidas, Barrington or Samba. I'd go shopping almost every week – Manchester, London, Leeds and Leicester were my favourite places. A young lad with money to burn, it was heaven.

At 17, I started taking driving lessons. Then one day I came home from work and got a clip around the ear from my dad.

'What's this?' he shouted, waving a wedge of around £400 around – he had found my hidden stash. 'No son of mine is going to gain money illegally,' he said.

What galled me was the fact that a couple of days later when I got home from work my grandad's car was parked on the front. I went in thinking he was visiting.

'Where's my grandad?' I asked.

'He's not here,' Papa Bear replied.

'Well, his car is.'

'Yes, I've bought you his car.'

'Dad, I haven't passed my test yet.'

'Well, when you do, you've got one now.'

He could just have easily have said, 'I've bought myself a car with your fiddle money.' The stealer was stolen from. He'd paid my grandad around £300 of my illegally gained income.

At Laver's, things continued in the same vein. I'd got into the violence at matches and the more I earned the more I spent on my addiction in life, shopping and fashion. At the age of 17 I met my future wife Debbie; you couldn't exactly say it was love at first sight. She worked across the road from me and we often found ourselves waiting for the same bus. One particular day, she broke the ice and asked me how long the bus was going to be.

'Twenty-seven foot,' I replied. To be honest, I didn't want to talk to her as she had Wednesday woollen gloves on. So, first impression (mine) – she's a Pig; hers – he's an ignorant twat.

We bumped into each other in the Bar Rio in town a couple of weeks later. Once I'd established the fact that the Wednesday gloves were her brother's, pleasantries were exchanged. She asked my mate Pez to ask me if I'd take her out. Pez, you're a twat – 26 years later and I'm still lumbered! Only kiddin', dear.

Debbie first realised I was a bit of a lad when a couple of months into our courting we were on the bus on the way home from town. Debbie was sat with me and her best mate Donna. Two lads kept looking back and digging me out.

I thought, who the fuck are these two nuggets? Debbie was panicking and told me they were going to jump me as I got off the bus because one of them wanted to go out with her. As my stop approached, I kissed Debbie goodbye and walked past Plum and Plummer giving them the dead eye I'd perfected. As I went down the stairs of the bus, I heard Debbie and her pal shouting at the two lads and the patter of feet following me as the bus pulled up.

I was right off the bus and into the waste bin. Tin can in hand, I crashed it straight into Plum One's face as he jumped off the platform, sending him crashing to the ground. Plum Two papped his pants and he and his mate slumped off into the night. Debbie soon got to know that I was into a bit of the bollocks. I also punched a big bearded geezer in the Rio when he grabbed her arse. I thought I'd fucked it when we got outside as the cunt was massive, but he thankfully apologised and saved me from smashing my face into his fists for a minute or two. The love Debbie and I felt for each other grew stronger and stronger.

I still needed a release, though, and that was football violence, the company of my mates and fashion. At Laver's, I'd got my feet well under the table and was earning a nice steady number; basically I was lumped up to fuck.

Then, one day, I got a bombshell. 'Steven, we've noticed that you've put a lot of effort in here and want to transfer you to Queen's Road,' a manager told me. 'You will be understudy to Harry Marsh who's slowing down to retirement. Your wage will double and we want you to start Monday.'

Fuck! The gravy train had ended. I'd also heard that this Harry Marsh was a grumpy old geezer. I couldn't exactly say, 'No thanks, I'm earning plenty here,' could I? So off I went to pastures new.

In the first six months I'd had six fights, probably more out of frustration at not earning a few shillings extra but, in reality, trouble drew itself to me. The first fight was with an older Wednesday fan I worked with who thought it would be funny to yank the United badge off my coat and throw it in the skip.

Bang, he's on his arse and two people had to pull me off the snorter. The Pig shat it: even though he was a lot older than me he knew he'd met his match.

The second fight was with a customer. I can't really remember what started it but I had a rumble in a woodpile.

The third was with a big skinhead. I was walking past

Cromford Street near the yard which was a rough street if ever there was one. I had a deerstalker hat on and an Adidas cagoule. The big skinhead had been staring at me every time I passed him and I admit I always dropped my gaze to the floor. Skins and trendies had been bang at it in town at the weekends so there was no love lost. Bear in mind I'm 18 or 19 and this bonehead's a big lad in his mid-twenties.

Enough was enough though, so this time as I walked towards him, I lifted my head and, instead of looking at the floor, I stared straight back. He tried to take the piss but I nutted him before he could get his words out. My deerstalker went flying and so did he; surprisingly, he bottled it and the next time I saw him he said, 'All right, mate.'

I got a big buzz out of that one because I'd been very wary of him – in truth, scared – but as I looked down at him sat on the seat of his arse I thought, if I can put that lump on his arse I can look after myself. One of the managers from the office had seen it all happen as he passed in his car and told all the staff about me planting a big bonehead on his arse. I was getting a bad/good name for myself.

I was put back in my place in my next scuffle. A group of lads were sat outside the sandwich shop as I walked up to greet Debbie in our lunch break. They were giving her and her mate some grief – 'tits out' and all that. I challenged them and a big lad gave me a tab warmer for my troubles. Not so invincible after all.

The fifth one in such a short period of time was because of a 'head-the-ball' bully called Bill. He was the foreman of the rough-sawn timbers at the top of the yard. Bill was an ex-paratrooper, one big strong fella but an obnoxious bullying cunt. I'd been serving a customer in a timber aisle when up walked Bill. He told me to tidy up a pile of wood that was all over the floor, thinking I'd left it that way.

'Bill I haven't been near it... These are 16-foot long and the ones on the floor are 18-footers,' I tried to reason. The customer backed me up but Bill told him to fuck off and grabbed me by the throat. I couldn't breathe as he lifted me up by the neck, my back pressed against a load of six-by-two inch timbers. He let go as the customer pleaded with him to back off, as I was turning blue. Bill let me go, and I gasped for air. After a few seconds, I got my senses together.

'Sorry, Bill, I'll shift it,' I said, walking towards him. As soon as I was in striking distance, I belted him with a right-hander. He fell back and, as he came up again, I planted my forehead into his nose. The customer was gobsmacked. He'd only gone to fetch a bit of timber but had copped for two rounds of entertainment. Bill held his nose as blood ran into his mouth; he picked up a three-by-two inch batten and came at me. I did one. When I got back down the yard, Harry (we called him 'H') could see I was a tad flustered. I told H what had happened and the customer backed up my story with, 'That idiot up there wants locking up.' Two minutes later, Bill's down the yard like a big grizzly bear that's had his salmon dinner snatched from him. He wants to rip me limb from limb. I was bouncing around tormenting him.

'Come on, old man, I'll fucking smash you in, you're past it, you Fuck Pig.'

H intervened and gave Bill a right old going over. 'You touch him and you'll have me to deal with,' he shouted.

This was the day I cemented a great friendship with happy Harry. He was staunch United and also ex-army. I ended up liking the man a lot, he was a right miserable so-and-so but we became close and I had developed a full respect for this man. He'd tell me of his army days and the sights he saw fighting for our country. He also worked at Bramall Lane and he told me all the latest news, which was handy because I could tell my mates who United were signing a few days before it happened. So H and I settled down as the timber sales master and his young disciple.

H was straight-ish and, although I made a few bits and bobs on the side, it was nowhere near in the league of the old place.

After a couple of years, his health deteriorated and he was forced to call it a day. A young lad called Neil was set on and he, too, was a Blade and became a good friend. With H gone I made a few more quid than when he was there. We'd got a nice steady number when news came through that the other yard was closing down and all the sales staff would be heading our way. That meant bent Dick and corrupt Foreman Pete would be winging their way down.

Another lad called Kav would also join the ranks and so started a great friendship. Kav was barking mad at times. His sense of humour was a little OTT but he was a great laugh to work with. I don't see much of Kav nowadays but he will always be remembered by me as one of the best mates a man can have. We soon forged a little sales posse and some of the laughs we had were nobody's business.

David Laver (the managing director) was a nice enough bloke; I got on really well with him but he was a little wary because he'd seen me bang at it at the back of the south stand with Bradford's Ointment mob. He started calling me 'Gunner Cowens', not because I'd suddenly turned to Arsenal but because he reckoned I was always 'Gunner do this' and 'Gunner do that'.

He had a good sense of humour but sometimes I pushed him too far. Once he came into the sales area and I'd told everyone that when he walks up the yard to get in a line behind and follow him; I'd seen it done on *Candid Camera*. He set off and I tucked in behind him followed by a snake of eight people. He realised we were behind him and spun around sharply. We just jumped to the nearest timber rack and started tidying up. He shook his head and continued his walk; straight away we were back in line. He realised we were behind him again and, without turning around, he bellowed, 'Fuck off!'

I had to laugh at Kav who shouted back, 'But how shall we fuck off, Oh Master?'

Another time I pushed that bit too far was when the management were having a meeting in the upstairs office. I'd found a huge dead crow that was in pretty good nick, so I stuck a long dowel that I'd pointed off with a Stanley knife up its arse and straight into its neck area to add stability to it.

As the meeting was under way, I held the stick up with the bird on the end and walked the crow along the window sill outside the office where the meeting was being held. The window was ajar and I heard someone shout, 'Jesus Christ!' I did one around the corner, carrying my eight-foot dowel with a black crow on the end as one of the management looked through the window. All the lads were pissing themselves laughing.

When the coast was clear, I headed back and got the bird in position on the window ledge then tapped on the window with the bird's beak. That was it, caught red-handed, as a manager opened the window and looked down at me with a long stick in my hand that had a dead bird on the end.

'Piss off, you idiot,' he barked.

Me and Kav were menaces, to put it mildly. If there was a laugh to be had then we were up for it.

It started getting very busy so around four new starters were set on. They were young lads and two in particular were both characters in their own way. Eddie Brown, God bless him, died later in a car crash aged only 19. He worked (and I use the term 'worked' loosely) in my department, hence I was his supervisor. I could never find him as he was always hidden in the wood stacks, smoking weed. He was a great lad, though, and was always coming out with trippy sayings like, 'I am the lizard king, I can do anything.' He was heavily into Jim Morrison and The Doors. That's when my interest in that mystical group began.

Another lad who started was John Wilkinson. He was 6ft 3in, a gangly, dopey, easily-led youth. I had him on that many wind-ups it was untrue; the usual things like sending him for a long stand, a bubble for the spirit level and some red-and-white-striped paint from the stores. The first time David Laver came into the yard after John had started, I sent John up to Laver and told him he was the taxman and needed to have a word as John wasn't paying any tax and he needed to know why, as it was a jailable offence. Laver told him not to listen to a word I said, I was daft as a brush.

In the first month of John's new career, I told all the lads to tell him to watch out for me as I was gay and would try it on if possible. Every time I talked to him, I gazed at him lovingly and talked as camp as I could without being too John Inman. If I could touch his hand on the counter, I would. He began to get really uneasy around me. Then, one day, he was putting timber stock away and had to stand it up in a tight corner. I'd told the lads I was having him. I dropped my trousers and pants and, as he got in the corner, I ran up behind him, bollocks bouncing in the breeze. His face was a picture when he turned around and saw me.

'Come on, John, no one's around, I like tall men...' I cooed.

He interrupted me in his panic. 'I think you've got the wrong idea... I'm not like that,' he said with his arm out, trying to keep me at bay.

That was it. I fell about laughing and all the lads were in bits.

Christmas was coming up and I had him on another wind-up that cost him his job and nearly cost me mine. I'd told John that on the last day before Christmas the newest starter – him – had to come dressed as Father Christmas and greet customers as they came in the yard. We gave him a tenner for the hire of the costume.

The last day came and we were all in the canteen waiting to start work when into the yard walked John fully togged up as Santa. I cried with laughter and we all had to compose ourselves before he came in the canteen. He'd even got a big sack and a bell to ring.

'Morning, John... You've never come on the bus like that?' I asked.

'No, my dad's dropped me off; he thinks it's all a wind-up but I've told him Richard did it last year... It's tradition.'

I could hardly hold back my laughter. He got into position to greet customers at the gate for 8.00am opening. As the customers were coming in, the big daft sod stood there ringing his bell shouting, 'Ho, ho, ho... Merry Christmas.' People talk about pissing themselves laughing – well, I did.

It turned sour when one of the managers came out and demanded he go straight to his office. He sacked him on the spot, the miserable twat. I thought he'd see the funny side but the festive spirit had deserted Scrooge. John went home in a flood of tears and all of a sudden it wasn't funny any more.

I went to see the manager and explained that it was my fault and that he was just a gullible lad who'd done nothing wrong. Later that day, a disciplinary meeting was rushed through and I had to go and stand in front of the manager and David Laver. Laver said, 'Maybe in your eyes we're being a little harsh, but I'm trying to run a business here, not a fucking grotto.'

It was all I could do not to smirk, because inside I was in tears, laughing. He went on to explain that John would be reinstated and that I would get a warning letter and to watch my future conduct. Fair enough, result. Laver later came out and had a laugh about it all. The one time I saw David Laver like a rabid dog was my entire fault. The Chesterfield to Sheffield train service ran right past our yard. To do a bit of free advertising for my club, I painted 'SHEFFIELD UNITED FC' on a long plank of piranha pine. It was the most expensive timber we did, £5 a metre

– nothing scrimped on my club, eh? Anyhow, David Laver must have seen it in passing on the train and came storming into the yard shouting, 'Cowens… Cowens!' I knew I was in the shit but I didn't know at the time what I'd done. He frogmarched me to the place where I'd wedged it up at the side of the train tracks. 'Who's put that up?' he barked.

'Dunno… what is it?'

Back to you again.

'It's a bloody sign with 'Sheffield United' wrote on it and I don't suppose you know anything about it,' he was fuming.

'No, I don't,' I said, lying through my teeth.

'Yeah, and I suppose you haven't wrote *that* either,' he said, pointing to a 'BLADES' sign I'd written on the side of the yard wall.

'Yes, I've wrote that but not that,' I said, pointing at the Sheffield United sign. He smashed his brolly down in anger, and it broke in half.

'Now look what you've made me do!' he yelled.

He was on a roll, so he took the opportunity to drag me around the yard pointing out everything that was wrong. He told me to smarten up or he would replace me. I got the bollocking of my life. For 20 minutes I couldn't get a word in edgeways as he went on and on about the state of this and that. When he eventually calmed down and I got the chance to speak, I asked, 'Apart from all that, is everything OK?'

He half-smiled and walked off muttering he was wasting his breath. To be honest, I liked the bloke and I think he liked me for what I was – different.

The lad I mentioned earlier called Neil became a good pal and we used to have a few beers together every now and again. One night we'd been down Woodseats and knocked the froth off about eight pints. I went back to Neil's to order a taxi. His mother was a magistrate and Neil must have already told her I was a togger [football] thug. She was fascinated and wanted to know all the ins and outs of why people like me got involved in a bit of terrace dancing. I told her the buzz was immense and the feeling of battle was second to none. I was pissed and let my tongue flap about in the wind too much and included a few stories of battles we'd had. Little did I know at the time that I'd meet her again, but that time she'd be on her throne and I'd be in the dock! But all that was to come.

At Laver's, I met a lot of people and quite a few characters. One was a bloke called Benny; he was, and still is, quite mad. I knew him through Sunday football as he played at a decent standard. One Monday morning, I'd gone in my Portakabin office. As I opened the door, the worst smell I've ever had the misfortune to inhale took my breath away.

'What the fuck's that smell? Something's dead in there,' one of the lads said as he was going into the canteen next door.

'Fuck knows, but someone is going to be dead when I find out who's responsible,' I replied with my face contorted with disgust. Pulling my jumper up over my nose, I ventured inside and looked around. Under my desk was a large plastic sandbag and I could see it was half full with shit, piss and tissue paper. I put on a glove, picked it up and threw it outside; I was heaving, I'll tell you. Some dirty bastard had stitched me up. I was going around the lads saying if I find out who's done that then I'd stick their head in it.

Around two days later, Benny came in. 'Heard you had a bad game on Sunday,' he said sarcastically.

'I've played better but I thought I'd had a decent game,' I replied, sticking up for myself.

'I've been told you were a bag of shit,' he went on.

The conversation carried on for a while and he kept saying 'bag of shit', whenever he could. I then tumbled it was that dirty bastard that had planted the unwelcome present in my office.

'Nice one, Benny, I owe you one.'

A few months later, I shat in a bag and put it under the seat of his van, but he never mentioned it. I bet it's still there now, all dried up.

Another time, he had his pants down, literally. One busy summer's day, I was serving a customer and the yard was full of people. There was an area around the saw and quite a queue of customers were milling around waiting for their timber to be cut. Then from around a corner came Benny carrying a piece of skirting board in one hand and he was as naked as the day when he was born, not even a sock on. Everyone just looked at him, astonished, as he strolled over to me and asked calmly, holding the wooden skirting in front of him, 'All right, Steve... Any chance of a bit of discount off this?'

I fell about laughing at the lunatic. Mad as a March hare is the only way to describe Benny. He's even worse when he gets together with his brother Melvin.

Another story about Benny had me absolutely creased. The man who told me is a builder and works with a lad called Richard who plays football for the team I run. Around a year ago, they were working at an old people's home. At the back of the home where the old dears sat in the summerhouse was a small pond. The tadpoles had just turned into small frogs. Richard was busy working when Benny walked up to him.

'Rich, I think I've got a problem down below. It's a bit embarrassing but I've caught something... there's a growth on the end of my knob that shouldn't be there. Just take a look and see what you reckon it is.'

Benny proceeded to pull down his shorts and took his cock in his hand. He slowly rolled his foreskin back as Richard watched on. Slowly, the eyes of small frog appeared, and it sat patiently on Benny's bell-end until, once free from his foreskin, it jumped off his cock. When Richard told us the story, talk about laugh...

Benny's totally obsessed with cocks. The first time I introduced him to my dad, Benny asked my poppa what his cock was like.

'I beg your pardon,' my dad said, laughing.

'I bet you've got a real strong veiny one, haven't you?'

That's Benny, always on about cocks. Once he got on about them he wouldn't shut up.

'Bryan Robson's got a great penis, a big, strong, fine-looking thing it is. Uriah Renni's is a beauty, an angry snarling pole that's got business written all over it,' he'd go on and on.

I knew a few of his old team-mates and they told me he was always asking if he could wash their privates for them in the showers. Any new players that signed on, Benny would always stand at the side of them, staring down at their nether regions saying stuff like, 'Not bad in length but a bit short in the girth department.' He's not gay, as he's married with a lovely daughter called Amy. Yes, Benny's one in a million... Or make that a billion.

I have fond memories from my time at Arnold Laver and I hope the people there enjoyed working with me because there wasn't a dull moment, that's for sure. My time at the company ended in a way which I'd probably deserved a few years earlier but the simple fact of the matter is not everything is painted in black and white, especially hidden CCTV footage. I was charged with four counts of theft.

I've no need to deny it now but the simple truth is that just because my forklift was caught on CCTV loading timber doesn't mean I'm the man doing the driving, especially when two of the thefts I was charged with occurred when I wasn't even at work. I knew who was responsible but kept my mouth firmly shut. At the time, I was off work, sick, but in truth I was off touring around watching The Beautiful South. My forklift stood out on CCTV because I'd had a 'BLADES' registration plate made for it.

I knew the case wouldn't stand up in court but Laver's (or, rather, a certain director) pressed on and refused my solicitor's request to see the clock cards that would have proven beyond doubt that I wasn't even at work when the thefts took place. A year and two months and three court appearances later, the CPS dropped the case. Just why it took them so long only they will know.

After Laver's, I went to work for my mate John Corker who had his own tarmac business. The trouble was that a lad called Macky also worked for him and we'd been enemies before, as he was a respected Wednesday lad and obviously I was United. To be fair, I didn't really think too much about it but our first meeting began with a grunt at each other rather than a conversation.

Macky had something to do with the Sportsman football team from Stannington. They were mainly Wednesday and I ran and played for the Denby Sportsman football team, which were mainly United. Prior to starting work with Corker's, we'd had a game abandoned against them. I say abandoned, but it never actually got started, and our team got a police escort all the 12 miles back to Sheffield – more of that later.

Anyhow, I settled in and met some great lads and became good pals with Macky. They were all top-notch blokes and I really enjoyed the company and laughs we all had working at Corker's, except when I had a shovel in my hand, which was every fuckin' day. The pay was shite as well; I don't know how people are expected to graft like that all day for the pittance they take home.

I was put with a lad called Kev Creaser to start with; he was sound but as daft as me. Every morning when I picked him up, he'd climb into the truck and fart while saying he was starving; that happened every morning for three months. I've seen him shit in places you can't imagine. That was the trouble with tarmacking – no shitting facilities – but to Kev it wasn't a problem. He'd often shit in a bucket in the lorry cabin but I used to go mad, as it stunk the cab out for ages.

Once, we were working in a posh cul-de-sac in Harrogate. Kev went missing, and then I realised he was in the cab having a plop. He's got the paper over his lap to cover his pride from the overlooking houses and had his back to the door as he squatted in the footwell of the cab.

A couple drove up and were getting their shopping out of their car so I sneaked around the side of the cab and opened the door to reveal Kev's arse mid-shit. The woman's face was a picture as she watched on in horror as Kev tried to cover his arse up as a Winston Churchill cigar was protruding from his butt. I've seen him shit everywhere, including a graveyard on a busy town-centre street, squatting with his back against a gravestone, no respect for the dead!

All the time I was at Corker's, I got up to no good. One day, I put kippers down the air vents in everyone's cabs. It was freezing so everyone had their heaters on so the kippers were gently cooked and the stink from them had everyone spewing. There were about ten lorries and all had a two-way radio system in them. Later in the afternoon I got a call – they'd all been in touch with each other and worked out who the culprit was, which wasn't hard really.

'You dirty bastard… What have you put in our cabs? It stinks vile. Where have you put it, you cunt, it smells like something has died.' They couldn't suss out where the smell was coming from. As usual, I pleaded my innocence saying that they were only blaming me because I was a Blade.

Another Blade called Chris Shaw worked at Corker's. I liked Chris a lot, mainly because he was one of the few Blades around, but he was also a funny and well-likeable man. He sadly died in February 2004 and I went to the funeral. It summed up really how stupid the rivalry goes in our city when the pallbearers down one side of the coffin had Blades shirts on and on the other Macky had his Wednesday one on; it sort of puts the rivalry into perspective in sombre moments like that. RIP Chris, mate.

Back at Corker's, I was now working with a top lad called Pat. He actually liked digging; must have been something in his Irish blood. Although he was a dirty Leeds fan he was sort of a half-Blade; in short, a good spud. If we finished early enough me and Pat used to go in a café at the top of Chapeltown which was two minutes from the yard. There was a bloke who worked in the café called Frank. He was a bit backward and his only word was 'Yip'. It was 'Yip' to everything. His job entailed clearing the plates away and a bit of washing up.

One day we were in the café and my mind started ticking. 'Frank, do you want a ride in the truck?'

'Yip.'

I asked his boss if we could take him for a spin. Frank climbed in and started bouncing around all excited like. He wore an old wool jumper with big holes in it that came to his knees and sandals with white socks and his big toe poking through a hole. I drove to the yard. Macky was unloading his lorry and looked at me with a 'What's he up to now?' expression as I coaxed Frank out of the cab. I took Frank in the office and sat him down in front of John Corker, who was still on the phone. I mouthed, 'He's come for a job' to John then beat a hasty retreat. I drove off pissing myself as I pictured John trying to talk to Frank. I hadn't got far when John's voice came over the two-way radio. 'What the fuck is this bloke doing in the office? He can only say "Yip",' he said, going crackers.

'I don't know, John... He jumped in the cab at Leeds and wouldn't get out. You'll have to ring the coppers.'

'Fuck off coppers! Get back here and take Yip Man back where you found him.'

Me and Pat were rolling about all over the place. I went back and took Yip Man back to the café.

I think, in the end, they were glad to see the back of me when I left. At least they could start to relax a bit. After Corker's, I went to work for a large tool-making firm. I've been pretty well behaved since, as I've got a responsible job where I can't be fuckin' around all the time. I still like a laugh, though, and keep people on their toes with the odd wind-up. One classic was when we were opening a package. The box was full of those polystyrene curly things that stop the goods getting damaged. They looked just like Wotsits, only a paler brown colour. My mind went into nuisance mode.

'Kez, have you got a packet of them shitty space invader curly snacks in your lunch box again?'

He had, so a plan was formed. We carefully opened the pack from the bottom and emptied the invaders out of the bag and filled it with the foam curls. I glued the bag back up perfectly and put them in my snap (lunch) box. A lad called Carl always sat next to me; he was a sound lad, but I call him 'Owt for Nowt' as he always ate anything that was left by anyone or took anything home that was being thrown away in the factory. Anyhow, we sat down at break time and I opened my snap box. I tucked into a sandwich and pulled the space invader pack from my box.

'I can't believe our lass has put the kids' crisps in... She knows I don't like them,' I said, tossing them on to the table in front of me. Carl was straight in there like I knew he would be.

'I'll have them,' he said as he opened the pack.

I was trying to keep as straight a face as I could, as was

everyone else who'd been told what I was up to. Carl stuffed a couple in his mouth. I thought he'd just gob them straight back out but, no, he's chewing away like he's got a Hubba Bubba in his mouth. He swallowed, then went for another. I couldn't hold back and collapsed all over the table.

'Fuckin' what are they? I thought they tasted a bit sketchy,' he said with his face all contorted.

'They're fuckin' polystyrene, you thick Wednesday bastard,' I said, tears rolling down my face. He'd swallowed two and gone back for more – priceless.

I've been in my current employment nine years now and have a manager's job, so I have a more responsible role but deep down the kid in me still lurks around – as my bosses find out every last day before Christmas!

So that's basically my working life – I've never been out of work or signed on since I left school at 16.

Bollocks! Spoke too soon as I've just got laid off!

SUNDAY FOOTBALL

I've been involved in playing or managing a Sunday football team since 1981. It's a great release and I've enjoyed it immensely. There is no substitute for playing but since I hung my boots up I've also enjoyed managing teams and I've been very successful at it. The trouble with me is sometimes I'm too passionate. That passion has brought a fair share of trouble my way, too.

In 1981, I began playing for the pub I drank in at the time, The Penny Black in town. A bunch of locals formed the team and we joined the Nomads league. In truth, we weren't a good side; in fact, shite's a word I'd use. We were a mix of United and Wednesday and that rivalry boiled over at one Hallowe'en 'do' as both sets traded punches, then spilled out into the road to take up a bit of street dancing. After a couple of years, the manager – Big Terry – called it a day and my dad took over as boss. Terry was a sound enough bloke but it was farcical in the changing rooms.

'Get changed lads,' he'd say. That was OK, but with 14–15 lads it was a free-for-all who got the numbers 2 to 11. My dad and I steadily got together a good side consisting mainly of Blades. Trouble was never far away from me as I was a bit of a hothead and spent a lot of time suspended. I actually had to sit in front of Geoff Thompson (the geezer who's now running the FA) in a disciplinary meeting after I'd knocked out a bloke's front teeth. He'd wanted to sue me so I sat with Thompson discussing my record, which didn't make good reading, but because I'd not even been cautioned for the teeth removal I knew there wasn't a lot they could do about it.

'How about offering to pay so much towards his dental fees, as a sort of goodwill gesture?' reasoned Thompson. I agreed to pay the bloke some money.

Gradually, I started calming down and realised that I didn't have to fight every opponent who said something to me or my team-mates. The old red mist still used to come down now and again, though.

The team now had some great characters – Shots, Mitch, Nobby, Kav, Norm, Housey, Sainey and Nudge – who were all involved with United's firm in those days and this often led to trouble.

Wednesday's main actors at the time had a team called

The Shakespeare. They met every Sunday morning on the steps just outside The Penny Black. One Sunday, they attacked a car being driven by one of our team, which was the last one to set off for our game. Baseball bats were used and the car was badly damaged. It was unfortunate for the owner of the vehicle – a lad who worked behind the bar – as he'd lent us the car because we didn't have enough transport to get to the ground.

He wasn't impressed when he saw the state of his car when we returned. The following week, I told everyone to bring a bat as we were going to 'do' Wednesday in a revenge attack. It was quite funny as our lot turned up with 'straight arms' due to bats being concealed up their coat sleeves. Not half as funny as Nobby, who walked in the pub carrying a six-foot boating oar.

'It's the only thing I could find,' he said, smiling through the gap in his teeth.

Thankfully, Wednesday didn't turn up. It was now 1986 and we were getting a decent side together. We won promotion to the first division but were always struggling with fund-raising. Two brothers, Richard and Paul Shaw, joined us. I worked with Richard; his dad Graham used to play for United and England. My dad filled me in on what an excellent player Graham Shaw used to be. Graham and his smashing wife Beryl had just bought The Sportsman Inn on Denby Street next to Bramall Lane.

It was a pub that was staunch United and they were looking for a team to play from there. We had a vote and a meeting with Graham and that was it, we were off to beautiful downtown Bramall Lane and the famous Denby Sportsman FC was born.

Denby Sportsman had a very successful first season but we nearly lost our place in the league due to a blatant bit of cheating from our promotion rivals. Eckington Activities and ourselves were pushing for promotion and the penultimate match at the end of the season saw us travel to Eckington for a game we needed to win to gain promotion. Before we went on the pitch, one of Eckington's officials came and explained that there had been a change of referee. We thought nothing more of it. As I tossed the coin in the air, I couldn't help but think I'd seen the ref before. Ten minutes into the game, it hit me – the bloke who was the referee actually played for them.

I'd been to watch them play a couple of weeks beforehand and the cunt had played up front for them. I shouted to my dad and told him of my concerns. He'd also twigged what was going on. I went up to the ref and said, 'You play for these, don't you?'

'No.'

'You fuckin' do... I watched you last week. Your name's Lawrence, isn't it?'

To cut it short, they had worked us one by cancelling the proper ref and having one of their own players ref the game. The game progressed and we were too strong for them and took a 2–0 lead into the last 15 minutes of the game. Then the Cheating Bastard from Cheatsville took over. We were on the attack when the ref blew the whistle.

'Your goalkeeper's just called me a cheat,' he said, marching back up the pitch with the ball tucked under his arm. He gave a free kick on the edge of our box and booked Chaz, our goalie, who was bewildered by it all. They scored from the free kick and the ref sent one of our players off for protesting. I got booked, as did Zuey. He then sent Andy off for a tackle. In the last minute, with us still winning 2–1, our full-back jockeyed a ball out of play for a goal kick to us.

'Corner,' pointed the cheating twat. They scored from it and not only did the full-time whistle go but so did the lot. We all started fighting the nearest opposition player to us as their goalie had admitted the ref played for them and that he was ashamed of what had gone off. The ref ran off, as we had lost the plot. Their players were chased into the changing rooms and their door was smashed down with a wooden bench. We were fined £200 and warned about our conduct. Mr Cheat had put a report in that he was asked to do the game at short notice and had informed us that he played for them – bullshit.

Years later, I actually became good friends with a lot of the lads who played for Eckington that day. I've had a few chats and they all remember the day when they had to barricade themselves in the changing rooms. All admit they were embarrassed about the cheating that went on. Despite that, we were promoted, but not as champions, which we really deserved.

The following summer saw us training earlier than normal; we trained in Norfolk Park, which is close to the city centre. During that summer, my uncle Edwin had come over from Canada on a surprise visit. Only my nan knew he was coming over, and as we sat at a party arranged at my nan's house, a strange figure sat in the corner with the worst wig I've ever seen sat on his head. After a few minutes, we realised that it was my uncle Ed; we hadn't seen him for a few years so it was hugs and tears all round.

The wig had to be made use of somehow, as it was so bad. It was there and then that me and my dad hatched a plan. The following Wednesday at training, we were warming up so I explained that my dad and mum had split up and my dad had got himself a new bird. 'Trouble is, lads, he's started wearing a wig and a bad wig at that. He's very touchy about it so when he comes later, watch what you say, OK?'

Shotgun and a few others were having none of it. As usual, lazy Norman was late; he liked to avoid the two-mile run around the park that we did. We were doing some shuttles as Norm sat on the grass embankment, putting his boots on as slowly as possible. Then my dad came walking down behind him from over the hill, complete with the ill-fitting divot on his noddle.

'Fuckin' hell,' said Shotgun as he stifled his laugh.

'Remember, lads, he's really fuckin' touchy about it, so try not to say anything,' I repeated. My dad sidled up alongside Norm, who hadn't a clue, as he'd missed my warning. Norm looked up. 'Fuck me, Dave, what's that you've got on your head?' he asked.

With a totally straight face, my dad shouted, 'Get down there and get training you lazy little black cunt.'

I was crying inside with laughter; the look on the lads' faces was a picture as a rather hurt Norman joined us.

'I told you. Sorry, Norm, he's a bit touchy about it, he's started wearing it all the time. I know he looks a twat but he's fuckin' serious.'

We trained, then went to the pub; no one would travel in my car with my dad as they couldn't keep a straight face. When we walked in The Sportsman, Beryl, the landlady, fell to the floor behind the bar. Leaning on the bar was Roger, a pal of my dad's, the pair of them went fishing together. Roger had no idea my dad had started wearing a wig. As he turned and caught my dad's eye, quick as a flash he said, 'All right, Dave... I didn't recognise you without your glasses on.'

That was it for me, I had to go outside and was doubled up, I'd kept up the straight face all through it but I'd cracked up big time.

It was a period in time my life when me and my dad were at our closest; we both loved the football and the drinks that followed. We developed a bond that, in truth, had been missing in our relationship. The bond didn't stop me playing practical jokes on him, though. Sometimes I wondered why he even bothered to talk to me.

One time, he'd left his freshly packed pipe on the table in The Sportsman. When he went to the toilet, I quickly shouted Fitzy over and asked him for a small bud of the very strong skunk weed he had on him. I removed some of the baccy from Dad's pipe and put the skunk in carefully, covering it with the baccy. Dad came back from the toilet, pulled out his Zippo lighter and sparked up his pipe. We were all creased up as he puffed away, nonplussed. Then the sweet smell of cannabis hit the air. Still he puffed away until the whole pub stunk of the stuff. Beryl and Graham came over to us, the landlord wanting to know who was smoking the 'tricky tackle' as he called it. I pointed at Dad. He was just sat wide-eyed, then slumped back in his seat looking rather stoned.

'You bastard... What have you done to me?' he accused. He was stoned as a badger. His legs wouldn't move and I helped him get in the car to take him home to Mum's. All the way home I was laughing as he laid across the back seat slurring his words but saying he was starving: 'munchies time'. He got home, ate his dinner and went to bed.

I played a few more tricks on him over the next few weeks, including taking the ham out of his sandwich, one of those which the landlady had prepared for the football team. I replaced it with a beer mat. As he fought to bite into it, he pulled his false teeth clean out of his mouth. Everyone in the pub was falling all over the place.

The following week he was well on his guard, announcing, 'You're not having me this week, ya cunt.' That only made me more determined, so, as he got up to get a quick half to top his drink up before we went, I grabbed the cling film that had been covering the sandwiches. I covered the top of his pint pot as neatly as I could with the film. When he sat back down next to me, the lads waited with anticipation.

'I've just been saying, Dad, that you've learnt your lesson and we'll never be able to get you with a wind-up.'

'Yeah, too right... I'm on my guard now.' And with that he poured his half pint on to the top of the cling film and all over his bollocks. Talk about laugh! He threw the remnants from the glass at me as I beat a hasty retreat in fits of hysterics. My dad's always been a good sport, though, and even accepted that at the end of every presentation night, I would pick him up above my shoulders and spin him around until he was really dizzy then put him down and watch him tumble over the tables to the floor. This practice later stopped, as one night after I'd done it he spewed up all over the gaff.

Mum said it was one spin too many and demanded an end to the ritual.

Without sounding too bigheaded, I was a decent player, the type that every central midfield needed – strong, physical, a good talker but, above all, I could play football.

They say everyone has an Achilles heel, well, mine's an Achilles tendon. Our team had been winning league and cups for two or three years so the plan was that at the end of the season we would apply to join the Meadowhall league, which is the highest standard of Sunday football in Yorkshire, if not the country. The likes of Chris Waddle, John Beresford, Billy Whitehouse and Chris Wilder have all played in the league. So as I was in my late twenties and in my prime, I couldn't wait to get stuck into this new challenge. Then with only a couple of games left in the season and the league almost won, I snapped my left Achilles for the first time just after I'd scored in a game we won 2–0 against Ridgeway Athletic. I went down while running and the noise it made was horrendous.

Now if you have ever snapped your Achilles, then you will testify that it's one painful injury and is worse by far than a broken leg – ask former Man United and England star Neil Webb: it finished his career. I actually went out on the night I snapped it; I was in fuckin' agony all night and hardly slept a wink.

The next day, my dad took me to Rotherham Hospital and the doctor confirmed I'd snapped it and I would need an operation. He asked when I'd done it and when I said, 'Yesterday playing football,' he looked at me a bit puzzled.

'How have you managed to get to hospital?' he asked. 'You can't walk when you rupture your Achilles.'

'I went out last night,' I replied.

He thought I was taking the piss but I wasn't. I had an operation that day and was in hospital for three days. After the op, I was in plaster for 12 weeks and had a limp for a year. I was told I wouldn't play again and at only 29 I was gutted. I managed to turn my misfortune into a bit of mischief, though.

The *Green 'Un* – the South Yorkshire Saturday sports paper – was running a new competition called the 'Predator player of the month'. Predator boots were just about to come out, designed by former Liverpool striker Craig Johnston; the boots were on every player's wanted list but at £120 they were out of a lot of lads' reach.

That weekend at football I informed our team in the changing rooms that I was going to be the '*Green 'Un* Player of the Month', and I'd have a pair of Predators before anyone else. I limped off on my crutches with a smile on my face leaving all the lads thinking I was nuts.

A lad called John Mcfazdean played for us; he was well known in football circles in Sheffield and was some player. John had been on Rotherham's books and always played at a very high standard; not as high as he should have, though, as he was a brilliant player but had shit for brains. Anyhow, I penned a letter to the *Green 'Un* pretending I was Mac.

A week later, I received a phone call from Sheffield Newspapers informing me I was the first Predator Player of the Month and could they send a photographer around to my house. That Saturday's *Green 'Un* carried an article with me sat looking forlorn in my living room, fully potted up (in plaster). The article went like this:

DENBY SPORTSMAN'S player-manager Steve Cowens has a special incentive to recover from a ruptured Achilles tendon – to try on the new pair of boots he has won as the first Green 'Un Predator Player of the Month *in November. Steve was nominated by team-mate John Mcfazdean. He snapped his Achilles after scoring in a recent Nomads Sunday game against Ridgeway. 'He had an operation and was in hospital for three days and has been told he will never play again,' said Mcfazdean. 'But he still came in our changing room the following week saying, "You lot are going to struggle without me carrying you, but I'll be back next season." That's typical of his attitude; he is touching 30 and has played almost 400 games for the club, scoring 97 goals. He has played for Denby since he was 16 and his commitment and loyalty to the club are unreal. I have played for Altringham, Rotherham and now Alfreton Town and I have never seen a player give so much... He goes for every ball as if his life depends on it. He is determined to play again and if he wins the boots it will help him on his way to fitness.'*

Steve led his team to the league title and league cup final and hopes to join the region's top Sunday league, the Meadowhall, next season.

It would have brought a tear to a glass eye, would that. Next day, all the lads at football were pissing themselves as they read the *Green 'Un*, especially Mac who thought it was the best con he'd ever seen.

Even though I had a pot on and crutches, I still managed to get myself sent off a couple of weeks later when we entertained our bitter rivals Chapeltown. They, like us, were a good side and, like us, they were physical. Most of the games had gone our way but this was a crucial game to more or less decide the championship.

To cut the story short, it kicked off big time after a bad Chapeltown tackle. As all the players and spectators slugged it out, I set off on the long hobble across the pitch. I was fucked when I got to the scene, puffing and panting, but I still had enough energy to smash my crutch over a Chapeltown player's head. Two players – one from each side – were sent off, then I rightly got my marching – or should I say limping – orders. I still hadn't learnt my lesson and went for one of their players again.

I actually get on with the Chapeltown lot now and have a laugh about what happened that day. Looking back, I was an idiot at times; my temper and commitment in sticking up for myself and my team-mates always got me in trouble. The Predator boots were used again as I fought my way back to fitness and got back into the team again. Every game was a bonus for me after being told I wouldn't play again.

Our first game in the Meadowhall, as luck would have it, was away at Sportsman, a team from Stannington, a district in the north of Sheffield and a Wednesday stronghold. I knew a Wednesday lad called Mack had something to do with running them and that they were mostly of the blue-and-white persuasion. In the build-up to the game, we'd heard rumours that Wednesday were turning a firm out for us, even though we had a few Wednesday lads in our side.

It left us with a predicament – do we go up to Stannington firmed up or do we just take the team? It was our first game in a new league and I could see it kicking off, leading to us being kicked out of the league before we'd begun. So much hard work had been done in the pre-season to get us into a position where we could compete not only on the pitch but also financially.

A lot of United lads had got wind of Wednesday turning out for us and my mobile received quite a few offers of help, including one from our Main Man Lester Divers, who offered to bring his 'team' up, as he called them. We decided to go up with just the football team and to treat it as another game. Well, almost, as on the day everyone had a rounders bat in his bag. I'd told them that they were for protection only and not to pull them out unless they had to.

It was a Thursday evening game and we had to make our way across Sheffield in the rush hour. Their ground was 12 miles from the city centre. We tried to keep together but I lost the rest of the lads and then got lost on the way to the ground. I pulled into a side road just after Stannington to try and get my bearings as we headed out of Sheffield towards Dungworth. The side road had six police riot vans and two dog vans parked together; I didn't think anything of it as the area wasn't familiar to me. I just thought there must have been a cop shop on the road. I later found out those bizzies were for us. I read my street map and got my shit together then drove the two miles to the ground. On the way my mobile went.

'Steve, you better get here quick… There's loads of them and a few are tooled up.'

Good job we'd got the bats, I thought. I pulled into the car park of the ground and quickly got out of the car. My 'straight arm' was caused by the bat I had concealed.

Our opposition stood 30-handed on a bank and some numpty was stood there swinging nunchucks around like a pissed-up Bruce Lee. I stood in front of them posing like Eubank used to do. A few motioned my way, so I prepared for kick-off. It was then Bally shouted, 'Steve, watch it.'

I thought some more were coming up behind but it wasn't that… No, it was the plod who were hid in the bushes filming events with a camcorder. Then police appeared from everywhere, it was well over the top. Raggy and a few others walked up to my car and threw their bats on to my back seat, which was good of them. The referee had heard about the impending trouble and had decided not to come. The police, however, were keen to get the game out of the way so one bobby offered to ref it for us! I didn't fancy playing with more police than spectators around the pitch; to be honest, I wanted out of there as my car was full of bats.

'We've had to set up a special operation for this,' one copper moaned to me.

'I can't help the fact that these idiots have forgot we are supposed to be playing a game of football,' I replied.

We set off back to Sheffield with an escort Kenneth Noye would have been proud of. Every time I went around a bend, I threw another bat out of the window, much to the amusement of Tubs and Fitz who were in the car behind me. So that was that, our first game called off and an eight-vehicle police escort back to Sheffield.

Back at the pub, I phoned the Sportsman at Stannington and asked for Macky. Someone came on the phone and started having a chirp. 'Look, just because I run the side doesn't mean all the lads are BBC – far from it. Don't forget, you've got to play at our ground; we've come in this league to play football, nothing else. Let's make sure that next time we play there's none of that shit... OK?'

He agreed.

When we played them at home later in the season, the police came but kept a low profile. There was no trouble and our opponents came and had a beer with us after the game. The ice had been broken and we could get on with the football again. Little did we know at the time, the rearranged game would be the last match of the season and would decide who got promotion – us or them.

During that game, we only needed a draw and I scored a tremendous scissor-kicked goal from the edge of the area that had the watching Don Hutchison (ex-Liverpool, West Ham and, of course, the Blades) suitably impressed. The ball flew in like a bullet and I thought that I'd sent us up. Unfortunately for us they equalised then scored the winner in the last few minutes to win 2–1. We'd had enough chances to win four games but it wasn't to be.

I'm always gracious in defeat and I took two bottles of champagne into their dressing room and I actually forged a lot of friendships with them, and to think only seven months earlier we were going to knock seven shades of shit out of each other.

To finish off a really bad day, in the early hours of

Monday morning the taxi that was carrying John Mac and myself home crashed; it was a fuckin' crash-and-a-half and went on for 40 yards, smashing a letter box into the air and ploughing into a brick wall. The taxi had skidded on the newly-laid tram tracks, and the fact that it was pissing it down didn't help... And I suppose the taxi driver doing over 50 mph on wet tram tracks was probably a contributing factor. Anyhow, despite being cut by shards of glass and a bit shook up, I was eventually two-and-a-half grand better off when the compo came through.

I'd had my fair share of scrapes during that season, which included knocking a Woodhouse player out. I'd tried my best to avoid the confrontation but he was giving me consistent verbals and so I snapped. Then, later in the season, I had a strangling match with a big Rasta called Custer. Now this geezer is very well known in Sheffield and is not the type to mess about with, but I had to stick up for myself. I ended up being booked for the wrestling match and, despite Custer starting it by grabbing me by the throat, he escaped a caution because the ref bottled it. I went to see Custer after the game and, to be fair, he just shook my hand and we now get on quite well. The referee, incidentally, has never given me or my team a thing and he's still that way today.

At this point in my playing days, I really calmed down a lot. I'd spent a lot of my footballing days either suspended or fighting people who I really should have just laughed at. It suddenly dawned on me after my injury, when I thought I'd never play again, that at the age of 32 I should enjoy the rest of my playing days, and I did.

The following season we won the league. It was always

my goal to play in the Meadowhall premier league but we fell short by one division and the following season we folded as a club. I'd had enough of trying to raise money and running the club; I needed a break and had a year off from Sunday football.

Towards the end of the season, a good mate called Fridgo asked me to go and have a look at the side he was playing for. I went along and they had the usual bad habits that Sunday pub teams have. The following season, I took over and brought in five new players, including a good 'keeper. To cut it short, we went on to win everything. I still played now and again but I wanted to concentrate on managing.

The curse of the Achilles then struck again, this time in the other leg. It was probably the worst feeling I've ever had as I, for one, knew straight away what I had done. What's more we had a family holiday booked to Tenerife the following week so I knew that not only had I got 12–14 weeks in plaster to look forward to, but I also had to tell my family at home that their holiday abroad would have to be cancelled.

That was it for me – my boots were hung on a six-inch nail in the garage. I'd had a good go but, in truth, I was coming to the end of my tether and had all but retired. I hate players who play on and think they can still do a job when, in fact, they are struggling big time. It's like they can't face up to the fact they are past it.

When you finally hang your boots up, it leaves a big void in your life. The enjoyment I got from playing football was immense. It's a great feeling walking on to a pitch with your mates and giving everything you've got. I've always been a winner and hated losing, it used to take me three days to get over a defeat, I took it that bad.

These characteristics have followed me into management. I expect my team to have the mentality that I had as a player. It's difficult for some lads to accept that winning is everything, but I think that the lads who have played under me realise that I want to see them play with spirit, determination and, above all, courage. I am a serious person when it comes to football; I don't do anything by halves – it's full-on or nothing.

I've always liked a laugh and get up to mischief and joke when I can to lighten things up. A typical example of that comes from the 2004/05 season. We'd won our old league and cup two years on the trot and I wanted a new challenge, so we applied successfully to join the Meadowhall league.

Our first league game was against High Noon FC, quite an appropriate name as it happened. The High Noon lads are mainly United and actually play in the Blades kit so I didn't expect any trouble, especially as I knew a few of them pretty well. Anyhow, the ref let too much go and, as the game wore on, it became evident that it was going to go off. The straw that broke the camel's back came when we scored to make it 6–2 with only five minutes to go. One of their players threw a punch and it kicked off near the corner flag and I was a good 60 yards away. I was quite happy to let the ref sort it until a few of their touchline lads joined in and a couple of my players were hit by sidewinders. So I set off on a 60-yard dash to help out. When I got there, everyone was fighting and I saw one of the Noon players punch one of our players from behind. I lost control and got involved. It all calmed down and the ref said if anything else happened the game would be abandoned. The game finished without further incident.

I couldn't believe it when, two weeks later, I got a letter from the local Football Association asking me to explain my actions. The ref had just reported me out of all the two dozen people who were fighting. I knew it was because I am who I am but that didn't mean I was guiltier than the rest. I was banned from managing football for eight weeks and fined over 100 quid; it totally pissed on my bonfire and I seriously thought about knocking Sunday football on the head. It didn't feel worth it. In my position as manager, I did wrong, I know that, but I felt at the time I had to defend my team and I had done nothing the other's hadn't done.

On the first game of my ban, we were at home to Sharrow United, so I popped in the changing room half-an-hour before kick-off to wish the lads the best of luck. I told them I was going to watch one of our rivals and I'd see them in the pub later. What they didn't know was that I had no intention of watching another game as I had plans of my own. I'd been and hired a furry fox outfit from the fancy dress shop and had everything organised. I went into the trees behind one of the goals and started to get changed into my fox outfit.

Just as I was about to put on my fox head I noticed a bloke watching me from his bedroom window. He was on the phone and looking at me all perplexed. I waved, he waved back, and then I put my head on and got into position. Next thing, I hear a voice.

'Here, mate, what you up to?' It was the bloke from the

house and he had the phone in his hand. He'd been saying to his workmate, 'You're not going to believe this but there's a big bloke getting dressed as a fox at the bottom of our garden.'

His mate was still on the phone so he passed it to me and I had to tell him what it was all about. By now, our team were warming up so I cut it short so as not to blow my cover.

Anyhow, ten minutes into the game, Sharrow got a corner and the ball rolled into the bushes just in front of me. This is my chance, I thought. As the Sharrow player was bending down to pick the ball up, I ran out of my den and pounced.

'That's my ball,' I screamed as I jumped out at him. The poor lad shat himself, screamed and threw the ball at me while back-pedalling. Everyone in our team realised it was me and fell all over the place laughing, except for a couple of our not-so-bright brigade.

The ref was pissing himself, even though he was being assessed that day. The assessor later came over to me and asked what the crack was.

'I'm banned, mate.'

'What you doing here then?'

'I'm a fox now,' I replied. He just looked at me as if I was barking.

'I've been watching football games for 20 years and I've not seen anything as funny as that... You've made my day,' he said as he walked off chuckling to himself.

That's me, though. I like a laugh and want my team to be serious about winning, but I enjoy having fun along the way.

We finished up getting promoted in our first year in the

new league. The following season we beat all the odds to lift the first division title. We had done what I wanted to do as a player and that was to play in the Premier against the best. The team and I would be pitting our wits in the best standard of football in South Yorkshire.

As manager, I'm really proud of our achievements as a club. Eight years ago, we had no money and played in the second division of a poor league. Our club has since won everything and now has two adult teams, an Under-18s and seven junior teams. I want Mosborough FC to be the biggest and best setup in Sheffield.

I have really enjoyed managing. Obviously, nothing beats playing but when you get a set of lads who will give you everything, it's very satisfying. What I have drummed into my team is discipline. It's something I never had, so I speak from experience. The trouble is, my team get tarred with the same brush as me and that's not on. We are a very good side and, contrary to what people believe, we have a lot of Wednesday fans playing for us and they are very good pals of mine. I do feel guilty that an honest bunch of lads are sometimes treated like they are and it's all because I run the side. People in power notice my name and see the club in a bad light as a result. We have one of the best disciplinary records around and that's with two adult teams. Football is everything to me and if I can put something back into the game then I'm a happy man. My son also plays for Mosborough Juniors and one day I hope he makes it into the first team.

We are a very close bunch of lads and, in March 2008, 28 of us went to Ibiza on one of our team's stag nights. It turned out to be a trip that deserves its own diary section:

IBIZA UNCOVERED 2008

Day 1

I decided to go on my mate Stinky's stag do. I wasn't initially going but thought it would do me good to get away for a bit with the lads. I'd had a bad time of it lately. Three days in Ibiza sounded like it was not long enough but, trust me, the way we were hard at it, it was plenty. Well, my liver thought so, anyhow.

We met at 2.30am, with two vans ferrying 28 of us to East Midlands Airport; we were straight into the drinking. I literally bumped into Gary Cahill, who is now at Bolton but spent three months on loan at the Lane while on loan from Villa. He was actually on our flight and we came across him in a bar two days later; top man was Gary, as I talked to him about his time and his wholehearted displays for our team. He's actually a Sheffield lad so his down-to-earthness should have been expected, what with him being from our great city.

We eventually got to our hotel at 10.15am Spanish time. By 11.00am we were on to the booze and supped ourselves well into the early hours of the next day. I've got to say it's probably the best crack I've had with the lads; so much happened and at times my side ached with laughter. The first night's highlight will live with me forever.

We were absolutely shit-faced at around 1.00am. I was starving as I'd hardly had anything to eat. Miffer told me about a good kebab place bang opposite the bar we were in so we headed unsteadily across to it. At the counter stood a cockney battle-axe; she was around 50 and looked hardened to most things Ibiza had to offer. Well, she wasn't ready for what Miffer was about to throw her way.

Being drunk is great but being as pissed as a cunt is not so great, as generally it all ends in tears. Anyhow, we ordered two kebabs and Battle-axe went in the back and started carving that big piece of brown dripping fat that is supposed to be some kind of meat. Miff was playing with a 10-euro note and, as he leant forward on the counter, I flicked the note over the worktop, a childish, pissed-up act. Miff just looked at me all disgusted and started to lean over the wooden surface to reach for it. As his feet dangled off the floor, I couldn't resist and grabbed his legs and threw him head-first over the counter, like mates do! He went flying and, to be honest, I thought I'd gone too far, as his legs went over the top of his body and he smashed into a load of pans and cardboard takeaway boxes.

Miff jumped up as I stood there laughing like a big kid. Then, just as Battle-axe was hotfooting *it to see what all the commotion was, Miff turned and saw a huge pan of curry. Fuck knows why (probably because of the 25 drinks we'd had) but Miff looked left, then right, and plunged his head into the curry right up to his neck. He came back up gasping for air and looked like a swamp-monster, as curry completely covered his head. I was rolling with laughter as the cockney woman started screaming at him.*

'What the fack are you doing, you fackin' idiot… I've jast made that fackin' curry.'

'I'm suing… where's there's blame there's a claim,' Miffer spluttered back as he unintentionally spat curry in her face and stumbled about behind the counter, totally blinded by the spicy concoction, as chunks of chicken rolled off his nut. By this time, I was in absolute hysterics; I couldn't talk and tears were rolling down my face as I watched the woman slipping and sliding on the curry-covered floor trying to get Miff back around the counter. Then Miff slipped in the mess and fell on his arse, almost dragging Battle-axe with him. That was it for me and I fell to the floor laughing uncontrollably while holding on to my cock, trying to stop piss coming out.

The woman pressed some kind of alarm and, within seconds, two burly geezers had got hold of the blinded Miffer and were manhandling him back around the counter. It was at this point I came round and demanded they let go of him and opened the hatch and took my mate by the arm while telling the security geezers to let go.

We stumbled into the street and sat on a bench. I got some paper towels and Miff wiped the curry from his face. His white G-Star shirt was now bright orange (I fuckin' hate G-Star by the way). As Miff's face reappeared from under the gunk, I started laughing again and, to be fair, so did he; we sat there laughing for what seemed like ages as people walked past, staring at us.

A few of the lads came out of the bar to see what all the fuss was about and asked me what had happened. I was still unable to talk but Miff mumbled through his laughter that I had thrown him over the counter. Yeah, I did, but I didn't stick his head in a big pan of curry, the daft twat! It could have been red-hot for all he knew, and scalded his nut off.

After that, I retired for the night as a few of the lads went clubbing. Fuck that! Sixty euros to go in a club to pay another fifteen euros for a drink!

My mate, Ravy-Davy-Gravy, stumbled back to our apartment at around 5.00am, promptly collapsed on the bed and fell into what I thought was a deep sleep. No such chance – the cunt started raving in his sleep. He was knocking some shapes out like there was no tomorrow. I tried to ignore his sleep-dancing but after ten minutes I turned and gave him a dig in the ribs which seemed to work a treat.

Next day, Ravy-Gravy woke up and was holding his ribs, mumbling that he must have fell over. If yesterday was anything to go by then today should be fun.

Day 2 – Gay Day!

The plan for today was to meet poolside at 11.00am. Everyone was a little tender from yesterday's exploits but by 11.15am we were all there and back on the piss. Stinky had to wear his 'mankini'... His balls struggled to stay in place all day. His best men, showing solidarity, went out and bought the tightest thongs known to man. A few others joined in, most notably Casper, who came back wearing a tight leopard skin number.

A fat bloke sat on a sun-lounger watched the goings on with a little more interest than he should have. It was Ludwig, a German who ended up tagging along with us. Casper walked to the bar hand in hand with Ludwig, his thong nearly cutting him in two. He then slipped his hand on Ludwig's arse as they walked to the bar. Ludwig returned the compliment by slipping his hand on to Casper's bare bum-cheek. We all creased up as they both disappeared into the bar with a hand on each other's arses... Gay Day had begun.

We decided to go out to the bars, watch the impending Portsmouth v Cardiff FA Cup Final then go back, get changed and go straight back out. It was like Gay Pride day as thonged-up blokes walked hand in hand along San Antonio front. We settled in a bar there and treated a couple of little shirt-wearing Blades fans to a standing ovation and a chorus of 'The Greasy Chip Butty' as they walked past with their ever-so-proud parents. Bare arses were slapped so hard they bled as we walked down to a cockney bar to watch the match. A few of the lads were rattling as they had had no drugs and were on the lookout for some staying-awake gear, or 'marching powder' as football lads call it. We settled in the cockney bar and awaited kick-off. Chip returned from the bar clutching a load of sweets.

'Fuckin' hell, Chip... I haven't seen one of those in ages, I thought they'd stopped making them, sherbet fountains, they bring back childhood memories,' I said as he dipped his liquorice into the sherbet. It was then it came to me, my mind being like it is and all that. I went to the bar and got some paper; discreetly, I made a paper wrap and asked Chip to pass me the sherbet fountain. I poured a bit of the sherbet in and neatly folded it up. All the rest of the lads were playing pool so no one knew what was going off except around five of us.

'Watch this,' I said as I followed Kenny into the bogs. I brushed past him as he stood having a piss and went into the cubicle. I quickly sniffed up as loud as I could so Kenny would hear me, then exited, deliberately wiping my nose in front of Ken as I passed him. He followed me out and went straight over to Titus. I sat down and waited... The bait had been thrown in so I waited for the bite. This fisherman didn't have long to wait as Titus was straight over.

'You got some sniff?'

'Yeah, I got it off a cockney inside the bar... Want to try some?'

'Too right! How much is it?'

'Sixty euros.'

Titus beckoned Kenny and off they shot into the bogs. Out of interest I had to sneak in and listen to the events. They were both locked inside the cubicle as I heard the first sniff, then another, so I quickly went and sat down with the four lads who knew what was going off.

'Don't fuckin' laugh... Keep a straight face when they come back,' I demanded.

Titus sidled up at the side of me and discreetly slipped the wrap back into my hand. 'Cheers, Steve... Who's selling it?'

'Sit down and I'll sort you some out. What do you reckon? Do you think it's good gear?' I asked, keeping a straight face.

'Yeah, sound,' Titus said while returning to his seat with Kenny and the rest of the lads, who were all oblivious to the events. I asked Chip to give me the rest of the Sherbet Fountain. As we looked over, the two numpties were telling everyone else about the pretend coke they'd had. I headed straight over and asked them for 60 euros. As they fumbled in their pockets, I pulled out the sherbet and emptied the contents out of the tube in a massive line on the table in front of them.

'Here, get that down you, it's what you've just had,' I said as everyone cracked up. They both just sat there with daft expressions on their half-smiling faces. The landlord was collecting glasses and had seen what was going off.

''ERE, no drugs in here... Fackin' snorting off my tables, you're taking the fackin' piss,' he shouted, then turned away laughing.

There was still time for Burt Bacharach to nearly kill himself as he leant back in his plastic chair, only for it to buckle and send him crashing backwards down a set of steps and slashing his arms with broken glass in the process. It was getting to the stage where everyone was getting too pissed, so after the match we went back to the apartments to get changed and put an end to Gay Day.

Ten of us and a football went to the pool and decided to have a game of keep ball, 5 v 5, baldies v hairies. I'm receding slightly so went with the baldies! We sorted the rules, ten unopposed thrown passes was a goal. Everyone was drunk after the 12 pints we'd each had. I dived in, as did everyone else. Dicko, being Dicko, dived in the shallow end and smashed his nut on the bottom; he came back up completely *dazed, blood running from his forehead, nose and chin!*

We started the game and the baldies quickly built up an impressive 2-0 lead with Biscuit-Mack having a fine game for the baldies even though he's trying to hang on to his ever-decreasing hairline, which looks like a fanny bush on his nut, hence the nickname 'Minge Fringe'. I'd swallowed too much water and was feeling a little rough. Then the ball was thrown to me, I tried to fend off Dicko who was all over me like a rash trying to get a hand on the ball, and I swallowed another gobful of water. God, I'm gonna be sick, I thought. I know, I'll spew on Dicko. I immediately turned and Ralphed up on him. His face was a picture as I power-spewed on him. He backed off with a look of horror on his face. Ludwig was still poolside and chuckling away to himself as he watched events unfold. He must have been thinking, ze fookin' English are crazy!

After five minutes we were all knackered and the baldies had won 3-0 plus one sick assault to nil. As we headed to the showers, Ludwig walked alongside Casper, who was still in his leopard skin thong.

'You have good body,' Ludwig said, looking admiringly at Casp. We all laughed... Casp had pulled!

Shitted, shaved and shampooed we all met back up and went back on it. As you can imagine, the drinking binge soon caught up with us and it wasn't long before we were falling about all over the shop again. A few lightweights (Wednesday fans) couldn't take it and retired early, leaving the rest of us to represent Sheffield. We did so in style with a fine rendition of 'The Greasy Chip Butty'. Ludwig had tagged along and you could see on his face that he thought we were all crackers, as a few of the lads took it in turns to suck at a cylinder of laughing gas. I was creased up as the lads who inhaled it fell about laughing hysterically. I don't know what chemical is in that shit but one thing I do know – it fuckin' works.

A few of the lads had found a sketchy geezer who was selling the disco biscuits (Es) and they indulged. I'm not one for that shit but each to their own. Titus walked up to me with a wrap of coke in one hand and two Es in the other. 'Cheese 'n' biscuits,' he said with a manic smile on his face. It was going to turn into a mad one.

Then as we walked across a square that had a few fountains in it, Miffer ran and jumped into the air and came back down in dive mode straight into a fountain. The only trouble was it was empty and he hit the concrete bottom with an almighty slap. It had about a four-foot drop and we all looked at each other with a shocked expression. It would have done many a good man in but Miffer is made from kryptonite. He was totally off his trolley on the

disco biscuits and didn't know what fuckin'
day it was.

Twelve of us headed for the Eden nightclub.
We hadn't even got a drink when one of the lads
came over and said Miff had been thrown out.
Me and Dicko went to see if we could get him
back in. Miff was in the street with a manic look
on his face and was gurning like there was no
tomorrow. I asked the bouncers if he could come
back in and we'd babysit him.

'Look, mate, he's just asked us if we've got
some Class As as he's come in and then gone and
got his cock out so, no, he's not coming back in,'
the bouncer said, half-smiling.

'Miff!' I shouted through the entrance door of
the club. Miff came running over, thinking he was
back in.

'You can come back in, mate, but only if you
can find a straitjacket to wear... See you later,' I
said, laughing as we walked back into the club.
When we left two hours later, Miff was still
outside and still off his head. I'm glad I don't
bother with that shit, I thought, as we made our
way back.

Ibiza 2008 – the best laugh I've had in ages.
Quality, lads.

3
TROUBLE NEVER FAR AWAY

I don't know whether it's just bad luck but trouble never seems too far away from me. If truth be known, I've had enough of all the shit and just want to settle down and get on with the rest of my days in peace. I'm 43 now and it's an age where you should start to relax and do things 43-year-olds do.

'BOY GORGE TO THE RESCUE – FLATTENED'

A strange front-page headline in the *Sheffield Star*, but it was a strange night all right. Shotgun, Mitch, Richard and myself had been up Handsworth for a night out. We were well oiled by the end of the night and decided to get a taxi into town and go to a club. We set off walking. Sheffield was – and still is, for that matter – one shit place for taxis, so we'd walked right into Darnall which is a good mile from Handsworth. Darnall is a tough area and home to some very tasty United lads. Last orders had been called and the pubs were turning out and the streets were quite busy. I walked in front trying to flag a cab. As we walked past the Wellington pub, Shots shouted me back: 'Steve, I think it's going to kick off.'

I walked back, only to see Richard squaring up to a well-set geezer dressed as a sailor. Without further ado, the sailor steamed into Rich and they fought each other. I was just wondering what the fuck was going on as the two rolled about on the floor when the sailor's mates, all in fancy dress, came charging across the road. As they jumped over the crash barrier towards us, I said, 'Leave them, it's one on one.'

No chance. A huge geezer dressed as Boy George headed towards me but I didn't think he was going to do anything. Think again! Mr 'Do You Really Want to Hurt Me?' hurt me by crashing his huge forehead into my face. I reeled back, senses gone in the wind.

It was a good job the Wellington's wall was behind me as I would have fallen over, but I backed up on to it. The rest of them steamed into us, including some fuckin' goddamn crazy women. I looked up through watering eyes just in time to see Boy George coming to finish me off. I don't know where I got it from, but I threw one of the best punches I've ever thrown – Bingo – right on the button. I suppose it's the survival instinct: when you're in big trouble you seem to dig deeper into your reserves. Anyhow, Boy George was sent reeling with a great punch. He went crashing to the tarmac. It was mad, as fists were flying everywhere and it was a confused situation. I joined my pals who were backing up the path. A woman dressed as a witch tried to glass me then hit me on the head with a stick. Boy George was getting to his feet so I half-volleyed him back down again. I thought it best that he didn't rejoin the action!

They cornered me and I received a few punches as I struggled free. My 'Aqua' jacket was ripped right down the side. Richie was on his arse so we went to help, more punches were thrown and the fight eventually started to calm. Two blokes with them were laid out on the footpath. I suggested we fucked off before the OB came. We walked down Stanniforth road towards Attercliffe. I knew that we needed to get the fuck out of there but we still couldn't get a taxi.

Looking back, we were stupid to stick together and walk down a main road after a major off but we just thought it would be a case of them and us going home. As we got into Attercliffe, though, a copper pulled up and jumped out towards us. 'What's happened to you lads?' he asked.

'Nowt,' I said, just as Rich said we'd been jumped by some pikeys. I had blood all over my face and my jacket ripped off; Richie was covered in blood from a bad nosebleed. It was pretty obvious we'd been bang at it.

'There's been a serious assault in Darnall; I don't suppose you lads know anything about it?' the bizzy asked. Another cop car pulled up and asked if we would hang around a few minutes until the assaulted man came to identify us. We obliged, knowing we had no fucking option. Two bizzy vans pulled up and we were taken to the back of one. The doors opened and there sat Boy George absolutely covered in blood and holding on to a blood-red bandage. He went demented when he saw us and it took about five police to hold him back.

'I'll kill you bastards, you're dead, you're fucking dead!'

All right, we get your drift, I thought. I was a bit puzzled, though, as to where all that claret had come from. OK, I'd punched him and gave him a dig with my size nines but he was covered head to toe in blood and his head was bandaged, all very Terry Butcher. He was still going shit-pot crazy as the cops tried to restrain him.

The bizzies bundled us into another van and took us to Attercliffe nick. In the station, the usual pre-lock-up ritual went on. Then before we were taken to the cells, a copper said, 'There's no point you all taking the rap, boys... This is a serious assault so you'd better own up to whoever did it.'

The usual silence filled the air. Rich and I were put in one cell and Shots and Mitch in the other. In the cell laid asleep across the only bench was a huge Pakistani bloke. I tried to wake him from his slumber but he was away with the fairies. I rolled him off the bench and on to the floor, and it was then the smell hit us – he'd shat himself. Quick as a flash, I'm ringing the bell while gipping up. The custody officer sauntered down after five minutes.

'What's up, lads, you've only just come in and, no, you're not having a drink.'

'Fuck a drink, this dirty twat's shit himself, it hums in here,' I pleaded.

'Tough shit,' he said, walking away laughing. We sat down; it was the first time Rich had been locked up.

'Our old man's going to kill me,' he sighed.

'Fuck me, Rich, your old man's gonna kill me an' all,' I replied. We sat trying to work out how Boy George had ended up like he had.

'I've twatted him, Rich, but that's not a punch that's

done that…' It then dawned on me he may have banged his head as he fell. The fat Pakistani awoke from his slumber and tried to get to his feet but only succeeded in falling and banging his head on the closet. Blood ran down his face and he was mumbling away like a good 'un. Once again, I rang the bell and as all you who have been locked up will know, the plod don't exactly come a'running, do they?

We'd all been put in a cell together with these words ringing in our ears: 'That man's had 38 stitches in his head… This is serious. You'd better get together and sort out who did what. You've got ten minutes to get it sorted.'

I now knew that it wasn't me that had done it, unless Edward Scissorhands was some relation. Rich thought I'd done it but said he'd admit to fighting so we could get out.

By this time it was Sunday morning and we were charged with malicious wounding and let out at 10.15am. Our Sunday football team were four players light. Rich was remanded in custody and we all had to be in court at 10.00am on Monday morning. Later that morning, I had the unenviable task of phoning Rich's dad, Graham Shaw. He was a good friend of the family's and was a straight-talking bloke.

I loved the fella but I knew he would blame me as he knew I was into the bollocks at football. When I spoke to him he gave me a right round of fucks. I couldn't really get a word in but I could understand his anger. I felt like saying it was your Rich that started it all and what did you want me to do, leave him to get hammered? But I didn't.

On Monday morning I went to work and had to tell the gaffer that Rich wouldn't be in today and that I had to go at half-eight as we were both in court. He wasn't impressed at all and later that week I was warned that if I got involved in any more trouble I'd be sacked.

In court, Rich was brought in from the cells. He looked as rough as a bear's arse.

'Stand up for the judge,' the clerk said. Enter Neil's (the lad from Laver's) magistrate mother, the same woman who I'd drunkenly told about the buzz of football violence over a coffee at Neil's. I knew it was going to be an adjournment so it didn't perturb me too much. The clerk went through all the rigmarole. I was stood nearest the judge as our names were read out.

'Are you Richie Harry Shaw?' It was the first time we'd heard each other's middle names so we smiled at Richie.

'Are you Alan Edwin Noble?' Again, a smile at Edwin. Then it came. 'Are you Mitcham Frank Spencer?'

That was it... We all cracked up. Fuckin' Frank Spencer – Ooooh, Betty! What was his mother thinking? Mitch just stood staring ahead with his tongue pushing on the side of his cheek. We got bollocked off the clerk who rattled on about contempt of court. Thank fuck I didn't have a middle name when they asked.

We were bailed. Later, I found out the truth about what happened to the bloke who'd got 38 stitches. In the fracas, Mitch had run around the corner and returned with a full crate of milk bottles. Unbeknown to us, Boy George had copped the crate over the head. Mitch reluctantly stuck his hand up to it and the charges against Richie and the rest of us were dropped. Mitch got 100 hours' Community Service in court and that evening's *Sheffield Star* front-page headline was 'BOY GEORGE TO THE RESCUE – FLATTENED'.

OLD BIDDY BURGLAR, BASHED

As I've said, trouble seems to attract itself to me far too easily. For instance, there's only me that can get involved in a load of bollocks just going to the pictures with our new neighbours.

Around 14 years ago, we'd just moved to our new home after five years in a two-bedroom town house, and with one child here and another one planned, we moved into a three-bedroom house. We didn't know anyone but my daughter Stacey made friends with a girl called Amy who lived two doors up from us. Debbie – my wife – and Amy's mum got on pretty well and we decided to have a night out with our new neighbours.

We went to the cinema and then popped into the local for a couple of pints. In the pub's kids' room sat a bloke I knew vaguely; he was with a few pals and a couple of women. I say I knew him but that doesn't mean to say I had time for him. He was, and probably still is, a cunt. He made his living as one of nature's lowest life forms – by robbing old people. A lot of the lads I drank with knew him and he sometimes flitted around in the same company as me. I'd never had a single word with him as I knew what he got up to.

It was just before Christmas and he'd been bragging about taking £8,000 off some old dear. He used to get dressed up as a gas man and blag his way into old people's houses and rob them; in short, he was scum.

Anyhow, he and his mates were showing off in the kids' room, chucking bottles about and generally being a pain in the arse. It was nothing to do with me but I knew the landlord pretty well and he looked a bit on edge. At last orders, we got up to walk the short journey home, and I went to point Percy at the porcelain before I left. Mid-piss, the landlord ran in saying, 'Steve, you'd better get outside... Your wife's in trouble.'

My wife's in trouble? She's never in all her life been in any kind of trouble. I ran out of the pub to see my neighbour being attacked by two blokes and Debbie struggling with two women. I ran over and pulled the OAP burglar off my neighbour. He started giving it the, 'Who the fuck are you?' I explained that I knew him and that I knew he was a cunt. He started getting aggressive so I held his arms by his side. He started giving me grief about what he was going to do to me. Then the old red mist came down. Bam – cop for that, I planted my head into his face, the force behind it was for all the old folk that this vermin had robbed. He went down like a sack of spuds.

The other two came at me and there was a lot of dancing and screaming going off. Out of the corner of my eye, I saw 'Cunt' staggering back to his feet and heading to the boot of his car so I shrugged off my attackers and ran over. I thought if he gets a weapon out of his boot someone could get seriously hurt. I pummelled him into his boot. The others in turn pummelled me but I was prioritising my work.

My neighbour was neither use nor ornament but that's no slight on him as he was just a normal bloke caught up in something totally alien to him. I did one around the pub and collected my wife and neighbours and hurried home. My mum was babysitting and, as Debbie told her we had been in trouble, I grabbed a claw hammer from the garage, then returned to the pub. They were still outside the pub kicking the doors as the landlord had locked them out.

I went up to The Cunt, his mouth covered in blood. He'd actually lost all four front teeth, courtesy of my butt. He turned on me and started shouting that I was a dead man and that he was spending £1,000 on having me shot. 'I'll find out who you are and you're dead,' he screamed.

'That £8,000 you stole off an old lady... Burning a hole in your pocket is it, you twat?' I countered. He was taken aback at that; it knocked him off his stride. He didn't know me and was perplexed as to how I knew he had robbed the money. The landlord shouted over that the police were on their way. So he and his cronies jumped into two cars and left.

'Thanks, Steve,' the landlord said.

'It's not over yet... Wait until tomorrow when he's sober. He's copping it.'

The next day, 'Cunt' went around to two of my pals' houses and asked if they knew a lad – stocky, balding, rough-shaven, handsome (well, maybe not the last bit!). My pals knew straight away it was me and told him who I was. He still insisted I was getting done in. My pals phoned and warned me. I knew where he lived but I don't go to houses; he'd got kids after all.

A few days later, my worried wife greeted my return home from work with 'I thought you said that bloke wouldn't want to know. He's been in the pub threatening to come for you with a gun.'

It transpired that the husband of one of Debbie's best friends, who was a regular at the pub it had happened in, had told his missus who, in turn, had told my wife. I was 'on one'. I jumped in the car and went around to 'Cunt's' house; see, I don't go to houses. As I screeched up outside his home, he clocked me and ran and closed the curtains. I banged on the door. 'Get out here, you fuckin' pig, I'll fuckin' smash your noodle in.'

I waited but he wouldn't come out to dance. I went to see the landlord of the pub, who informed me that it was a load of shit; the bloke hadn't been in at all, adding that he was barred for life. I was fuming; I'd been around to someone's house on the strength of a bullshitter.

About two weeks later, I walked into the Golden Keys in Westfield. All the lads were playing cards and I sat down with them. There was a strange atmosphere as I made small talk. Something was amiss. 'Cunt' was at the end of the bar and I hadn't seen him. I got up and went for the bastard. He's shouting, 'Steve, I don't want no bother,' as he ducked under the hatch and behind the bar.

'You've already got some,' I snarled.

Billy the landlord tried to force him back out, saying he had to go and face the music. To cut it short, he left the pub out the other doorway and later moved away from the area.

Sheffield's Westfield estate has more than its fair share of smack rats, and the rabbit-warren setup of the estate means the police struggle to get any results. I fuckin' hate dirty needle diggers. To me, anyone peddling smack should be jailed for at least ten years. It fucks me off when you read the court review. There's smackheads caught with heroin getting a smaller fine than someone with a bit of puff.

Around 13 years ago, we had our house burgled. My wife had returned home with my then two-year-old son and my seven-year-old daughter. They thought I'd come home from the pub early because the lights were on in the bedroom. My daughter ran upstairs shouting 'Daddy' only to be screamed back down by my wife who'd seen the video and SEGA Mega Drive in the middle of the room and had sussed out what had happened.

I got a call at the pub and ran home. All my family were in a right state. As the CID went through everything I wasn't listening; I wanted to get out of the house and smash the first smack-head I saw. The CID bloke knew me through Arnold Laver's – his name was Gordon Simmonite, and he'd once played professional football for Wednesday, if you can call Wednesday professional. He's a sound enough bloke, though. His parting words were, 'Steve, don't do anything stupid.'

As soon as they pulled off our front, I got my mountain bike out, tucked a baseball bat into the back of my jeans and told my wife I'd see her in five years. Someone had to pay for my family's upset, especially for my daughter Stacey, who took over a year to settle back into her own bedroom. I pedalled off towards the Westfield estate.

Now, a lot of the smack-rats around there are just young deadbeats. I wanted a name but I couldn't go around smashing young lads in, I'd get called a bully. So I decided that the oldest smack-head there was the one I'd go for. He was in his late twenties and had a younger brother who was bang at the robbing.

When I screeched up on the Westfield shop fronts, two smack-heads known to me were just coming out of the chippy. I pulled the bat out even though I knew that they weren't responsible, as I'd seen them earlier.

'You two, come here,' I demanded but they just dropped their chips and legged it. Both have since lost their lives through smack. Just then, Scratch came running around the corner in just his shorts. Debbie had rung him and told him to try and talk some sense into me. He did, but I wasn't letting it go.

I found out where the big smack-head lived. While I was waiting at the end of his road one night, he came around the corner. He sussed me and legged it into the house. His mam came out and gave me the usual: 'Get off my property or I'll phone the police.'

I didn't realise he lived with his mum. So I walked back down the path saying, 'Yes, love, I'll get off your property because I've got respect for other people's homes, not like them two dirty twats you've got for sons.'

I knew my time would come, and one day it did. I was walking to the Mill pub to meet my pals when two smack-heads were walking towards me. Another lad was walking backwards with his hood up. I could see by the expression on their faces that the lad walking backwards was big smack-rat. I grabbed a hold of him and – Bingo – it was him. I punched him to the floor then smashed him over the head with the carrier bag full of tinnies he was carrying. The other two protested but hadn't even got the balls to help him as I told them if they came one step nearer me then they were having it.

Looking back, I don't think any of the Westfield smack-heads had anything to do with my house but, to me, if you do dirty things then dirty things will haunt you. They all piss in the same pot.

About two months later, I had a laugh walking home from the pub. I bumped into a well-known smack-head who was totally off his face. He came up to me trying to

76

talk but he was that monged out he just slurred. I grabbed him and lifted him clean off his feet then threw him over a four-foot wall. I can still see him now bouncing down that garden path. I walked home chuckling away to myself.

Not all lads on the Westfield are bad 'uns and I've got a lot of pals on there who are just working lads who like a drink and a smoke. One lad who used to drink in the same circles as me was a lad called the 'Quiet 'Un'. He was a brickie by trade and a bit of a character. One day the local minimarket had been burgled by the Westfield hole-in-the-wall gang. They'd actually spent all night chiselling their way through the minimarket's wall and robbed all the drink. So next day, the owner asked the 'Quiet 'Un' if he'd rebuild the wall. He did exactly that but put hardly any cement in the mix then told the lads who'd robbed it that they could go back and the wall would just push in. That's exactly what they did, so the shop got robbed two nights running!

ENGLAND V ITALY 1997

I think there are only a few people could end up in a free-for-all after a night out with their club's players. We'd arranged to go to Hotshots to watch the Italy v England match from which England needed a point to qualify for France '98. On the same night, Naseem Hamed was fighting Jose Badillo next door at the Sheffield Arena. Also on the bill was 'Cwith' Eubank, whose fight with Joe Calzaghe was a mouth-watering clash. The plan was to watch the match in Hotshots then go to the Arena next door for the boxing.

While on the subject of Hamed, he's the only geezer I know that can manage to get his own city's people to dislike him. The man's arrogance knows no bounds.

On the flip side, it's great to have another world champion not only from Sheffield but from the area where I live. Clinton Woods is everything Naz isn't. Clinton has a massive heart and has improved over the years and that's mainly because he hasn't changed a jot as a person in the decade or so I've known him. He's a great geezer, down to earth and even despite his blue-and-white persuasion I am chuffed to bits for the bloke and his mentor Dennis Hobson, whom I've also known for a long time.

Mitch Ward, who played for the 'red-and-white wizards' at the time and is a good pal of mine, arranged to meet up with us, along with the rest of United's players.

Hotshots was a massive bowling alley with around 20 American pool tables. When we arrived, quite a few of the Blades players were playing pool. We went over and Mitch introduced us to the few players who didn't know us. One of these players was teetotal (not that it's a sin) and I got the impression that the other players saw him as a bit strange. I'd also got quite pally with a lad called Mark Beard who was a former Millwall player who'd signed for the Blades. He was one sound lad with a lovely family and I often went out with him.

The bar at Hotshots was rammed and the place itself was chocker with England fans awaiting the kick-off. We were doubling the drinks up at the bar to save time.

It was my round and the bar was four-deep. I noticed one United player (I'll not name him for legal reasons) getting served; it was queue-jump time.

'Get us four lagers, mate,' I asked. He did, but passed me a Coke first and said, 'Have a taste of that and see if it tastes strange.'

It was frothing away like some brew that Frankenstein would drink. When it had settled down I had a little sip. 'It tastes a bit strange but it's sweet enough.'

He said that this drink was for the teetotaller.

As we walked back to the area where the United players were, he told me that he'd spiked the drink with some coke (the sniffing type) and some whizz.

'You can't do that... He's an international, for fuck's sake! What if he gets tested?' I reasoned.

'Fuck him,' came the Blades player's reply. He laughed as the guy took a drink then went to play his pool shot none the wiser. All my pals and the United players were playing 'killer' for a fiver a go. There was only me, Dane Whitehouse, Don Hutch and Bally left in and there was a good £100 on the table. Dane then missed so he was out then I was left with a terrible shot so, nodding Bally's way, I attempted a double that left Don with an impossible shot and Bally potted to win.

We didn't see it as cheating, just a way of getting a bit of our season-ticket money back from the overpaid grabbers. We settled down to watch a fine, spirited England performance which gained a 0–0 draw, and thus qualification for France '98. With five minutes to go, the place was electric as everyone was roaring England on.

Mitch nudged me. 'Look at that twat,' he said pointing over at the player whose drink had been spiked, who was stood on a table with eyes like saucers singing, 'Eng-er-land... Eng-er-land...' with all his might. He even knocked out a couple of aeroplane moves that he famously did when he hit the onion bag. He was off his nut.

Incidentally, when the big screen showed police baton-charging England fans, quite a few nuggets surged towards the screen and started throwing bottles at it, like it was going to have an effect over there!

After the match, we headed off to the boxing. The Blades players, being the big-time Charlies that footballers are, were sat ringside while us paupers were stuck up in the heavens. On the under-card, Sheffield's Ryan Rhodes had just finished his fight and we were having a bit of banter with a few Barnsley lads we knew that were sat around ten rows in front of us. Being completely pissed, none of us had noticed around 15 well-dressed lads sat bang behind us. Then, just as Raggy was shouting about Barnsley getting run by United, a voice from the back piped up, 'You weren't mouthing off when Birmingham ran you all over the other week.'

It was like, 'I beg your pardon?' as we turned to face these lads. There were eight of us sat together and that included Bally's dad and his best mate, Frank. Raggy started arguing with the lads behind us. Raggy was five seats on from me and he gave me the look. I gave him the 'I'm in' look back.

That was it – we waded into them. I punched one over the seats then grabbed another and punched him back into his chair. There were a few punches thrown back but we soon had them spilling over the rows. In less than a minute, we'd steamed these lads right out of the area. It was then I realised that half of Sheffield arena were watching the action, including all the United players.

Raggy told me afterwards that the lads were Wednesday. We sat back down and watched the rest of the boxing with 15 spare seats behind us. Later, we went on to a club where Mitch told me that Fjortoft was off his tits at the show and was shadow-boxing in his seat.

Speaking of Raggy, we have been in a few scrapes together over the years; we've shared a friendship that has lasted two decades so here's a few tales about him from over the years.

PETER, PETER, PUMPKIN EATER

One Monday morning at work, I checked out the BBC website – the Blades Business Crew one, not the TV lot. There had been some trouble outside the Casbah nightclub in town. I read that one Wednesday lad boasted that Father Christmas had been dropped in the mêlée. I knew immediately who Father Christmas was – it was my mate Rag. Raggy's beard has turned grey over the years but it's not through lack of sleep, I'll tell you. The cunt could sleep on a washing line.

I phoned Raggy up straight away. 'Were you in the Casbah on Saturday?'

'Yes, I ended up fighting with Wednesday.'

'I know, it's on the Internet... They've put that Father Christmas got dropped.'

He laughed and told me what had happened. Raggy had gone in with a lad called Ian. Ian was a retired Blade hoolie and a good mate of mine and Raggy's; he's also game as a badger by the way. Inside the club were around 12 Wednesday lads and Raggy started arguing with one. The challenge was on.

The head bouncer – Clem – is well known to me and Raggy. As Raggy and Ian stood outside waiting, all the Wednesday lads were trying to get out. Clem was holding them back when Raggy said, 'Let 'em out.' Ian and Raggy had a right pop but the odds were stacked and Raggy got put on his arse, no disgrace. Unbeknown to Wednesday, Tap, Stiles and a couple of other United lads were just coming out of Charles Street (a club just around the corner from the Casbah). They'd seen the scuffling and had gone for a nosey only to realise that it was Raggy and Ian at it with a dozen Wednesday men.

Tap and the rest steamed in and Wednesday didn't fancy it now. They legged it up the road taking their belts off and turning briefly before going on the run again. By the way, Wendy lads – you're supposed to use the buckle end of the belt, not hold on to it. It's kinky the other way, though, I suppose.

One Friday night, Raggy, myself and a lad called Dave went down London Road for a drink. We were well pissed by last orders so Raggy and Dave went in the Italian restaurant.

I'm not a big lover of Italian food, so I went further down London Road to the Indian. I knew the owners and had done them a few favours, so I always got a freebie. They sat me in a private booth and I tucked in. Around 20 minutes later, as my chicken madras arrived, so did Raggy and Dave, who both plonked themselves opposite me. It all went tits up from there onwards. Raggy, being the greedy cunt he is, started pinching food off my plate.

'Carry on, cunt, and the next time you're getting this,' I said, brandishing my fork. Sure enough, Raggy dipped in again so I tried to stab him in the back of his hand with the fork. He managed to get his hand out of the way so I stabbed a piece of chicken and flicked it at Raggy. It hit him on the head and dropped to the floor.

Dave and I laughed as madras sauce ran down our mate's forehead. With that, he leant forward and tipped the whole plate into my lap. He jumped up to make his escape, but I went after him brandishing the fork with madras all over me bollocks. I tried to stab Raggy in the back with my fork but he managed to get away, knocking the table over in his haste. The waiters were going mad.

'I'm going to kill that cunt,' I shouted. Dave was by now in absolute hysterics. To make matters worse, I'd got a white, pure wool Valentino jumper on that I'd bought that day at a cost of £130. It was covered in curry.

'Sorry about this, Mohamed, but I've got to dash, mate... Let me know if I owe you anything for the damage,' I shouted as I stepped out on to London Road.

'Look at the state of me,' I said, standing with my arms outstretched and a big orange stain from my stomach to my balls. Dave couldn't talk for laughing. We both walked up London Road and, from around a corner, I saw a Sam Torrance-type face appear; it was Raggy hiding up an alleyway.

'He's there... don't let on we've seen him. I'm having that twat,' I said.

I quickened my stride as I headed towards his hideout. Raggy must have sussed me and he bolted. I ran after him. As we both sprinted up London Road, I was around 30 yards behind him as a taxi was dropping someone off outside the Tramway pub. Raggy tried to hurry them out and was just about in the taxi when I grabbed him. He'd got one foot inside the cab but had his back to me. He hung on for dear life as I tried to pull him out. I managed to get in a punch to the ear hole. He fell face down as I punched the back of his head. The punches were semi-hard, not meant to hurt too much but enough to leave a bit of bruising – he was my mate after all!

Just then, two young United lads who were walking down London Road eating chips spotted me grappling with Raggy.

'Steve, what's up mate?' Neil asked.

'Fuckin' Wednesday,' I said, nodding down at Raggy, who still had his face to the floor. With that, the pair of them dropped their chips and started booting Raggy, not knowing they were actually booting one of their own! Raggy was shouting, 'Drive off... Drive off...' as the boots flew in. It was then I thought enough was enough but I didn't let go of him until I'd pulled a Timberland boot from his foot. The taxi driver screeched off into the night, Raggy scrambling inside.

'Who was it?' asked one of the young Beebs.

'Raggy Tash,' I replied, laughing. They both picked their chips back up and walked off chuckling to themselves. Dave was by now totally gone; he was laid on the pavement laughing uncontrollably. Then I started; we must have been laughing for ten minutes solid. People were walking past and looking strangely at us as the pair of us fell about.

That wasn't the end of it, though. United were at home the next day and, as I walked in the Pheasant, Raggy came over and said, 'What happened last night, you twat? I'm black-and-blue.'

'Inter Milan fan are you? You've fuckin' ruined my jumper, you space cadet,' I snarled.

Raggy carried on. 'Have you got my Timberland?'

'What you on about?' I pretended I hadn't a clue.

To cut it short, I had Raggy going down to the lost property at the taxi rank outside the train station. He laughed off suggestions that he ought to buy me a new jumper.

Anyhow, around three weeks later, after I'd had my jumper cleaned professionally and it had come up as good as new, I thought I'd give Rag an early-morning call. I was at work on Saturday morning and I knew he had been out clubbing with his wife Minnie, so I thought I'd get 'em up at 7.00am. After 25 rings, Minnie groggily answered. I asked for Raggy. I heard him mumble to her, 'What's that cunt want?' then he came on the phone

'What the fuck do you want at this time in the morning?' he spluttered, sounding as rough as fuck.

'I've got some great news for you, mate... My jumper's come clean.'

'Well, I'm right fuckin' chuffed for you,' he said with more than a hint of sarcasm.

'No, you don't understand... You can have your Timberland back now.'

'You bastard, I've lobbed the other one away now.'

I put the phone down, pissing myself with laughter.

It's not the first time me and Rag have had a to-do in an Indian restaurant. Another night we'd gone in the Shapla Indian late one Friday. The previous week, Rag had fallen asleep in the same restaurant and I had to pay for his meal; not only that, I'd dropped him off at Woodthorpe on my way back to Mosborough. He got out, dug in his pocket and gave me about 38p towards the fare, which would cost at least a tenner. So I was fucked off at getting ripped off twice by the Sleepy One.

So we're in the Shapla and King Prawn Raggy is off to slumberland again as the bill's about to come. I did my best to wake him but he was having none of it. I thought 'fuck this for a game of soldiers' as the bill landed on the table. I grabbed a tablespoon and emptied the pepper pot on to it. Holding it under Rag's nose, I twanged it straight up his hooter as he was breathing in: perfect timing. Trouble was, there was that much pepper on the spoon that it went all over his face. I slapped him quite hard across the cheek. Rag woke with a start, not surprising really. He couldn't see, as his eyes were streaming due to the pepper and he was sneezing at an alarming rate. I rolled back in my seat laughing.

'What have you done to me you idiot? I can't see... Aaaaah-chooooooh,' he sneezed again. I asked for some money to pay and he told me to fuck off, he hadn't got any. Now there was no way I was paying for him again so I stood up and wrestled him to the floor, trying to get some dough out of his pocket. Rag was blinded and was still sneezing like mad but put up a good fight to stop me getting in his pockets. Water was pouring from his eyes and the other diners must have wondered what the hell was going on. The staff were trying to get me off him.

'Mr Steve, please stop,' they reasoned.

I managed to pull a bank card from his pocket and decided to march him to the cash machine. So after paying the bill, I grabbed Rag outside and arrested him by ramming his arm up his back. He sneezed all the way to the machine, moaning that he was blind and that I was a fuckin' lunatic. He then started pressing the wrong numbers, saying he couldn't see. It came to the third and last go before his card was swallowed, so I shoved his arm right up his back and managed to force his pin number out of him. He drew £100 out and threw it at me, then walked off in a huff. I managed to collect all £100 as it blew off in different directions and caught up with Rag outside the Music Factory. We went inside after Rag had calmed back down and his eyes had cleared a bit. We both laughed it off but he was still sneezing in the taxi home.

Another time I had a laugh at Rags was when I put his four Stone Island coats in the free ads along with various other items at bargain prices. I'd left his mobile number for the contact. I got a phone call a couple of days later.

'I don't suppose you know anything about me selling my Stone Island coats do you?'

'Nope.'

'I must have had 70 phone calls, you twat.'

It was a fair cop, I owned up. Trouble was, Minnie thought that was funny but I then got the blame six months later when various sex aids kept being delivered to their house. She pulled me up, demanding, 'Will you stop having vibrators sent to our house?' I pleaded innocent but she was having none of it. I later found out who it was – Tiler. So I've grassed him up now.

It's amazing me and Rag still get on. Another time when he got stitched up by me was in the Pheasant. Minnie was pregnant with their first child and was about due to give birth. Someone behind the bar shouted, 'Is Raggy in?' It was chocker with our lads as we had a Cat-A match, that being a team with a good firm. I looked for Rag but couldn't see him so I went to answer the phone. It was Minnie and she was hysterical. I looked around and saw Rag coming out of the bogs.

'Rag, quick, it's Minnie and she's in a right state,' I called out.

We both thought the worst; I stood next to him as he listened for few seconds, then he said, with more than a hint of worry in his voice, 'I'm coming home now.'

We both rushed outside with me asking what the matter was. He was jumping around in the road trying frantically to get a taxi.

'Rag for fuck's sake, is the baby OK?' I asked, concerned.

'It's... It's... Er...'

'It's fuckin' what?'

'It's the cat... It's got run over,' he said sheepishly.

'You fuckin' what? I'm dancing around in the middle of the road and all that's happened is your cat's got splattered?' I was relieved it wasn't a problem with the baby.

'Minnie's in a right state – don't tell anyone will you?'

'Of course not.'

I headed back into the Pheasant. All the lads had seen the commotion so came to ask me if everything was all right. I waited until I'd got a decent audience, then told everyone that Rag's cat had got run over. Everyone laughed – a bit harsh, but there you go.

Around an hour later, Rag walked back into the Pheasant. He was greeted with a chorus of 'meows' from about 100 lads. He caught my eye, and if looks could kill... I just raised my eyebrows and smiled.

Me and Rag have been in some right scrapes; he's game as fuck and we know we won't leave each other's side if it kicks off. Once he started fighting with a Wednesday lad in the Limit when the two off us went in one night. He was getting hammered at first but somehow got back on top. I'd got my back to the fight as I tried to keep it one-on-one as there were a lot of Wednesday hovering over the pair. One Wednesday lad then booted Rag in the face, and I immediately chinned him.

The lot went, three bouncers lobbed Raggy and the other geezer out and left me to battle my way free. I was throwing punches at an alarming rate as I back-pedalled. I got dropped a couple of times but jumped back up and steamed in. The Limit had some steep stairs leading down to it so I thought I'd get to the top so me and Rag could have a pop as Wednesday came up the stairs. Trouble was, as I got up there, I saw Rag curled up in the middle of West Street, with three Wednesday playing football with his body. I had to think quickly and get into them. I managed to side-wind one to the floor and Rag got to his feet and we waded into them and had them on the move until reinforcements had us on the back foot.

We were battered already so we stood and traded. The plod pulled up and everyone scattered. Me and Rag ran down a dark alley at the back of the Dickens pub. We stood under a streetlight to assess the damage. Both of us had black eyes and our shirts were hanging from our backs; Raggy was worse off than me but he'd copped for a pair of size-nines in the clock. In the taxi home, I asked what had started it.

He told me it was Minnie's best mate, a girl called Samantha. The Wednesday lad had hit her when he went out with her. Fuck me, I thought, I've been brawling because of a lass I hardly know. Saying that, I don't like women-beaters. I've never laid a finger on our Gert in all the 24 years I've known her; felt like it sometimes, but haven't. The lass whose honour Rag was defending by the way, well she'd been on the TV show *Blind Date* and was shown on the beach abroad with the bloke she'd chosen as her date. As they splashed around in the sea, she came out with this beaut: 'Why does the water taste salty?' Jesus, why is it we get shown up every time someone from Sheffield goes on the television?

DAD'S PRIDE AND JOY SMASHED

My dad had been made redundant from the steelworks and had an idea about starting up his own business. So he bought a shop with living accommodation in Sharrow which is within shouting distance of London Road. At first, I thought it would be sound as I always drank in town or on London Road so my weekly taxi bill would disappear. Debbie and I were saving for our own house and she had all but moved in with us.

My dad had never had a new car in his life but, because the business needed a biggish vehicle to bring stock from the warehouse, he went out to look for one. I couldn't believe it when he pulled up outside our house in a brand-new orange Lada Riva. I wasn't so much fucked off about it being a Lada but, as my dad showed it off to me, I said, 'Dad, you're a fuckin' nesbitt... What the fuck's that?' I pointed at the registration plate. It began 'SWF'.

'Oh, I hadn't noticed,' he said, scratching his bald platter.

'Hadn't noticed? What kind of Blade are you? Wait until I tell my grandad.' The reg-plate was only missing the C and he'd be driving around with our bitter blue-and-white rivals stuck out in front.

Anyhow, this car was Papa Bear's pride and joy. He'd only had it around a month when, one night when he'd gone down to the pub, I asked my mam if I could go out in it.

'Yes, but be careful,' were her famous last words.

I went and picked Waz and Doyley up and we went for a few drinks in town. After we came out of the Yorkshire Grey and walked towards the adjacent car park, five blokes were just getting in a white XR3i. They took the piss a bit as we were getting into the Lada.

'We'll race you,' one said sarcastically as he shut the door. Then, as I started to drive out of the car park, the XR3i came up behind me. It was that close to me that I couldn't see his headlights. I slowed as if to say, 'Back the fuck up,' but his car ended up nudging into the back of my dad's.

That was it; I jumped out – Bang, Bang, Bang – three punches into the driver's Shirley Temple. Waz was giving the passenger the same treatment on the other side. Because it was only a two-door car the lads in the back couldn't get out, so they were doing their nuts.

Then – Crash – Doyley had launched a brick straight through the windscreen. One of the lads in the back had grabbed my arm and was trying to bite me as I continued to pummel the driver. A straight-fingered poke in the eye saw him release his grip and I fell backwards on to the floor. The driver punched out the glass from his windscreen and slammed his car into reverse. I'd got to my feet and was thinking, yeah, go on, fuck off you numpty, when the driver suddenly put it into first and drove straight at me. I tried to get out of the way but the car clipped my trailing leg and I spun around, all Torvill and Dean.

I stopped spinning and hit the deck just in time to see the XR3i slam straight into my dad's pride and joy. 'Fuck... fucky fuck... fuck...' it drove off with Waz and Doyley in hot pursuit and me sat on my arse, head now in my hands. My dad's going to go fucking ballistic, I thought.

To make matters worse, as if they possibly could, was the fact that the driver's door had been left open in my haste to get out, and it was now a crumpled mound of steel stuck on the side of the car. I drove home with a big hole in the side where the door should have been and a lump of twisted metal stuck on the car.

Luckily, when I got home my dad was still out and my mum, supportive as ever, hatched a plan after I'd told her what had happened. Let's just say I was very grateful to an old lady neighbour who came out of her house and told police she had seen two lads crash straight into the car while it was parked on our front: a quality piece of lying! I reckon my dad knows but, to this day, he hasn't said anything about it. So, Dad, after all these years, I'm sorry, mate.

Those three years down at Sharrow were the worst years I had while living with Mama and Papa. Our family life was nonexistent, mostly because the shop was an 'open-all-hours' setup. We couldn't even have tea together without eight interruptions, due to people coming into the shop. I hated it and spent most of my time in the sanctuary of my bedroom, which was that far up the house that Chris Bonnington would have got a nosebleed getting up to it.

When it was windy, the carpet used to lift six inches from the floor and it was like fucking Moscow up there.

Family life was piss poor. On top of that, we were burgled three times. Our trusty dog Casper had slept through it all but not a lot fazed him so no blame there and the cheeky burgling twats had even made themselves a sandwich and cup of tea while they screwed us. My car was constantly being vandalised and I ended up in trouble with a few Asians who I later found out had committed at least one of the break-ins.

It should have been heaven, really; London Road was a two-minute walk away and I was within touching distance of my spiritual home, beautiful downtown Bramall Lane. Debbie and I were saving for our first home and I couldn't get away quick enough.

Things went from bad to worse when one person who I respected and loved so much died – my grandad. I came home from work one day and, through his tears, my dad told me. I was absolutely devastated and I'm welling up now as I type. He was the man who had taken me to Bramall Lane week-in, week-out when I was a pup. He loved United like no one could ever love the club; he was so biased towards our team and we could lose 5-0 but it wasn't the red-and-white wizards' fault, no – the ref, the other team kicked us all over, anything to make an excuse up, that was my grandad, but now he was gone. I couldn't face going to the funeral, something I'll always regret, but, at that time, I had never been to one before and the thought of seeing my grandad buried horrified me.

Eventually, we found a perfect two-bedroom home in the south of Sheffield. This area was always going to be my first choice as I'd been brought up at that end of town and I've lived up there ever since. We married when we were both 24 and had a great day; I ruined the night late on, though, by not consummating the marriage, due to being absolutely shit-faced. I'd only had around six pints by 9.00pm but then I hit the Southern Comfort or, as I was calling it later on that night, Couthern Somfort. I supped a full bottle and then half a bottle of Pernod. I was history and have no recollection of anything later that night apart from shedding a tear or two because my grandad was not at the wedding.

The next morning I awoke to the fear that I was blind in one eye. I wasn't – it was a piece of ham stuck over my eyelid. I'd been sick all night and Debbie had been awake, as she thought I was going to choke to death on our first night of wedlock. I bet if she knew then what she knows now she would have let me choke all right.

Twelve months later I was a dad for the first time. My daughter Stacey was born and my world was almost complete. As any dad will tell you, watching your children being born is the greatest and most emotional feeling in the world. I was still earning a bit of spendo at the woodyard so we kitted the house out with the newest and latest of everything.

My mum and dad got rid of the shop and moved to a house not far from me. Every time I went round to see them, my mum told me about a lad who lived opposite; his name was Robert and he was always asking my mum if I'd go for a drink with him.

After a couple of conversations with Robert on my mum's front, I agreed to go for a beer one Friday. I knew quite a few lads from around that way; some, like Patch, were big Blades and no strangers to a bit of dancing in our firm's name. On the Friday I'd arranged to go out with Rob, we entered the Mill pub, I got the drinks at the bar and we headed over to the poolroom. There, laid spark out, was Patch. He was blindo and was having a power nap.

After about 20 minutes, a few of the lads who were out there decided to relieve Patch of his jeans and pants. It was around that time that I wondered what I'd let myself in for. Patch laid there with his family jewels on display, then his mates decided to go a step further by buying a packet of salted peanuts and, one by one, inserting them under his foreskin. To be fair, it was a tad funny as the peanuts disappeared under his helmet's coat. His cock started looking like a cross between a Topic and a caveman's club. Two girls wandered up into the poolroom and soon strolled back out again when they saw Patch laid asleep with his lumpy knob on display.

Then some bright spark called Chick had the idea of putting a half peanut into his Jap's eye. This was going too far – they were salted peanuts after all. With a lot of concentration and a few calls for quiet to the laughing onlookers, he managed to tap the peanut into the end of Patch's piss pipe. This was the start of my friendship with a new bunch of lads; these lads weren't football hooligans but would get stuck in if they had to. They were what I call 'barmies' and every club has 'barmies' following them. Space cadets might be a better way of describing the lads I met and became friends with. There was Dave the Beckton butcher, who was actually a pal of mine. He got a five-stretch for chopping at his neighbour with a machete.

Another loon was Gaz, or 'Nicely Brown' as everyone called him, as that was his catchphrase; if you asked him anything he'd simply reply, 'Nicely bloody brown.' As mad as a March hare was Gary.

I'll never forget the first time I went out with Drifter (the gaffer at a new place of work). We'd just got to the Mill car park when Nicely Brown screeched up in a car.

'Yeee-haaaaah,' he screamed as he walked over, holding the straps on his dungarees like he was doing bit of line dancing.

'All right, Brown?' I asked.

'Nicely bleeding brown... Coppers are after me. I've just set fire to the landlord in the East End.'

He wasn't kidding either. He'd gone over there armed with a can of hairspray; as soon as the landlord turned his back, he lit the spray from the can and burnt the landlord's bouffant. Another time, I was in the Golden Keys and Brown was gutted because all the lads were off abroad on holiday in two weeks' time and he had no holidays left. Then out of the blue he just got up and said, 'I've got it,' then walked over to the brick wall and punched it with all his might. Sure enough, Brown's hand was shattered and he was off on holiday with the lads, even though he had to have a pot on for eight weeks.

Then I remember the time he walked into the pub looking like he'd done 12 rounds with Sugar Ray. Apparently, the night before, Matt, Knocker and Brown were off their faces back at Brown's house. They bet him he couldn't dive off the kitchen side into the wheelie bin they'd brought in the house without it falling over. Brown dived headfirst into the bin three times and made a right mess of himself.

I was once walking through Westfield with him and he had a rather large spliff on the go. As we walked round the corner, driving towards us very slowly, was a police car. Quick as a flash, Brown was in the road with his arm up in halt mode. He'd spotted the police car had a light out on the front.

'STOP! Officer, you have a light out... I think it's best if you get back to the station and get it fixed before you run someone over,' he said blowing cannabis into the cop car, obviously taking the piss big-time.

The two brothers Matt and Knocker are both fruitcakes. In fact, Knocker is proper radio rental and, although it's hard to believe, the following story is 100 per cent true. Knocker had been in the Gatecrasher club in Sheffield and pulled an absolute stunning 19-year-old. Knocker's the body-builder type, big square jaw and that. The week after, he'd arranged to meet the girl in his local saying that they could have a few drinks then go to town. The girl, bless her, wasn't to know that Knocker was as mad as fuck. On the night in question, quite a few of the lads sat around in the pub when the girl and her two pals came walking in. Not knowing anyone, they sat in the corner. Ten minutes later, in walked Matt, absolutely crying with laughter. He stood at the bar giggling away to himself. Everyone knew that he was up to something but didn't expect what was to follow. A dark figure appeared through the glass in the door.

Without further ado, in walked a large bloke with an all-in-one diver's suit on – mask, flippers and snorkel, the works. To top it off, he was soaked from head to foot with water running from his wetsuit, due to him diving in Matt's koi carp pond for added effect.

Everyone in the pub fell about laughing; they knew it was Knocker but the poor girls were sat, just staring at this Jacques Cousteau figure stood at the bar ordering a pint. Knocker got his pint and flopped his way over to the horrified girls. He squeezed his way in between them and proceeded to lift his mask to reveal himself to his date.

He then threw the full pint into his own face and asked his date where she fancied going tonight. Needless to say, she got up and left without him, leaving Knocker and the rest of the pub crying with laughter.

I was once driving through Eckington and saw this 'woman thing' leaning on the wall outside the Angel public house. It was Knocker dressed as a prostitute, fishnets and all. That's what we're dealing with around our way.

Another lad from around our neck of the woods is called Chris; he smokes the green stuff like it's going out of fashion. He only seems happy when he's stoned. Well, he's mates with Knocker and one day, not so long ago, Chris was in a local pub with Knocker and he's ready for home because he's fucked on the skunk. In desperation, he asked Knocker if he knew anyone who would sort him out some staying-awake powder.

'Leave it with me,' Knocker said, as he walked over to a bloke in the corner of the pub and had a word in his ear. Ten minutes later, the bloke went to the toilet.

'Chris, go in the bogs now and that bloke will sort you out... It's a fiver for a wrap,' urged Knocker. Chris got up and followed the bloke in.

As Chris says, 'I've followed this bloke into the toilet and stood at the side of him with a fiver in my hand as he's pissing. He's looked at me as I stood there stoned, so I held out my fiver and asked him, "Can you sort me out with that gear?" The bloke's just putting his cock away and he's looking at me a bit puzzled.

'"What?" he asked. I'm stood with a fiver pointing towards him when he just said, "Have you been listening to that nutter Knocker?" He then walked past me, smiling. It turns out he's only an off-duty copper having a drink in his local and Knocker has had me around the corner big time. He was pissing himself when I sheepishly came out of the bog.'

There are a thousand stories to tell about the lads from my neck of the woods but it would fill a book on its own. And not all of them would leave a smile on your face. Local rivalry can be a serious business, and it doesn't take much for the isolated incidents to blow up, big time. And that's where we're going next.

4
LOCAL WARS AND MR BONES

Sheffield is a weird city when it comes to the red–blue divide. There are areas all over the city which are strongholds for both clubs. Some of these areas are often on each other's doorsteps. For instance, the area were I live is predominantly United, but the surrounding areas are mixed with a fair few Wednesday lads a stone's throw away. I've always been a believer in keeping hostilities away from your own doorstep, but some of my blue-and-white pals are of a different view. To me, it's a cock's game; anyone can mob up, go to a pub, kick off with a few individuals and leave claiming some sort of shite result.

Anyhow, this is how local wars can get out of hand and I confess to seeking out a few local rivals when they paid my local a visit, mobbed up and looking for two brothers who don't even drink round our way.

Around four years ago, one of United's younger lads worked behind the bar in the English Cedar pub situated in our village. He and his brother had been having bollocks with a few Wendy lads from the next village. There had been a few rumours about Wendy turning a firm out to sort these lads out but confirmation came via one of their own lads who thought it was out of order for a firm to turn up at the young United lads' place of work and kick off. He'd actually given us information before and was sort of a spy in the enemy's camp.

That Sunday, the football team I manage had clinched a place in the Cup Final and, as usual, we celebrated with a Leo Sayer (all-dayer). I was blindo by the time we walked through the doors of the English Cedar. Kippins (the young Blade) was behind the bar and there were around ten local United lads waiting for any attack on the pub. I wasn't arsed really – for one, I didn't think they'd turn up; and two, I was shit-faced.

Around half-an-hour later, in walked 15 of United's firm. I assured the nervous landlord and landlady that these lads hadn't come to cause trouble but to protect the pub. The pager behind the bar informed us that Wendy were indeed on the move towards us.

Within ten minutes of the United lads turning up, so did the OB (Old Bill – police) – two vans parked up outside full of coppers. That was the end of a chance for a bit of a dance, I thought. How wrong I was. I was sat near the doors and around half-a-dozen of our lot were outside. The OB drove off and, around a minute later, I heard one of our lot outside shout, 'They're here!'

I couldn't understand it, though, as I had a view up and down the road and couldn't see anyone. It soon became evident that they were, in fact, here, when our lot backed into the pub doors under a hail of bricks and bottles. I placed my drink down and ran to the doors, then outside. I immediately thought what a dumb cunt I was for not bringing my glass, as around 30 tooled-up Wendy bounced towards the pub. Our lot came rushing out and I, along with a few others, ran at Wendy.

The first lad to greet me was a smallish, unshaven, scruffy-looking twat who held out a bat and swung it around as I approached, while ducking and diving under the missiles. I didn't slow and his face was a picture as he pulled back his arm and actually threw the bat at me before hotfooting it back from whence he came.

I'd actually ran past Wendy's front line who were by now backing away from our lot. I ran across and side-winded one to the floor; another copped a pint pot on the noodle as he retreated, sending him to the canvas, then the roar went up and Wendy were off at a rapid rate. A couple were caught as the rest of their lads were diving through prickly bushes in a blind panic to get away. They had actually come from the fields at the back, so clearly had local knowledge.

Two Wendy were laid sparked out in the car park; one was under a tree, totally unconscious. What made it even more amusing for us was the sight of Merts coming out of the darkness with a baseball bat in one hand and Mr Bones straining at the leash in his other. Mr Bones was a massive Great Dane; Merts used to live near the English Cedar and, while walking the dog, he'd spotted Wendy tooling up and saying to each other what they were and weren't going to do. I imagined the look on their faces as we chased them back into the fields only for Merts and Mr Bones to scatter them as he came face to face with the fleeing snorters.

The OB screeched back up and, during the 3–4 minutes

they'd been gone, so had Wendy; business had been dealt with. We went back into the pub and I picked up the pint I'd left on the pool table. The OB came in and looked the familiar faces up and down. After a few minutes, I went outside to phone home as I was meeting our Gertrude later and I wanted to cancel our rendezvous for obvious reasons. As I stood in the doorway, an ambulance drove into the car park to tend to Mr Sparko. Two plod in a car pulled up opposite me and one leant out the window. 'Don't suppose you saw what went off, did you?' one said with more than a hint of sarcasm.

'No, I was snapping one off in the toilet at the time,' I replied. The bizzy was just about to move on when Gurder came out of the pub. 'Don't suppose you saw anything did you, Gurder?' again the bizzy asked.

Quick as a flash, Gurder replied, 'Yeah, mate, saw it all... That lad went up the tree to get some conkers, he slipped on a branch and nearly broke his neck.' I had to turn away as I cracked up laughing at Gurder's wit.

'I think you'll find it's not conker season, Gurder,' the plod replied, smirking.

'Even worse, then... must have been up that tree nicking birds' eggs. Serves him right then, dunnit?'

I started laughing and, to be fair, so did the plod. Gurder walked back inside with a wry smile. Gurder has been around for three decades now and his quick wit and sense of humour never cease to amaze me. His sharp edge has got him out of a lot of scrapes.

Before I left the English, I had a quick chat with Tap. 'Go steady on the net, Tap... you know the OB will be reading everything you put,' I reasoned.

'I know, I'm not putting anything on,' he replied.

Next morning, I checked out the United hoolie site and there, in all its glory, was Tap's rant about the day's events. He'd posted it at midnight while still pissed. I suppose a nice little result had to be told.

A couple of weeks after the English Cedar sketch, Gaz, a United fan, not a boy from around our way, was jumped by three Wendy as he staggered home from one of our locals. Prior to the attack, Gaz had a big cob the size of a half golfball just above his eyebrow; it required surgery to remove it. During the attack by the Wendy boys, he'd been booted in the head and, when the swelling went down, the lump had, to everyone's amusement, disappeared. 'Had to cancel the operation to have it removed... I must get that Finchy (Wendy lad) and his mates a drink next time I see 'em,' Gaz laughed.

Local rivalries can get silly. A typical example of that was in the mid-Nineties when three brothers who were Blades fell out with two brothers who were Wednesday. The tit-for-tat attacks got so out of hand that a 50-strong coachload of Wednesday actually stopped off at the Blades brothers' local in Hackenthorpe on their way home from Coventry.

Things escalated then one Saturday night; a rumour went around that Wednesday were planning another attack on the same pub. Within half-an-hour, 100 BBC (Blades Business Crew) were plotted up and waiting. When nothing happened, 15 BBC went looking for Wednesday at Frecheville; a few BBC attacked the Sheriff pub and one of the Wednesday brothers was badly beaten up in the toilets. A week or so later he had a heart attack, which the other brother blamed on the beating.

The trouble between the two groups went on for years; one of the Blades' brothers was even attacked while shopping with his wife in Meadowhall Shopping Mall. To me, it's stupid to cause trouble on your own doorstep. Sometimes, I've been dragged into things I felt I had to deal with locally but, to me, the rivalry should be left to match days and town.

FLYING YIDS AT THE FLYING SCOTSMAN

The Spurs firm had been bang at it around this time and most lads knew that Tottenham had become one of the best and most active firms in the capital. The rival cockney crew's views may differ but those were the noises coming out of the smoke. United had beaten QPR 2–1 and around 30–40 of United's old school had plotted up in the Flying Scotsman in King's Cross.

AJ remembers, 'The Scotsman is a favourite place for a lot of firms visiting London. It's not too far from the train station and for a quid in a pint pot – or 50p in my case – you can watch some scrubber reveal her saggy tits and bounce her baggy fanny in front of you. We'd actually gone there because we'd heard that Chelsea were around and figured they might be in. No such luck.

'Around half-an-hour later, one of our youngsters came running in with the shout that 40 boys were heading our way. We rushed to the doors just as the cockney firm came around the corner. They hurtled towards us with the usual football roar going up. It's at this point you need your bottle and we had it all right. We fanned and traded. Two lone coppers tried to stop it but they were pissing in the wind. We thought we were at it with Chelsea at first and it was only when one of their geezers shouted that we realised we were in combat with the 'front-wheel skids' – yids.

'I actually thought we'd do well to stand our ground because the Spurs lads were well up for it but the more we traded and waded in, the more ground we managed to gain. We got a good surge in together and Tottenham started to back off with some actually running. A few tried to hold it together but we'd got the upper hand now they were ready for off. "BBC... BBC... " we yelled, just to let them know who they'd got done by. Another chant and another wade in and they were off. One of ours got sparked by the OB who crashed a spring-loaded baton into his head.

'We chased Tottenham back to King's Cross and, like a dog with a bone, didn't stop until they were actually in the station. They turned and had a go but we just steamed them again; the victory was ours. We gained a lot of credit that day as the Yids had slight numbers on us and had more than enough game lads but we held it together and with the quality we had out, managed to claim a nice little result. As one of theirs said on a website: "Fair play, lads, you were up for it and got the result but that wasn't all our main firm." It's the usual excuse... But that wasn't all our main firm either.'

COVENTRY/DERBY 2002 – TWO CITIES IN ONE DAY

The first match of the 2002/03 season saw United travel to Coventry. The BBC had grown in numbers, mostly because of the youth now attaching themselves to us. I'd seen a large growth in the youth within United's firm in the previous season and, if these lads had been made welcome and groomed by the seasoned thugs, then the BBC's older lads could have slipped on the carpet slippers and let these eager youngsters tackle other firms. But, for one reason or another, they had fallen by the wayside.

Anyhow, I and several mates from our end booked a coach run by a lad who was a bit of an entrepreneur. I say entrepreneur – robbing twat is a better term. In fact, the coach was almost filled with lads from around our way. I didn't expect any trouble so I took my wife's friend's son, who was only 16. 'There won't be any trouble,' I assured her.

We set off in good time for a great drinking session, actually hitting Coventry city centre at midday. The pub we met up in was chocker with around 300 United, a big turn out. I was asked to sign a couple of shirts by virtue of minor celebrity status, which was a tad embarrassing but I don't like to be ignorant.

At about 2.00pm, everyone drank up and set off towards the ground. I stayed put with 20 close mates. The sight of 300 lads heading down the road looked impressive. News soon came through that the United firm had been at it with the plod and had attacked the police line only to be gassed and beaten back by the old 24-inch black rubber dongs that the OB use with relish. Coventry, with respect, don't have a large firm so the BBC had turned on the police, as frustration over the lack of opposition took over. The game itself passed quickly by.

We boarded the coach and set off for home, or so I thought. I was nodding off in my seat when I heard the robbing twat who ran the coach say we were having a couple of drinks in Derby. This is going to be trouble with a capital 'T', I thought. We'd no sooner got to the outskirts of the town centre when we saw the unmistakable sight of lads bang at it. It was kicking off around 200 yards down the road and everyone alighted sharpish and ran towards the set-to.

I stayed on the coach with the 16-year-old lad I was looking after. I could see from the vantage of the coach that around a 25-a-side fight was taking place outside a pub. The 50 or so from our coach ran to help but the United lads at it had already chased their opposition back into the pub. I walked up the road behind everyone else as another coachful of United hurtled up the road to swell the BBC's numbers to well over a hundred.

The first lads in Derby who had been at it were the Darnall lot and I can't think of a more solid bunch of lads that represent our club, game as pebbles to a man. As I got level with the first pub, it had been totalled, broken glass everywhere and stools from inside the pub strewn across the road. The BBC were 100 yards in front of us and a roar went up again. I could see punches being traded outside another pub. When I eventually got up there I noticed it was called the Neptune and was, in fact, Derby's hooligans' main boozer.

The BBC chased the Derby Lunatic Fringe (DLF) lads back inside and the pub suffered a couple of smashed windows. I looked around and noticed CCTV cameras everywhere. 'There's a few people going to do a bit of stir over this shit,' I informed the young lad with me. I shouted up to around five of my non-hoolie mates who were tagging along just in front of me, to come back towards us and away from the kick-off. As I turned around to walk back down the road away from the off, around 15 Derby were heading up from the first pub that had been ransacked. The camera down the street was pointing straight at us. The OB had arrived with snarling dogs and pushed our lot down the precinct.

Just as our little group got level with the Neptune, Derby poured out. Fronting was a huge fella with a blue Burberry shirt on, his face was covered in blood and his shirt was hanging from him. He was 'on one' and clocked our six or seven stragglers. Derby saw us and made a move but a few coppers with dogs got in between us and the pissed-off Derby lads and, as more bizzies came, we moved down the precinct to catch up with the rest who were all rounded up and backed against a wall ready to be Section 60'd. All I thought of was getting out of there, so as the lads with me joined the herded-up Blades, I jogged across the road to flag a taxi to the train station. Scotty drove past in his car with four other United lads in and stopped.

'What's gone off, Steve?' he asked.

'The lot's gone, pal... Any chance of squeezing me in and getting the fuck out of here, mate?'

I got in and off we headed back to sunny Sheffield. For the next couple of days, my phone was on fire. Newspapers and radio wanted an interview. I thought about blanking it but then realised that they may be told by the plod that I was around so I did a couple of interviews and said I'd inadvertently got caught up in it. One interview totally misquoted me and a few of the lads were a bit miffed about it and, to be honest, when I read the article I could see why. It taught me a lesson about what a lot of the press are about. I still do the odd interview but it's only with a few people I've learned I can trust, as they always put my point of view across rather than the general one-sided shit that the law seem to have written themselves.

Over the next two months, several United lads were nicked, but not in the numbers that police had threatened. 'Headline news', 'long stretch', 'stamping down', 'not tolerated', 'CCTV footage'... etc. In the end, only four lads were convicted and the worst they got was a bit of Community Service along with a three-year football ban; the rest then got all the charges dropped.

A couple of months later, ten United youngsters were attacked by Derby in a bar at Skegness. You had to admire their front when they were asked by Derby who they were. The answer ended with a few of them copping a few bumps and bruises but you should never ever shit out of telling anyone you are Sheffield United.

THE BATTLE OF THE SPORTSMAN

Just how South Yorkshire Police and the people who control their actions got away with the jailing of 12 lads, and the arrest of 11 others, God only knows. The actions that day were akin to a fascist state with no rules except the ones they make up. I wasn't there – fuckin' glad I wasn't, too, so I'll let the people who were tell their story.

The first witness began:

'This was it, Sheffield Wednesday v Sheffield United at Hillsborough. In short, the big one. This fixture wasn't one to miss and holidays abroad weren't booked until the fixture list was published. The workplace and pubs became different places as the red–blue divide argued their cause. It also saw the rival hooligan groups plan their day. The

September game meant we didn't have to wait long before we got it on with Wendy. United's lads had started the season in very active mode and had already been involved in major disturbances in Coventry, Derby and even the pups had been at it on Skegness seafront.

'On the day of the match, it was a bit of a rush due to the early kick-off time and the fact that my son was playing football that morning. I got a call from my mate Andy; he was in the Hanover pub around half-a-mile from Bramall Lane. So me and the lad went down to the Hanover to meet him.

'On arrival, the street outside was teeming with lads. There was designer clobber everywhere and it soon became apparent that United had turned a massive team out. The plod ushered the rest of United's lads out of the pub and the long walk to Hillsborough was on.

'It was a formidable sight as I walked behind with my young lad. My estimate was that the BBC were 400 strong and it looked like the majority were into their thirties; in short, a nasty firm of seasoned hoodlums. If the OCS (Owls Crime Squad) were around today, they were in for a torrid time, I thought. The mass of bodies snaked out over 500 yards as they flowed down the hillside between the University and Langsett Road. I could see lads moving off into small groups and shaking the plod off. The police were like a TV crew with cameras everywhere. It was evident the plod had no chance of keeping this torrent of lads in order as they tried to keep the bulk together.

'Eventually, the majority of the firm were stopped at the bottom of Langsett Road, but loads of lads had slipped the net. The plod were trying to fathom out what to do with such a large group. I had no problem in moving through the police blockade as I had my young son with me. As I got through, it started to get a bit heated as the Beeb pushed forward and lines of plod tried to hold them back.

'I eventually got to Hillsborough Corner to be greeted by another blockade of police. The scene was more akin to a war-torn no-go-zone as a dozen officers on horseback were backed up by riot police and dogs while the helicopter hovered just above street level. As I neared the ground, I saw a group of around 20 OCS surrounded by police; if only they knew what was heading their way, I thought.

'I learned through the mobile that United were at it with the police and a group of around 60–80 lads had broken away and got into Hillsborough Park.

'The game itself saw United batter Wednesday, only to lose unbelievably 2–0. It was later in the day that this game will go down in Sheffield's hooligan football folklore. There was sporadic fighting during the day and evening of the game, but what happened later had a lot to do with the police.'

Another Blade who was there that day offered his own perspective on the events as they unfolded:

'We'd been to Hillsborough with a huge mob and we'd basically had nothing but a few baton marks to show for our efforts. The elusive OCS had managed to vanish into thin air after the game again. It's the fourth time I've been to Hillsborough in the last eight years and I've yet to encounter our rivals. We show, they don't, end of. That's why the plod are always on our case but I didn't expect them to go as far as they did later in the night when the law turned lawless. We are obviously the fox and the plod are the hounds and, yes, they ripped us apart.

'The Sportsman is 100 yards from United's ground... We were drinking at basically a supporter's pub and there was no sign of trouble. In fact, only around 60 United lads were still out so the pub was mainly, as we call them, 'shirts'. Around another 100 United fans were only 200 yards away in the Cricketers. Wednesday had been up to their usual tricks, those being phoning us up and telling us they were in one place when, in fact, they were nowhere near. After a couple of wild-goose chases, everyone settled down. Just as I thought there was going to be no action that evening, I got a call from Billy. He and his pal had just been attacked by Wednesday down near the Leadmill. Two taxis had headed off to Intake to check if the Wednesday lads were in the Hall pub. We phoned them and they turned the taxis around and headed back down to the Leadmill. Around a dozen of us set off on foot. We met the lads that had been attacked outside the Royal Standard pub. We were informed that around 40 Wednesday were in the Dodgers pub near the train station. The two taxis arrived and we were 20-strong. The rest of United's lads were on the blower and informed us they were on the way. We wanted to get it on, so headed straight for the Dodgers without waiting for backup.

'Unfortunately for us, a police inspector in an unmarked car spotted us. The plod soon had us against a wall and arrested one of us for fuck all. We weren't having it and kicked off with plod. That culminated in five more of us getting nicked. One of my mates was accused of assault on the inspector – total bollocks – but at least he didn't get charged at the station.

'I headed back to the Sportsman. Inside, it was still full but mainly with 'normal' fans. I got a drink and went outside. There were around 20 lads there just drinking when the OB screeched up mob-handed. The riot police politely told us to move inside. From what I saw, everyone was heading indoors when the OB just flipped and started clubbing everyone. There was a crush to get inside as the batons were brought down on our heads. The plod had been waiting all day and didn't hold back. Blood ran from open head wounds. The lads inside were trying to attack the plod but we were stuck in the middle getting battered. Lads were going down under the blows of the batons and getting dragged inside by their collars. It went up as the attacking police were pelted with everything, including the kitchen sink. My back was burning due to strikes with batons; I had six welts across me. The police were backed away from the pub doors as everyone surged forward as the roar went up.

'I peered outside; there must have been around 100 plod in the road. Stalemate – we weren't going out and the plod weren't coming in. The standoff lasted an hour. Then the riot squad formed a tunnel. We were let out one at a time, filmed, then beaten in the tunnel. What got me was that there were loads of innocent fans in the pub and they copped it as they left, with even a woman being clubbed to the floor. It was bang out of order.

'I went out and braced myself. "Run, you fat bastard!" the first copper said. I don't run for no one, so I walked through the line of 30 police. I copped another four or five blows to my legs and arms. I was fuckin' black-and-blue but my pride and spirit remained intact.

'Two weeks later, 25 United fans were arrested and charged for the 'Battle of the Sportsman'. Of those arrested, ten were jailed for between 14–22 months. In my opinion, not only had the police started the whole affair, they actually got away with it, as the courts ignored massive amounts of evidence of police brutality. Even a family bloke aged 43 with no previous convictions copped two years in the clink. It was the worst piece of police brutality Sheffield had ever seen; a few miners might disagree but, to me, the worst hooligans that day were the plod. I hate the cunts with a passion now. When you've seen a disabled bloke get smashed in a tunnel of hate, when you've seen two young lads crying as their dad is beaten senseless, when you've seen a woman dragged by her hair ten yards down a road, it makes you burn inside.

'My mate got 22 months for that day; he is now banned from Sheffield city centre, and banned from England games. The worst of it all, though, is he's banned from Bramall Lane for six years. The police have been sued for thousands by various people for what happened that day. How can the courts give jail to people with one hand then give payouts because of police brutality with the other?'

THE SHEFFIELD DERBY 2002

Before the United and Wednesday derby at Bramall Lane, I agreed to do an interview for *Look North* (a local BBC news programme). I'd also asked Paul Heaton to say a few words about the hooligan scene. I met Paul and we went and had a quick drink with the United firm who had gathered in the Moorfoot Tavern. Outside was swarming with OB, inside was chocker with United's hooligans. One of the lads came over and tipped me off that the OB had mentioned my name on the radio, as one of the lads was at home listening to the scanner. Me and Paul walked up to the Lane to do the interview.

It was quite surreal as the TV crew filmed me leant on the corner flag pretending to read my own book. After the real BBC had got what they wanted, we headed back to the Sportsman pub. Rumour had it that Wendy were, for once, turning a decent mob out and would be coming to the game. With ten minutes to kick-off, police escorted around 30–40 lads up Bramall Lane. I tagged behind for a nosey. Once they got level with the Cricketers, they started singing football songs, a bit childish like. The OB had them well under wraps and United's onlooking firm at the side of the pub had no chance of a dance.

I managed to get through the police blockade as Wendy were ushered to the turnstiles on Bramall Lane. It was then I saw a couple of their main actors. They gave me a wave and a nod. I tried to talk to one of them, whose name was Dinga, but the mufty squad gave me a shove. Then this tall, bone-headed dresser started with the 'Cowens... You're a wanker!' He's surrounded by OB and giving it the big 'un. I stared him up and down, trying to see what clobber he wore, or some other way to recognise him later. The OB gave me another shove so I was off into the ground. G and H block in the South Stand were absolutely rammed with Blades boys.

It was a great atmosphere. Wednesday took the lead through Alan Quinn (who, incidentally, soon swapped his trotters and grew hands instead, and became the first ever player to score for both sides in a Sheffield derby when he scored the winner in a 1-0 win in 2006). We replied in style and ran out 3–1 winners, making me and thousands of others as happy as Larry.

That said, Larry wasn't that happy after getting a six-year stretch for a fight in town. He's a United lad and had been bottled (hit with a bottle) in a nightclub in town and had then waited outside. The assailant himself was then attacked with a glass, and Larry found himself locked up. During the trial, the local paper ran the story and Larry got four years for the assault and the judge gave him another two years on top for shouting that he was BBC to all and sundry, as he waited for the bloke who had attacked him.

'I'm giving you a further two years for admitting you're part of an organised football gang,' rang in Larry's ears as he was led to the cells.

Back to the match itself – during the game, three distress flares were fired from H block into the away end. This, coupled up with a few other incidents, gave the police all the ammo they needed to force a closure of G and H block. A £100,000 fine hung over the club. With the closure of G and H, the atmosphere at the Lane suffered. That area of the ground had become a no-go zone for police and stewards and the coppers openly admitted that they couldn't look after the area. Two United fans were jailed for their part in the firework display.

As the South Stand emptied on to Bramall Lane, there were United lads everywhere. The 40 or so Wendy won't be singing now, I thought, as I walked. Outside the away end, hundreds of hooligans were waiting and the OB were at it with the batons, dogs and horses. Outside one exit stood around 15 Wendy surrounded by OB; this was the remnants of what was left of their firm.

To be fair, you have to give those lads credit, as the previous season Wendy simply hadn't showed and got so much stick for it that at least this time they had come, even though the reports of them turning a couple of hundred out were way off the mark. It was bedlam on Bramall Lane as the OB tried to move on the waiting hordes. It was then that I saw a face that had me thinking: where have I seen you before?

Then, despite seven pints of Nelson Mandela (Stella) before the game, it registered – it was big-mouth Pig from before the game. He'd slipped on a baseball cap and was trying to slip away in the crowd. I tucked in behind him and followed. As soon as we're away from the plod, he's copping for one, I thought. I followed and he was nervous, looking this way and that as he tried to get away from the ground unscathed. Past the petrol station, I thought, this is my chance... I walked quickly past my tormentor then turned to face him.

'How do, big mouth...' I said.

His face was a picture but, to be fair, he was thinking on his feet all right as he bolted to the side of me, pulling a passer-by into my path as he ran. Then – Dink – in his panic, he ran across St Mary's roundabout and a car clipped his back leg. He fell, but was back up and off like an Olympic sprinter.

I turned to walk back towards the Lane. There were mobs of United everywhere. In the darkness, I spotted a group of around five young lads of around 16–17, tops. They were obviously together but trying to walk separately.

Following behind them were Brian and a few other United hoodlums; they'd sussed this little group of young Wednesday and were closing in. As the young Owls realised they had been rumbled, they just stood at the roundabout like startled rabbits in the headlights. I went over to them.

'Come with me lads,' I beckoned them across towards the church. They wouldn't move and looked terrified. This sounds a bit knob-headish but I took one by the arm.

'Look, I'm not going to touch you... I'm Steve Cowens. Come with me and I'll make sure you're all right, lads.'

Brian and his little posse soon realised how young these lads were and the fact that they were shitting themselves, so they watched on as I took the young lads across the road and to safety. Not one of the Owls pups said a word, but the tallest lad just nodded my way as they disappeared towards town.

A bit later, the OB had around ten lads wrapped up. These were a few of Wendy's main actors and what was left of their firm. The OB didn't seem to know what to do with them, as large groups of United were everywhere and the atmosphere was ugly. The plod took the few Wendy towards town.

They were completely surrounded by Beeb; across the road, the Darnall lot made a charge at the police escort. The OB struck out with batons as they were nearly overwhelmed. I had to laugh at Tap; he's stood toe-to-toe with one of United's football intelligence and, as the copper tried to hit him, he's bouncing around giving him loads. Sometimes, there are lads who are too game for their own good and Tap comes into that bracket.

Anyhow, a few United lads were forced over a bridge directly above the excuse for an escort. Then the loudest bang I've ever heard came from the middle of the escort and had the police horses on their back legs bucking-bronco style. That was no firework, I thought. United saw this as the chance to have another surge at the startled police. Dogs and batons kept United at bay. I later found out the explosion was an army stun grenade, and also who had thrown it.

I'd kept out of it all and just walked behind, watching and taking it all in. My phone rang and it was Paul asking where I was. He was outside the Sportsman way back at the Lane. I turned to walk back to the Sportsman and got a wry smile off Harold, another United football officer. He's been on the scene years now and I'll never forget the first time we encountered him and other football intelligence officers. It was at Hull and 50 of us had settled in a town centre pub when in walked two geezers with green Barbour coats on. They tried to have a drink and blend in but they were that obvious they may as well have had their helmets on. The thing with Harold is he's actually a big Blades fan and from what I've seen he's by far the best plod that's kept an eye on our thugs.

Not long after the Wednesday game, a DVD came out called *Fists and Style*; Wednesday's little mob were actually shown on it while being escorted away from Bramall Lane, filmed by a camera situated in a multistorey car park. Everyone thinks I made the DVD but that's a long way from the truth.

I suppose when you get involved with the media, certain lessons need to be taken on board and I have learned the hard way. At first it's sound; a few extra dollars for talking about your past, no problem. I actually had Japanese TV crews flying over and paying between £500–£600 quid for an interview before the World Cup over there. I did TV, radio, newspaper and local news interviews. Then I got stitched up a bit by a newspaper after United had been involved in trouble at Coventry and Derby in the same day. Basically, what I said was twisted and turned. It made me realise that by giving the press interviews, I was setting myself up for a fall, so I stopped doing it.

I did go on the *Trisha* show, though, as the money they offered was simply too good to turn down. That was an experience, I'll tell you. I was booed on set by Liberal knobheads before I'd even had chance to speak. They weren't prepared to listen to what I had to say before they made up their minds, so with a smile I invited the whole audience out to have a fight in the car park. After that, they listened to me and actually clapped me in the end.

Anyhow, this DVD came about because a geezer I've known through other people who wanted to make a documentary about my life and involvement with the BBC. He was a United fan who was always hanging around players and so on – you know the type. To be honest, I was unsure about the venture. The money I would earn was going to be just under three quid for every DVD sold. At first, the DVD was going to be about my life, or so he said, but it slowly turned into something different.

To cut a long story short, I did an interview with his very aptly-named company. It was then he started doing things behind my back, like filming with a covert camera at matches, putting Paul Heaton's face on the cover of the

DVDs, and using my Internet name for the DVD title. He'd got pound signs in his eyes and was unscrupulous in his efforts to get this film out.

I ended up saying that I wanted no more to do with this bullshitting cunt and his company and pulled the plug. It probably cost me quite a bit of money but at least I could look my good friend Paul Heaton and the other lads in the face. That's all that mattered to me.

Billy Bullshit was supposed to have captured the police assaults on lads on covert camera outside the Sportsman and told everyone who would listen that he would release the covert footage to get lads off their charges. It never happened and a few Blades got jail while Billy Bullshit sat at home counting his cash. On the DVD, he slags Leeds lads and refers to Wednesday lads as numpties, all this from a lad who has never thrown a punch in his life for Sheffield United. I suppose you live and learn, eh.

WEST HAM AWAY 2003

West Ham away was a fixture that had shivers running down your spine in the Eighties and early Nineties. A tough area, some tough geezers and a well respected firm, known to all as the ICF (Inter-City Firm). God, how it's changed. To be fair, a lot of grounds have lost the intimidation factor for one reason or another. It does my nut in when you go away and the stands at the side of the away end are full of nuggets in Aqua caps gesturing all through the game. We had G and H shut at the away end of the South Stand. Why? Simple – the OB couldn't control the area. They wouldn't set foot in it, as sometimes there were as many as 1,800 lads in there for games like Leeds, Wendy and

Liverpool. Bramall Lane was a proper intimidating place to visit. Three sides of the ground making one hell of a racket. This coincided with our best home form in years; the fans were like a goal start.

West Ham was the same, only promotion via a play-off win over Preston has breathed life into a ground that was like a morgue, but it used to be a deafening, intimidating place to visit.

So...West Ham away, and a chance to meet up with Cass Pennant, a good day on the pop and hopefully three points. I travelled down on the train with a few close mates. On the journey down, we were entertained through the speaker system by some geezer who made Julian Clary sound like Arthur Mullard. He was camp with a capital 'C'. He had us pissing ourselves, though, with some of the shit he was coming out with: 'I hope you've all packed your flip-flops as it's going to be an absolutely gorgeous day in the capital... ' and 'I recommend the nice warm sausage rolls from the very friendly kiosk. They are cooked to perfection and ooze sensuality...' and so on.

Once in the smoke, I had a couple of jars with United's lads, who numbered around 50. 'Boro, who were at Arsenal that day, had a firm further up the road and a couple had asked one of ours if I was around, and if I was, I was welcome to join them for a beer. We split from our firm and went for a drink on our own. Later, as I walked down the side of the ground, I saw a figure that I recognised instantly: West Ham's own One-Eyed Bob. I ran across to him and his mates, saying, 'Come on, we're here.'

Bob's mates looked a little startled, then he realised who the spaceman was and came and shook my hand. I'd met

Bob at a film premiere in London. Dave Jones, one of the Cardiff lads who wrote the Soul Crew book, was also there, as was his mate who, surprisingly, was called Gareth. He was starring in the film. They were spot-on lads and we had a great night, apart from a few Andy Warhol types knocking around, but I suppose you get that with these sketches.

When I went for a piss at the film premiere I nearly zipped my cock off as a transvestite lobbed his knob out of his tights at the side of me – fuck that!

Anyhow, Bob's a well-known face around Upton Park and he's a sound geezer as well. The game was a dull 0-0 draw. I tried to get West Ham midfielder Don Hutchison's attention as he came over to the corner where we sat. I'd had a couple of great nights out with Don when he was at Sheffield. He's a great character and I liked the fella.

After the match, myself and Wilb turned right outside the ground and Sheffield's football spotters stopped us, calling out, 'Where you off to, Steve?'

'Off to the same place we've been before the game… I'm going for a drink,' I reasoned. They let us go and we went in the pub to be joined later by around 20 non-hoolie mates. The last train from St Pancras to Sheffield was at 9.30pm.

We headed to King's Cross and met up with some other lads in a bar opposite the station. I got a drink and sat in the window and was promptly entertained by a Charles Bronson lookalike. Charlie B went around and around the pub on a bike with a huge smile on his face. He must have gone around 40 times until a taxi nearly skittled him.

One of the lad's mobiles went. 'It's Wednesday,' he said as he answered it. I switched off as I was a tad stoned.

'You fuckin' clowns… what you doing down there when we're at West Ham? It's not even our boozer… hang around until we get back, you fuckin' plum…' It was Claws giving a Wendy lad the verbals. It turned out that 100 Wendy had settled themselves down in the Moorfoot Tavern which, although it's not a Blades pub, is close to London Road.

Everyone's mood changed. Getting back to Sheffield was priority number one. As we walked towards the train station, I bumped into a well known non-hoolie Blade called Shred (the best, most loyal Blades supporter that has ever lived). He made me laugh as he said, 'Oh no, not again,' referring to when he helped us repel an attack from Grimsby's boys on the platform of the station in 1984. He suffered a bad beating that day and was arrested with the rest of us but that's all been documented in the BBC book.

Even worse news came through on the blower from Tap, one of the BBC's main actors. 'Have you heard about Mally?' he said.

'No, what's up with him?' I asked.

'He's been battered by Wednesday… Fuckin' on his own in the Moorfoot and they've proper smashed him up – he's in hospital,' he went on.

Mally was in the Moorfoot when Wendy had entered. To be fair, some of their main lads had told him to leave which, at first, he was going to. Now Mally is one of the gamest lads around but the daft cunt went back in and gave a bit of the verbals out. Wendy, in response, smashed him up; some clown thought that smashing him in the face with a bottle would be fun. They then threw glasses and stools over the bar at the terrified pub staff while chanting:

'Wendy... Wendy... ' I know a lot of their top boys were suitably embarrassed by the whole affair, but I'll tell you this: nothing like that would have happened if the boot had been on the other foot. If they think that's what football violence is all about, then they want to call it a day.

The train journey home wasn't dull; a couple of Blade-on-Blade fights, sing-songs and enough coke snorted to keep Escobar and his henchmen high for a few weeks. It was turned midnight when we eventually got back to Sheffield. Wilb and I headed for a pub where around 25 United boys outside were on one, big time. They'd been scouring town in cars checking out if Wendy were around. The nightclub they usually went in had been checked, to no avail.

Mally then turned up at the pub straight from hospital. He was in a bad, bad way; there was no doubt he'd suffered a severe beating. Everyone went 'on one' now they'd seen the state of him. All Mally kept saying was, 'They can't hurt me, the blue 'n' white bastards, I fuckin' hate the cunts.' In truth, he had been badly hurt but I admired his take on it.

'See what they do... Fuck it, the gloves are off, no rules, fuck the code, if you see one on his own from now on, he gets it,' Tap argued. He continued his rant, turning to me. 'See, Steve, this is our payback... You leave them when the numbers aren't right and this is what you get in return,' he reasoned.

Tap was right and I thought about an incident from a month earlier when I'd been on Sheffield's Ecclesall Road celebrating my pal's stag night. Later that evening, around 40 of us had gone into a club that Wednesday sometimes frequent. The 40 were mostly Blades but I have quite a few pals who support the grunters and they are sound lads and good friends. We'd been in the club around half-an-hour when one of my mates came over. 'That Dweeby is in the corner with a few Wednesday.'

I knew Dweeby from the days when he used to drink around our way; he could be a trouble-causing cunt at the best of times and always seemed to be getting twatted but he didn't really bother me in the slightest.

At the request of a member of his family, I'd even sent him a book up to Leeds where he lives now. Trouble was, in the Leadmill a couple of months earlier, he'd spat at a girl who goes in our local, and he'd also thrown his drink on her because she had a United pendant on her gold chain.

I waltzed over. He stuck out his hand to shake mine, saying, 'All right, Steve, thanks for the book.'

SLAP.

'Fuck the book,' I said as I slapped him hard across the face, girly style. I sometimes think a slap is more degrading than a punch; I didn't want to hit him anyway, as I knew the fella, and there were only five or six of them.

'What you doing spitting on girls, you pleb? We're all rivals but you cunts always have to take it too far,' I reasoned.

'I made a right idiot of myself that day,' he explained.

SLAP.

'Say it again!'

He did.

'There's no need to go off like that. What chance have we with the conduct when nuggets like you are pulling strokes like that?' I argued. He nodded and I went back to enjoying my night.

Some United boys came in the club later and, when they realised that a few Wendy were in the corner, went for them. I ran across and jumped in the way. Dweeby had picked up a chair. I suppose he had to really, as they were backed up in the corner.

'Put that fuckin' chair down,' I told him, before turning to the handful of United that had gone over. 'Leave it out... There's only a few of them.' Our lot left them and the bouncers thanked me. I went back to my pals and our night continued.

So you see that's why Tap was right; I'd helped a few Wendy out and then this is what happens to Mally. He was right – maybe next time I'll step to one side and watch it go off.

This wasn't the end of it. Next day, a pub was targeted by the BBC. Fifteen main lads went to the Hall Inn on Sunday afternoon. The Hall Inn is a Wendy watering hole and is also camera'd up. This didn't stop United's lads storming in and the few OCS that didn't manage to get out the back got mullered. One of these was Errol, an older, respected Wendy lad. He was hospitalised, as were a couple of other lads.

I got to hear about what had happened later that day. At last orders, 30 Wendy went to a pub I drink in; just what for, I don't know. The Wendy knew that I'd had nothing to do with what had happened earlier in the day and it wasn't my style. I puzzled it out.

Why had Wednesday gone to this pub, when they knew the United boys who'd attacked the Hall Inn were on London Road? A cop-out on their part?

I was on one, big time, and searched out a Wendy lad who's the mobile organiser for their crew. When I eventually got him on the blower, he explained that I wasn't the target but, to be honest, I haven't a clue who they were looking for, as no lads from round our way had been involved in the earlier attack. I was well fucked off. The OCS knew where the Beeb were: eight miles away on London Road.

At 11.30ish, a few OCS pulled up on London Road in two cars and threw a couple of bricks through the pub windows and sped off.

Things in Sheffield were tetchy for a while with rumours of visits to rival pubs. Things got out of hand simply because bullying had occurred. No one was arrested for the attack on the Hall Inn, despite police announcing that the perpetrators would be dealt with.

Around three weeks later, I had a phone call from a good source saying that Wednesday were planning to come to a pub in the village and kick off. On the night in question, around 20 United lads waited in the pub. I didn't involve the BBC, as I didn't think we'd need them. By 11.30pm there were just five of us left in the pub, since the others had gone home because the chance of a ruck looked unlikely. Then Claws got a call that Wednesday were making their way to a meeting point not far from us. I was well oiled by this time but in no mood to take this shit.

'Right, let's go and greet them,' I reasoned. 'But I'm warning you – I'm not going anywhere, no matter what the numbers are. If you come, then you have to stand.'

Claws is as game as fuck and he nodded.

After we made a phone call to get some transport, eight

of us went to their meet. They weren't around so we went looking. Somehow, our two cars got split up, and then the news came through that they knew we were about and wanted to meet us on a quiet road outside an abattoir. Sound, I thought, a great place for a dead Pig to be laid to rest.

The car I was in headed straight there without waiting for the other. Outside the meet, a car was parked up with five lads in it. We pulled alongside. The look on their faces was a picture. As we started to get out of the car, a Wednesday lad called Qauz screamed, 'GO... GO... GO.' The car reversed down the road at breakneck speed. Our other car was speeding up and tried to cut off their escape. The cars collided and I watched as they sped off into the night. We again waited in vain then drove around for an hour searching, but to no avail. It had been a silly night and I wondered why I had got so involved, but if Wednesday feel the need to cause bollocks on our doorstep then they have to be met head on.

CARDIFF 2003

There had been a lot of hype leading up to this fixture. The mobiles among United's firm were red-hot. There's no doubt that Cardiff are Wales's number-one firm; they, indeed, class themselves as *Britain's* numero-uno firm. I don't really think they live up to the hype they give themselves. Yes, they have a big firm; yes, they have some game lads and quite a few looney tunes among them; but they big themselves up too much. I know all football firms think they are the dog's bollocks but Cardiff, along with Leeds and Chelsea, seem to have never run, never had a turnover, and basically rule the roost over anyone who dares to mention that they themselves have had a result or challenged the Welsh firm, home or away. I suppose Cardiff get a bit frustrated because there's not many teams have turned a firm out at Ninian Park. If United's ticket arrangements for the match at Cardiff were anything to go by, you've either got to be a vicar or a choirboy to have any chance of getting a ticket for Ninian Park.

Rumours of what Cardiff had planned for their visit did the rounds. The only one I believed was that they would be arriving in Chapeltown, which is about eight miles outside Sheffield city centre. On the day, the BBC turned out a number that, apart from derby games, hadn't been seen for a while. The numbers ranged from 350–500, depending on who you talked to. I had it down as around 400 and the OB outside the Sportsman said we'd wasted our time, as Cardiff hadn't come into town and wouldn't be at the game until after kick-off.

At around 2.55pm, around 150 Cardiff were escorted past the Cricketers. Most of them didn't look like a football firm but they had their fair share of grizzlers with them. I personally kept out of the way but had a good nosey at what was going off.

The game was a right ding-dong affair ending 5–3 to us. When United scored their fifth, the ground erupted into chants of 'Eng-er-land', and the taffs weren't happy.

After the match, the plod made everyone from the south stand turn left as they had totally closed Bramall Lane; everyone then headed onto the backstreets. Our main hooligan firm had gone to the other exit of the stand to meet in a hidden area behind St Mary's church.

As I walked around the corner of the Railway pub, a roar went up; it was the unmistakable sound of the tear-up starting. The street that led down to Bramall Lane filled with Cardiff and it went off for a while. To be honest, the ruck wasn't worth the hype that the papers reported, with the bizzies saying it was the worst violence they'd seen at Bramall Lane for decades. Give over! The police were probably trying to justify having 9,700 officers on duty!

United's main firm, numbering around 120, had hidden in the church grounds and attacked the Cardiff escort as it headed for the station. The escort was broken and a few punches were thrown, but nothing major, before the plod had the old batons in full swing. So, yes, the day had been interesting, Cardiff had come but not with the numbers or boys that United had expected. For the BBC's part they had not only turned out big numbers but the quality of lads on show was top drawer.

If only it was like the old days. The game saw the return to action for Boney M, as game a Blades lad as they come. His ban of three years had just been completed. Two weeks later, he copped another three-year ban because of his love of the Welsh and his actions that day.

CUPS RUNNETH EMPTY

Is your cup half empty or half full? As a Blade, you would have to say half empty!

The 2002/03 season was an amazing experience for our club and its supporters. The Cup drew up interesting ties for our hooligan element as well – Leeds in both the FA and Worthington, knocking them out of both 1–0 and

2–1 respectively. Then there was Liverpool and Arsenal in both semis.

So to the first Leeds game. It's very true that Sheffield and Leeds don't have much time for each other; bit of an understatement, really. Wednesday hate Leeds as much as United but Leeds, of course, hate Man United, so it's a second hatred for them. So when we drew each other in the League Cup, the build-up and Internet propaganda began. Would Leeds show? Surely they would. Leeds had been pretty quiet on the violence front for a few years and this was the chance for them to get their old heads out and prove they could still turn a mob out for the big games.

Not many would argue that the Leeds firm in the Eighties was one of the best around. Leeds showed up, but by train, which effectively ended any hopes of combat. Around 200 Leeds were escorted to Bramall Lane by a massive police presence. I was having a drink with my brother-in-law in the Royal Standard. I'd got my son with me so violence was a long way from my thoughts. United's firm were in the London Road area and were 300 strong. Around an hour before the match, Leeds were escorted along Shoreham Street near to the Standard; I went out and watched them pass.

After supping up, I went back out and headed to the ground, only to see police on horseback and foot trying to stop a large group of lads heading up St Mary's Gate. At first I thought it was Leeds who had another firm of around 100, as the last I'd heard was that the BBC were on London Road. Missiles rained down on police and, as I got closer, I saw a few familiar faces; it was our lot trying to attack the back end of the escort. The police managed to beat them back and I walked up behind the Leeds escort. The OB had stopped the escort on the St Mary's roundabout and I and my son had to walk through them.

It was then I realised that the escort was a mix of fans and lads. I'd say around 100 boys were in it, which is a fair crew. I saw a bird; I'll not call her a 'lady' as I saw her on the news footage throwing seats down on United fans after the final whistle. She must have been going out with one of their lads.

When I got through, the escort police were trying to clear a large mob of Blades from the side of the Cricketer's pub. I got in the ground and watched an up-for-it United side turn over a spineless Leeds team 2–1. At the final whistle, a few hundred Sheffield invaded the pitch to taunt their 2,000 Yorkshire rivals in the top tier of the away end. True to form, the seat smashers began smashing seats and hurling them at the Sheffield fans below. The mood was very much Eighties. Outside, the Leeds and Sheffield rivals managed to have a pop but not a firm-on-firm sketch. Leeds took pride in the fact that they turned a decent team out and, fair play, they came even though they were wrapped up like grandad's slippers at Christmas.

A TASTE OF SCOUSE 2003

The Cup Run had been unreal, and now Liverpool stood in the way of our first final since 1936. The game at the Lane saw a sellout crowd see United win 2–1 courtesy of Michael Tonge's finest – and some would argue, only – hour. After the match, a few Liverpool got clipped and some of the visiting coaches were attacked by an ever-growing BBC hooligan element. A lot of these new breed were excitable and just wanted to get it on. The south stand's H and G block had been filled with big turnouts of lads. The Leeds, Wendy and Liverpool matches had seen over 1,000 lads, with the Wendy game more like the 2,000 mark. Granted, not all these lads were proper boys, but a lot were and they were awesome turnouts. On the Net, the hoolie sites were filled with Liverpool lads moaning about what had happened after the game. I don't really know what happened but it was a bit rich for the Stanley-knife merchants to moan about a few clips.

The second leg of the semifinal at Anfield saw us run a coach from our local. It was filled in days and we would pick Mr Heaton up in Manchester on the way through. The BBC, for their part, were travelling in various modes of transport. We stopped off at the Rocket pub once we were in Liverpool. The driver moaned about the fact that he was breaking police regulations. A few more United lads joined us and we made our way to Anfield. We had no plans of a meeting with our scouse counterparts but the Beeb were 60-strong in one city-centre pub and one of them phoned me to try and get a number from one of my Everton pals for one of the Liverpool lads.

I wasn't really interested in getting involved as I didn't want to hassle my toffee buddies. When we got to the pub where I'd arranged to meet Bruce (Everton), Mark, an old-school Evertonian, told me Liverpool were in so-and-so pub, and were tooled up and on one because they said their shirts had been attacked at the Lane. More and more United lads came in and the numbers swelled to around 150. One of the Everton lads said that Liverpool had just been on the blower wanting to know where the Beeb were.

I'd like to bullshit and say I tried to get it on, but that's simply not the case. I wasn't interested, even though we had a big turnout and some high-quality lads with us. I just wanted to have a beer with my Everton pals, then go and enjoy the match; after all, I'd retired. The lads, on the other hand, were irritable and wanted some action. We were only just around the corner from the Arkle, and if Liverpool had attacked the pub we were in rather than the Arkle, they would have had a big surprise.

Around ten minutes prior to kick-off, we moved en masse; it was then I realised how big our numbers were. As the Arkle came into view, we knew something had just kicked off and ran towards the pub. A couple of non-hooligan Blades told me the pub had just come under attack from Liverpool's lads and pointed to the police on horseback who were obviously moving the Liverpool contingent to the ground.

We followed and a few Liverpool lads clocked us and must have wondered where the fuck we had sprung from. At the gates of Anfield, United attacked and ran at a few Liverpool; no result, as the numbers were firmly on our side. The bizzies on horseback charged at us and it was a bit mad in the crush.

The game itself saw our slender 2–1 lead wiped out in the first half, but a gallant show from United saw us take the game to extra time. In the last minute of normal play, Chris Kirkland, the Liverpool 'keeper, kung-fu kicked our striker Tommy Mooney while desperately trying to stop him scoring. Not only that, he caught the ball outside his area, which should have been a certain sending off, but clubs don't get decisions like that at Anfield, Old Trafford or the Emirates. No refs have got the bollocks to upset the big boys. Michael Owen scored in extra-time and we were out.

Outside, there was a bit of dancing but nothing major, just a few Blades venting their frustration. Quite a few supporters' coaches travelled home without windows due to them little scouse scallywags smashing them. I've never seen as many scruffy fuckers outside a football ground, and to think that Liverpool lads used to be one of the fashion flag-carriers in the early Eighties.

Unbelievably, we lost our second semifinal of the season when Arsenal beat us 1–0 at Old Trafford. The game is remembered for two things – Graham Poll's influence in Arsenal's goal and David Seaman's unbelievable save from Pesky.

That season ended with a play-off final defeat at the hands of Wolves at Cardiff. A season that had promised so much had ended and had left me with an empty feeling and an empty pocket. I felt totally deflated, but knew that one day we'd win something and, when that day arrived, then, boy, was I going to savour it.

THE BATTLE ON THE WATERFRONT – BRISTOL 2003

In the days leading up to the play-off final at Cardiff's Millennium Stadium, I'd been in two minds what to do. In fact, make that three. Going into Cardiff the day before the match was a nonstarter, as all the hotels had been booked up well in advance, hence a lot of United lads went to Weston-super-Mare and around 250 others went to Bristol prior to the game.

Anyhow, we still hadn't made our minds up about what

we were doing until the Friday before the match. Mr Heaton phoned and told me he was staying in Bristol on Saturday night with his fiancée, and did I fancy meeting up? That sorted it, really; out went going down on the day and out went Weston-super-Mare, so worzel-land, here we come! I arranged to travel down with three pals: Gravy would be driving along with DJ and the Ched-eye Warrior, who would be taking his girlfriend, Joanne.

To be totally honest, I didn't know that many of United's lads were heading to Bristol; I certainly didn't expect what was going to happen later in the day. We managed to find a decent hotel by midday. Shitted, shaved and shampooed, we went down to the bar to catch the QPR v Cardiff play-off final. The trouble with Bristol is it's a big rugby union place, and every bar we went in had the egg-chasing matches on. We went along the waterfront, which is one nice place to sink a few vessels.

After seven pints of Stella, we decided to have one more drink and go and get changed as I had arranged to meet Paul later that evening. We clocked a pub across the water; it looked like a place where we could catch the end of the match, so we headed across the bridge. Little did I know at the time, but this bridge was going to be the scene of one of the best tear-ups Blades have seen in recent years.

As we approached the bridge I saw a few familiar faces. Around 20 BBC stood outside with another ten or so inside. There were also plenty of other 'normal' Blades in the pub. I hadn't knocked the froth off my pint when, just as I got out the door, someone shouted, 'They're here.' I looked back across the bridge and saw around 30 lads heading over, some dragging steel-framed chairs by their sides. Straight away, I thought of CCTV and asked one of our more experienced lads, 'Cameras... Any cameras?'

'Yeah, there,' he said, pointing at our end of the bridge. 'They're at the other end as well.'

Right, I thought, if it kicks off stay clear of the bridge and keep out of CCTV's way. At the front of the Bristol's firm was a gypsy/pirate-type character. He appeared to be in his mid-forties but also looked up for it. He mouthed words that may as well have been in Chinese, because no one could understand anything the worzel said. I moved forward to within a metre of him. We squared up like two prizefighters.

'What's up? Lost your ship?' I asked.

'You're shit, Sheffield,' snarled Jack Sparrow as more Bristol came up beside him. It was going to kick off but everyone was shouting, 'Stay off the bridge... Cameras!'

It was going to be impossible to have them off without going on to the bridge and, as more and more Bristol lads came to swell their ranks, I and a few others realised that if we didn't get into them now, we might end up getting done. A roar went up and punches were traded. Bristol stood as glasses rained down from both sides. The bridge was only wide enough for around six or seven people to actually fight. That suited us, as our main actors fronted.

One big cunt from Bristol was dropped and, after another roar and surge from our lot, Bristol turned and ran. Sheffield ended up on their side of the bridge, which must have had a span of around 60–70 metres. Our lot realised they had got carried away and walked back, covering their faces; a bit late for that, I thought. I glanced around to see our true numbers – 40, tops – and too many hanging around the pub door for my liking.

Bristol came again and this time they were tight together and carrying various weaponry, ranging from bottles and glasses to steel chairs and the big umbrellas found outside boozers. Our lot seemed a bit hesitant to meet them on the bridge but mobbed up at the end. As Bristol approached, I realised we didn't have enough numbers around the entrance to the bridge. I glanced behind me, and saw that around half of our numbers were stood 20 yards behind us near the pub doors. I screamed at them, 'Fuckin' get up here or we'll end up getting done.'

The men fronting for United were good lads but I knew with the numbers and quality that Bristol had pouring over at us that our front line had to stand and trade or we would be ragged. Bristol roared and threw the kitchen sink but we stood firm; then a mass of bodies steamed into each other. A fuckin' beaut of an off; two sides slugged it out, trying not to lose an inch of territory. I was in the thick of it and the same lad who'd been dropped earlier on copped for my right cross to the temple. Again he went down, and this time he stayed down as a half-volley to the chin from one of ours put paid to him getting back on his feet. We had them moving again as we steamed in with an avalanche of fists and boots.

Then the usual roar went up: 'Come on!' The worzels were on the back foot as we pushed forward again and they started to turn and run. Quite a few of the Bristol lads were game as fuck and tried to hold the line but it was too much, as wave after wave waded into them. They were off and the glorious sight of 60 lads in retreat still has the same feeling and meaning as it did when I was 17.

Although some might not think this is funny, I had to laugh at the time. The big Bristol lad who'd copped a pummelling must have dropped his mobile as he got to his feet and ran. He'd got left behind and copped a few slaps from some of ours who, by now, were in the middle of the bridge. One of our lot had picked up the worzel's phone.

'Nar then, mate… your mobile… here,' he said, walking towards the Bristol lad whose boat-race was covered in claret. He gingerly walked over.

'Ta, mate.' He stuck out his hand and, just as he was about to grab it, Mark flicked it off the bridge and into the murky water 30 feet below.

'No!' cried the lad, as his mobile hit the drink with a splosh.

Our laughing was cut short as Bristol had regrouped and came charging back at us. This time we stood in the middle of the bridge. I'll remember this for ever, as one of United's so-called 'retired' hoolies – who will remain nameless – pulled up a steel folding chair. He opened it and sat down three yards in front of us. As Bristol swarmed across at us hurling glasses a'plenty, the daft twat just sat there shouting with his hand in front of him, as if to say 'Stop!'

'I claim this bridge in the name of Sheffield United. This is our bridge and we will not be moved,' he shouted while glasses smashed all around him. Bristol were only five yards away, but he was still sat there with his hand held up to stop them as we ran past him and got stuck into Bristol again. I'm convinced he'd still be there now living on handouts and still claiming the bridge was ours if we had not chaired him off after moving Bristol on again. It's hilarious, looking back.

The plod came but it had been ten minutes of to-ing and fro-ing across that bridge and, to be honest, I think both sides were fucking knackered; I was anyway. My fitness levels had dropped considerably since the early Eighties, when I could have fought all day and night. I headed straight off into town and jumped into a taxi with my pal. I was still puffing and panting and sweating like a greenhouse gardener when the blower went. The name 'Cass' lit up on the display on my phone.

'All right, mate,' I said.

'Where are you?' Cass shouted in an excited state.

'Bristol… It's quiet here – not!'

'Fack off… I've just been watching fackin' running battles on a bridge for ten minutes.' Unbeknown to me, Cass was with Bristol's lads doing a couple of interviews for his book *Terrace Legends* which was published in 2004, and for which I actually contributed a piece. I told Cass I'd ring him later and meet up when things had calmed down.

At the hotel, I got showered and changed but my mind was racing. You fuckin' idiot, I thought, I've kept out of trouble for ages and this could be Roy Orbison (over) for me now. How could I defend myself in court? The plod could just chuck the book down and say, 'That's him, Your Honour, a thug of 20 years' standing…' Leopard, spots and all that.

Fuckin' hell. I'd promised myself and my wife I'd keep out of trouble, but when push came to shove, I shoved hard. Don't get me wrong, I loved it, big time, but I have retired – not semi-retired, fully retired – from the scene, but when it came along it was *business as usual*.

I got a few phone calls and arranged to meet Paul in the Fishmonger's pub. When we pulled up in the taxi, shoed and shirted up, there were around 40 United outside. It was handshakes all round; I went inside and it was chocker with BBC, around 200 plus. Most had got the giddies on because they'd all missed the battle of the Bridge on the River Kwai. Paul wasn't inside so I ordered a drink and ten of us sat in the corner. Cass came in and looked impressed at our firm.

Dutch, a United lad from around our way, came and asked if I had been on the bridge earlier and explained that a film crew had captured the whole incident. Dutch had been on the Bristol side of the bridge but further down, and the film crew had been doing some filming on the waterfront when it kicked off. They spun the camera around and caught the whole battle. Fuck, I thought.

It wasn't long before someone came in shouting, 'Come on, they're here.' I got out the back door and looked down the road as the street filled up with BBC swarming out of the pub. At the bottom of the road, I could see around 20 City lads. Bristol had come for a nosey but as 200-plus United walked calmly down the street towards them, they jogged off back to the waterfront. I went back in and was asked, 'Not going down, Steve?'

'No, I think there's enough to sort it, don't you?'

Now, I've got to say that, by all accounts, Bristol had some very game lads who did their best to hold their ground and stood with pride. A lot of United's lads gave Bristol a lot of credit, but they got done. United's lads waded through a thin police line and, after Bristol had a pop, ran them from one end of the waterfront to the other.

I just sat in the pub with around 20 others and, within two minutes, Paul had walked in with his better half and a couple of his close pals.

'Where is everyone?' he asked as I shook his hand.

'They've gone hunting.'

Ten minutes later, the huge mob came back and, boy, had they got the Johnny Gidmans on (i.e. they were a bit giddy).

'We've gone through the bizzies and swam 'em all over,' one excitedly told me. Not surprisingly, the staff said they were not serving any more and the pub was shutting. Everyone was milling about outside so our little group of 20 went out the back and up an alley to a pub which had a lovely friendly sign in the window: 'Double vodka and Red Bull – £2.60'. We'll have some of that, we thought.

Some other Blades from Swallownest (an area on the outskirts of Sheffield) were in there. I knew a couple of them well; they were big on following England and had travelled the world with our national side. They were also lads who'd done a bit with United over the years.

After a couple of hours, Paul went to his hotel and we continued to get shit-faced. We'd sat laughing as we watched police run past the window, then back down, then back up. This seemed to go on and on and even the bizzies started waving as we cheered them after another dash past the pub; Keystone Cops sprang to mind.

Bristol that night was like a war zone with overstretched police at breaking point. It was then that the situation went tits up again. We had three women with us, so we were just out for a beer and wanted to avoid any trouble – some chance. A well-built lad was heading for the toilet when he knocked straight into a lad who was out with us; he went flying. My pal spilt his drink all over himself. It wasn't your normal drunken stumble into someone, but more like a fuckin' shift-out-of-my-way barge. My pal said, 'Watch what you're doing, mate,' then the geezer just turned and stuck the nut in.

I went mad and promptly nutted the nutter. It all went Pete Tong as I pummelled into the bloke and all his mates rushed over. Like I said, I knew a few of them but this bloke was out of order big time and I wouldn't let go despite all the pushing and pulling. We ended up in the street and, to be fair to my opponent, he was strong. Brand, one of the lads I knew, did his best to calm things down. I was covered in blood from a cut on my head that I did when I stuck the nut in. His nose looked bust and I let go; things calmed down, as the plod were approaching.

'Look, mate, you're bang out of order... We're all Blades here and there was no need for that. We're all blindo... Let's just put it down to too much beer, eh?' I said.

We all mooched off to the big hotel that Cass was stopping in. The mobile went; 'Housey' lit up the display. What's up with the strawberry blond, I thought.

'All right, mate,' I said.

'No, fuckin' hell, Steve... What am I doing at my age? I'm not bothered any more... I shouldn't...' Housey was talking complete nonsense and was in a bit of a state. I calmed him down and asked what the fuck he was blabbering on about.

'It's Wolves... We've just had it with their lads. I've twatted a couple with an ashtray. What the fuck am I doing, Steve? I don't need this...'

He explained that Wolves, including their most famous

thug, had piled into the boozer the Blades were in at Weston-super-Mare. Wolves were very lucky that United's firm had gone to Bristol and not Weston, as this had been suggested a few times. There's no way Wolves would have been able to cope with the numbers and quality that the Beeb had out in Bristol. It's a shame, really, because out of the two of them, Wolves deserved a tonking rather than Bristol.

Around 25 of United's old school had gone to Weston with their wives and kids. They'd ended up having it off with Wolves' main firm and Housey had been in the thick of it. (According to Gilly in his Wolves book, he apparently says that Wolves had it with, – and did – 80 of United's main firm in Weston that night. Everyone knows the Beeb were in Bristol, but then again anything with Martin King behind it has to include its fair share of bollocks).

'Look, Housey, if you could see the state of me, it's not been exactly a bed of roses here either, mate,' I pointed out. I was worried about him because he was in some sort of drunken incoherent state and very upset. I was his Best Man and he's godfather to my son so we're like brothers. I'll ring him in the morning, I thought.

When we got inside the hotel, it was packed with Blades all having a fair old sing-song: *'We're by far the greatest team...The world has ever seen... And It's Sheff United... Sheff United FC...'*

If only!

I'd got three-king sized Rizlas (cigarette papers) stuck on my head to stop the flow of blood. My smart Hugo Boss shirt was covered in the stuff. I was in a right state and, looking around, so was everyone else. The hotel staff had their work cut out as pissed-up fans were either passing out, falling over or spewing. We left at around 3.00am as the bar was closing, and jumped into a taxi back to our hotel. What a mad day, I thought, as the haze of a major drinking binge began to clear. It wasn't over yet, because as we entered our hotel around eight lads were sat having a quiet drink. I walked through, Rizlas still stuck on my noodle and covered in blood.

'Who are you?' one asked in a Midlands drawl.

'Sheff United,' was my proud reply.

'You're gonna get battered tomorrow,' a clever cunt retorted.

'Not off the pitch we won't,' I said, then walked off to follow the others down the corridor. Around 15 paces later I heard the sound of footsteps behind us.

'You what?' One of them made a gesture. Gravy turned and planted his leathery nut into the face of the Wolves lad. We went towards them and they were off from whence they came. We all went into one room and skinned up a couple of skunk 'send me to sleeper' joints. I went off to our quarters, filled the bath and lobbed my blood-soaked shirt in; as soon as I got in feather, I drifted into a deep sleep.

Next morning, I awoke with a massive hangover. The strange feeling between my legs was an orange that my mate Gravy had stuck down my boxers; he thought it might be funny. It wasn't. He also thought it was funny to piss in the shampoo. Luckily – or unluckily, depending on how you see it – I don't need shampoo any more, so it was DJ who copped the piss on the head sketch. I felt like a piece of shit as I sat at breakfast in my boxers, my hangover taking away the excitement of the big day.

The local news was on the TV and reports of the previous night's trouble were the headlines; they even had footage of all the to-ing and fro-ing on the bridge. Predictably, they harped on about pre-arranged this and organised that. Bullshit. Not one of our lads had been in contact with Bristol prior to the set-to on the bridge. It had just happened; two sets bumped into each other and – hey presto – it was beano time. If you want to call something organised, then Bristol's stopoff in Sheffield the following year was extremely organised. Wednesday had been down to Bristol earlier in the 2003/04 season for a League One game and, according to them, they'd had results all over the gaff!

The mouthing off had Bristol's lads fizzing, so when the return game at Hillsborough came in 2004, Bristol and Wendy had obviously got their shit together and arranged a dance well away from Hillsborough. In fact, it was in my fuckin' back yard. Bristol brought 50 quality geezers in a couple of vans and a few cars. They'd gone bang to where they were asked to go – the Navigation pub in Killamarsh. Wendy were up to their usual tricks, saying that they were here, there and everywhere.

Bristol set off to find a pub and plotted up in the Gypsy Queen at the side of Crystal Peaks Shopping Mall. It's not the best place to pick as it's covered by CCTV but, like most places that cater for meals, the cameras are more for show than clocking some cunt lagging up the wall or breaking into someone's motor in the car park. Bristol got on the blower to Wendy and called it on. To be fair to my blue-and-white pals, they turned up 60-strong and with most of their main faces in tow. My mate Bunny (who's since died of a heart attack) picks up the story from here, since he worked as head chef in the Queen:

'Bristol's lads weren't muppets,' Bunny began. 'I've been a lad myself but retired from the scene a long time ago, but I know a good set of thugs when I see them. These lads were all mid-thirties to forty, seasoned boys. I knew the score as soon as I saw them. They were on the mobiles and I knew it was going down, but I didn't expect it at the pub. I just thought they'd stopped off for a livener. I heard one of them on the mobile to a Wednesday lad, saying, "Look, we've been to where you said go, and then you've fucked us about by not turning up. We're in the Gypsy Queen and we're not fuckin' shifting... it's your call. We're on your patch so don't let us down."

'Around a half-hour later, Wednesday arrived and Bristol got caught out at first, as Wednesday got to the pub before Bristol realised. Wednesday were tooled up and it kicked off in the doorway. At first, I thought Bristol were going to get done but they soon had Wednesday backing away and then running full pelt. The sight of Wednesday in retreat had me chuckling and a couple got pulled to the floor and ragged a bit. Bristol marched back to the pub.'

RIP, Bunny, mate.

I've met two sets of Bristol lads who were there that day; one lot at Gloucester before a Beautiful South gig, and the others at the Green Street film premiere in London. Both sets of lads were good company and talked the talk. I quite like Bristol City's lads; they don't seem bullshit merchants like some. Fair play to both the Bristol and Wednesday lads for getting it on without the OB having an inkling. The police moaned about organised hooligans but that's what it's come to now that the plod have driven it to desperate measures.

Anyhow, as soon as we landed in Cardiff, we parked at the side of Ninian Park. I know Bramall Lane doesn't exactly have the nicest surroundings but the road that led from Cardiff's ground to the Millennium Stadium was, without doubt, the worst street I've ever walked up. It smelt like a skunk's ring-piece; litter was strewn everywhere, including nappies that had been thrown in the road and splattered open by passing cars. There were old settees in front of the terraced houses... In short, a shit-hole. Joanne still had time to drop a classic in. She'd stopped to look down at what she said was a dead baby mouse. I walked back to look.

'It's a baby bird, Jo,' I said.

'How d'yer know that then?' she quizzed.

'Well, the yellow beak and wings sort of give it away, flower.' I walked on as she pointed to the sky saying it had fallen from above. Well, it's not dug its way up through the fuckin' concrete, I thought to myself. God she's one dizzy bird.

We had a beer outside the ground. I got a few calls that United were mobbed up in the town centre and they were around 100 strong. I had met my wife and kids so any trouble was to be avoided at all costs. I saw the lad who we'd had trouble with the night before. He was fully panda'd up with his black eyes and looked more than a little rough with his puffed-up face. I was going to talk to him but I thought if he started the kids were with me and I didn't need it, to be fair.

The Millennium Stadium is very impressive but, as we

took our seats, which were bang at the side of United's dugout, I turned to DJ and said, 'No, it's not gonna happen today, mate... I can sense it. The players' body language isn't right.'

My doubts proved correct and Wolves were leading 3–0 at half-time. United had simply not turned up and something was not right that day. Steve Claridge was sat just behind the United dugout and he was doing my head in. Every time Wolves scored, the cock was bouncing around like Zebedee on E. He must have had a couple of grand on them, the gambling twat.

Any hopes of a comeback were dashed five minutes into the second half when Michael Brown hit a tame penalty which the 'keeper saved comfortably. I upped my family and left with five minutes to go. I couldn't watch the Wolves fans celebrating. As we left the ground, I gave my ten-year-old son a little cuddle as he looked close to tears.

'Look, son, you're a Blade and you'd better get used to failure... You better remember this season as you won't see a better one while you've a hole in your arse,' I reassured him. In truth, he had just witnessed a season to treasure. We'd got to two semifinals in the FA and the then-named Worthington Cup against Arsenal and Liverpool respectively, and a play-off final but, at the end of the day, we'd won fuck all. It was the sixth time I'd seen United lose vital games. The three aforementioned games were a 2–1 FA Cup semifinal defeat in 1993 to Wednesday, of all people; a 1–0 play-off final defeat to a last-minute Crystal Palace goal at Wembley in 1997; and a 1–0 defeat in 1998 to Newcastle at Old Trafford in another FA Cup semi. All part and parcel of being a Blade, eh!

Nearly every Blade I spoke to before the last match of the 2006/07 season said we would lose to Wigan and West Ham would win at Man United. All were proved right, as the Blades lost 2–1 and West Ham unbelievably won 1–0 (through Tevez) at Old Trafford. The results sent us crashing out of the premiership on goal average. A legal battle ensued between the two clubs with what has become known by the media as the 'Tevez affair'. (Kevin McCabe has since won his legal battle with West Ham and won £25 million in damages). In my view, United lost their premiership status on the pitch and not off it. Our negative approach away from home cost us; we only scored eight goals on the road all season. Warnock got his tactics drastically wrong in playing one up-front away from home. Look at how Hull have approached the 2008/09 season (and survived). They have played with no fear and respect for no one, and their approach at away games has been refreshing. Phil Brown seems to have decided that they may as well have a go at teams rather than sit back, and it's paid dividends for them. West Ham were wrong to do what they did and the lies they told afterwards proved that they knew they were in the wrong. They will (eventually) face up to the fact that they will have to pay heavily for what they did, but to use the Tevez affair as an excuse for our relegation is a smoke screen, as we had the chance to seal our own fate but blew it.

LOCKED UP AGAIN IN 2004

I'm rarely in town on a Saturday night nowadays; it's simply not worth the hassle. I believed the OB would have me locked up for anything – you know, belching in a built-up area, not walking in a straight line, anything – because I've written a book and pissed them off a bit. So when I was dragged out of a bar in town and locked up for the night it came as no surprise.

United and Wednesday were supposed to be having a bit of a tear-up but why go into the most camera'd-up town centre in Yorkshire looking for your rivals when a phone call can be made and a meet away from CCTV can be arranged? Simple – it takes two to tango and the Beeb have been on that many wild-goose chases that they don't believe a word Wednesday say now.

A typical example happened around 18 months ago when the two groups were on the blower to each other one Saturday evening. A meet was arranged at a place I'll not mention in case it's used again, but when a few BBC headed there in cars and on foot, Wednesday were nowhere to be seen. The OCS had apparently turned up but, according to them, they were hiding in bushes. Now, if they did turn up and hid themselves, fair play, better than hanging around the streets attracting OB, but at least let the Beeb know so they are not trying to meet an invisible enemy. The Internet is now the biggest bullshitting ground around; it's not worth a wank, as claim and counterclaim makes firms look like kiddy mugs.

Anyhow, this night in town the rumour mill goes around that Wednesday are turning out for a dance; to be fair, I treated it with the contempt it deserved. The Beeb have been on more wild-goose chases over the years than Elmer Fudd. So, like I said earlier, the rumours circulating about a set-to with the snorters fell on deaf ears with me. Sheffield's CCTV system is perhaps the most hi-tech in the country; a lot of United lads have learned the hard way and are now banned from the city on match days and, worst of all, from Bramall Lane. I've watched the video evidence that saw six of United's main lads get locked up and eventually banned for three years

The night I got nicked, I should have seen it coming. There had been trouble between two groups of Blades around six months earlier and that included myself. Without going into the details, it culminated in a mass brawl in a pub in town.

It's not good for a firm to be at each other's throats like that and I've always hated in-firm fallouts, as you need to be tight as a mob and trust the people you have to stand side by side with. A mob with internals going off is a mob that isn't as strong as it could be.

In my view, it was at this period in time that the BBC was in danger of self-destructing. The tightness of the firm was nowhere near as close as it should have been and the firm was very much split and in turmoil. Too many lads had let politics, bitterness and one-upmanship take over. A lot of things needed to be sorted out and, thankfully, they have been, and United's firm is once again as strong as ever – they are once again *united*. I hope people have learnt from their mistakes in the past and our firm stays tight in future.

Anyway, on the day United had a home game with Bolton and it was on Sky TV. I balanced the merits of about £23 for a match ticket, or £23 spent on Stella (lager), and the Belgian economy won. I went up to the Sheldon and sat with a few of the lads with whom I'd had run-ins in the aforementioned trouble. A few of these lads I've known for years and I used to be quite close to them. Everyone was man enough to forget about the grief and rightly so.

Later that evening, United went into town for the previously mentioned rendezvous with our good friends the OCS and their new breed called ITI (which stands for 'I'm Twelve Innit'). ITI actually stands for 'Is That It', a piss-take, so I've heard. I fuckin' hope so!

In town, the OB were all over United like a rash. As usual, I kept a low profile. Later on, United headed for the VP bar. The OB surrounded the gaff like ants on a caterpillar. As I walked through the massed lines of OB outside the bar, I heard my name mentioned. Wilb told me to watch it as he overheard the plod saying, 'Watch him, it's Steve Cowens.' I was watched all right, even videoed through the pub windows – celeb or what!

Well, ten minutes later it turned into 'I'm a celebrity… Drag me out of here!' There were a few words exchanged, then the OB charged in the pub mob-handed, including United's football geezer. I was pulled to the floor, handcuffed and dragged outside, but not before one copper smashed my head into the wall on the way out, the clever cunt.

I'm not moaning. They can take liberties like that and get away with it, I think it's all a game to them just like it is with us and, deep down, some of them love the violence as much as the lads do. It's just that they can get away with it.

I was the only one arrested and was back in the familiar surroundings of Bridge Street nick. I sat in the cells, head in hands. What seemed like an endless stream of plod came to the peep door for a chat and a nosey. I felt like a zoo animal. To my astonishment, I was charged. They may as well have said, 'This is for writing a book, you clever twat.'

Once again, I could not moan about it; I'd got away with enough in the past. The cell door closed and I once again sat with my thoughts. My wife, family and kids deserved better.

On the day of my court case, I went along with one of Sheffield's premier solicitors and was preparing to go 'not guilty' all the way to whatever charge plod wanted to throw my way. I was worried that the police could simply throw my book to the judge and say, 'That's him, who's now all innocent,' but my brief assured me they could not do that. In the end, the plod offered me a caution, which I accepted; after all, I'd done fuck all, Your Honour. Even I could keep out of trouble for the six months if I had to; if not, I would be automatically fined £200.

The internal rumblings in the Blades' ranks seem to have been sorted now and I hope the Blades firm continues to be united because a disunited firm leaves the door open.

Recently, one of our old-school lads developed a form of cancer behind his eye. A few of us came up with the idea of having a charity night for him and over 250 Blades lads turned out on the night. Local bands Section 60 and The Stoops entertained our boys, and we raised well over three grand for our mate. Our special guest was Cass Pennant, and he commented on how tight our firm was and I think everyone who turned out that night was proud to be a Blades lad, and long may that attitude remain.

5
FOR ST GEORGE AND ENGLAND

It's finally happened – a major football tournament that has passed off without the so-called 'English disease' ruining everything. The press have finally realised not to portray any little scuffle involving England fans as the Battle of the Somme. The 2006 World Cup in Germany passed without the usual headlines of drunken Englishmen on the rampage. The English at the tournament were not treated like animals but welcomed, and responded appropriately. Push an Englishman and he'll push back twice as hard; that's the mentality we have bred into our systems. Treat the same people with respect and the respect will come back tenfold.

OK, England had over 3,400 lads banned from travelling and this may or may not have stopped some trouble, but 3,400 lads is a spit in the ocean when it comes to the amount of men up and down the country who are willing to fight for their club and country. Putting it into perspective, that amount of banning orders constitutes around 12 clubs' firms.

It's also true that England has a new style of supporter in the face-painted, flag-waving variety, making our fans very much like the fun-loving Jocks and Irish. It is estimated that over 340,000 English fans headed into Germany at some point or another and only 1,600 of our fellow countrymen were arrested, with hardly any being charged with an offence. We are now a nation viewed by many as the Number One in terms of being the best and most loyal supporters in the world, rather than the worst fans, due to our hooligan reputation.

For years, the English abroad have been seen as an invading army of drunken thugs, and incidents over the years have made that a fair comment but, on the flip side, the English have been attacked, stabbed and slashed, gassed and beaten with batons. Thousands of innocent fans have been arrested en masse and treated like scum, and small numbers of English have been attacked by gangs of immigrants. Not once has our government or press reflected this in public statements or in print. I have travelled abroad with England and you feel about as welcome as Pete Doherty or Amy Winehouse at a nun's birthday party. One of the main problems with England abroad is the internal club rivalries that often explode into violence. The following accounts are supplied by lads who have been on the front line, not only for England but also for Sheffield United.

WEMBLEY REGAINED – 1983

Like most English youngsters at that time, I used to hate watching the jocks take over Wembley every time England played Scotland. I'd sit there thinking, 'Where's all the

England fans?' as the TV cameras panned around the ground showing masses of tartan and ginger.

In 1975, I watched *World of Sport* as Trevor Brooking and Kevin Keegan tore the Scots apart in a 5–1 win that hardly any English witnessed in the flesh. As an 11-year-old, I couldn't understand why our national stadium could be taken over so easily and why the English never turned out for this fixture; after all, an Englishman's home is supposed to be his castle.

That frustration as a youngster erupted into a punch on the settee's arm, as two years later thousands of sweaties swarmed on to our hallowed turf and wrecked the joint after beating us 2–1. I remember thinking that one day I would go and defend England's home, even if no one else could be arsed. So, with that thought in mind, in June 1983 I set off along with two Sheffield United boys in my Morris Marina, our destination Wembley, our opponents Scotland.

I'd put my ('This time we'll get it right') England shirt on under my Munsingwear jumper. I'd been to the dentist's the previous day as I'd got an abscess under a tooth and I was in agony. My face had swelled up to John Merrick-sized proportions but I put this to one side as I went to defend England's manor from the invading hordes that came down from chilly jocko land.

When we arrived, it was a real eye-opener as the sweaty socks were everywhere. We'd been told by an English lad that a big firm of Chelsea were at Euston and an even bigger firm of West Ham were at Leicester Square. Sound, I thought, as we headed off to find an English firm that would allow three 19-year-olds to tag along with them.

We saw Chelsea on the Tube interchange; they looked

over 200 strong but we missed them as they were on the other side of the platform. My mate Doyley insisted that we head back to Wembley; he figured that was where Chelsea were heading and didn't want to miss any action with the Tartan Army.

Once we got back to Wembley, I took off my jumper and walked out of the station into the sunshine. What greeted me were hundreds of Scots singing, '*Spot the looney... spot the looney...* They were all pointing at me as they sang, the cunts. I gave them the one-fingered salute in return; it was the best I could muster. By now, I was itching for some action.

'Where the fuck are all the English? This is wank... The jocks are taking the piss and there's no one here to stop it,' I grumbled as we walked up Wembley way. To be fair to the kilt-wearers, they could have mullered us but they preferred to take the piss. One pissed-up jock even asked for a photo with me as he said I was the first Englishman he'd seen in his three previous visits to London. Quite a few jocks even asked if I was all right, thinking my swollen face was the result of a battering.

Then we heard the unmistakable sound of a firm's roar prior to battle. We glanced back down Wembley Way to see the Scottish scattering all over the place as a large group of English had come piling out of the Tube station and had immediately called it on. We were too far away to help our fellow countrymen but, by the look of it, they were doing OK without the help of three skinny teenagers. We waited as the 300-strong English firm bounced up Wembley Way. Sporadic fighting broke out as they walked.

'This must be that Chelsea firm,' I mumbled to Doyley as

they approached. Wrong – they were mainly West Ham with other firms' lads mixed in. We tagged along. At the top of Wembley Way, thousands of Scots were charged on the concourse by the English firm. There wasn't much resistance; this is the bollocks, I thought. The Scots I'd met beforehand didn't seem aggressive; they just took the piss a bit. So when hundreds of English hooligans started chasing them about, I didn't class it as a result. As far as I was concerned, they were like 'shirters' (i.e. your ordinary supporters who weren't fair game) but, at the same time, enough was enough and England had to start to defend its manor. The OB charged around not really knowing which way to turn; there would have been arrests galore if it had been now.

I was pleased to see a lot of the English lads start to enter the same part of the ground we had to go in – the tunnel end. Inside, the jocks were everywhere and it took the English a good part of the first half to get a big enough mob together to get stuck in. England scored and I was pleased to see there were more English in the ground than I first thought. It kicked off to our right and this was the big Chelsea firm in action; they swatted the jocks down the terracing without much problem. Then the English around us waded in. It was now a free-for-all. Punches were exchanged but the English were going down the terracing and the Scots were overpowered. 'ENGLAND... ENGLAND...' rang out loudly. I remember the feeling was immense. We'd put up a fight and this was the final time that the Scots took over Wembley without a fight. I felt proud that we'd been part of England's fightback. England topped the day off by winning 2–0.

On the way home, my tyre blew out in the third lane. A lorry nearly hit us as I careered across the motorway lanes towards the hard shoulder. I'd got no car jack so I had to drive around three miles to the nearest service station where a van full of Scots manually lifted my car and changed the tyre for me. I felt a little guilty because every Scotsman I'd met that day had been so friendly, even when taking the piss, but England had regained control of Wembley and I was proud to have had a part in it. The only question that needed asking was how the Scots had taken over in the first place.

SCOTLAND 1987

The following incidents are the accounts of GJ, a long-term United hooligan who has travelled the world following England. GJ has been arrested eight times at football; he is now retired from the scene but, in his prime, was what I would describe as a 'boss boy': a backward step never entered his mind and he was always one of the first into battle. In short, he was game as fuck.

GJ's reminiscences began like this:

'I've been all over with England to places like Poland, Yugoslavia, Turkey, Germany, Switzerland, Ireland and Croatia to name but a few. Going away with England sometimes means you need to have nerves of steel. The Polish have a reputation for violence but when I went there for the European Championship qualifier in 1991, England absolutely took the piss. I travelled with ten Blades hooligans and every England fan that day was a thug.

'Like most England lads, I used to cringe at the jocks' invasion of Wembley so, in 1987, the chance came along to travel to Hampden Park and show the jocks who was boss and that was too good to miss for me and many others. I hired a 12-seater minibus but the 12 that were setting off at midnight became 17 as our ranks swelled as the beer flowed. Some of the lads woke from their slumber as we got into Glasgow at five in the morning; I think a few of them were thinking, "Where the fuck are we?" wondering if they had made the correct decision. We headed for the Barrowlands as it was one place were you could get a beer at silly hours. Our van had Sheffield written all over it and, as we were parking up, a lot of our lads had got the giddies on and were singing Blades songs.

'The last man hadn't even got out of the van when a firm of thugs came bowling over. Their numbers looked 30ish and they all looked the part, all touching 30. They fronted us up so we squared up, not knowing who we were about to kick off with. A Greek-looking geezer was their main man; he carried a menacing-looking walking stick and the lack of a limp said it all. He barked out in cockney, "Who are you?" We looked at each other and shouted back, "Sheff United."

'Their menacing mood turned into an "All right, lads," but I have no idea why they thought we were OK. This business-looking firm was West Ham and they were well up for some bollocks, be it with the English or Scots. Anyhow, we were welcomed into their fold and sort of tagged on, without getting too much in their face. Then a coach pulled up; it was Birmingham. Surprisingly, there was a few Villa with them (I don't think that would happen nowadays). I recognised a few of the Villa lads, I think they were all from Tamworth. Anyhow, West Ham were straight into them – no messing.

'Birmingham ran... We didn't really get involved but watched from behind, thinking, we've come for the jocks, what's this all about? That was the trouble with England in the early years – too much infighting. West Ham were really revved up so when around 150 Bolton came around another corner, I thought, here we go again. West Ham went straight through Bolton; it was a bad atmosphere and I knew we had to step away from this mad ICF firm. Later on, as the beer flowed, the English lads seemed to settle down a bit and started talking rather than eyeballing each other.

'England had mobs all over Barrowlands but no jock firm was to be seen. We thought we'd seen the last of the ICF mob but, as we chatted to other England fans, all the pub windows came in. Yes, it was the bubble blowers again. A couple of Wednesday lads, one who now runs with Millwall called Shaun, went outside with us and asked what the fuck was going on. The men on the pavement explained that they thought Chelsea were in and mooched off.

'Before kick-off we walked to the ground with a mob of around 50 English lads. We steamed every pub all the way to the ground. The jocks just barricaded themselves inside and the few that did try to have a go got steamed by this angry English mob. A coach of jocks drove past giving us the rods; unfortunately for them, the traffic lights changed and we smashed that coach to smithereens.

'Firms of English, notably Forest and Carlisle, were also making a nuisance of themselves and the OB didn't know which way to turn. It was funny when a biker with his tartan scarf flapping in the wind was kung-fu kicked off his bike, causing him to skid 20 yards down the road on the seat of his pants.

'A car screeched up and out jumped two plain-clothes coppers. They arrested an English lad but, as they tried to put him in the car, they came under attack from the rest of the mob and the car windscreen went through. Further up the road, we encountered the first mob of Scottish casuals. They were Hibs; we went straight into them and they scattered to the winds.

'At the ground, thousands of jocks were milling around. Like Moses, our mob parted them with anyone not moving far enough away copping for a punch or kick. Unusually, we had to go into the Scottish end and make our way across the terracing to the England end. Around 2,000 England had congregated and, of that 2,000, almost all were boys.

'After the game, we were held in for half-an-hour and, during that time, we came under a hail of bricks from outside. This just wound the English up even more and we steamed the gates and charged out. In the waste ground car park outside the English group got up as one and headed towards a jock mob that was waiting down the road. Police on horseback tried in vain to head us off as England marched towards the enemy. They tried to force the English down on to a train station. We headed back to Barrowlands through the piercing screech of police sirens. On the way back, we stopped at Lockerbie; the locals were sound and we had a good chat with them. We'd had enough bollocks for one day.

'Two years later, I travelled up again and was among over 200 English that were arrested. I was fined £500 and had the privilege of my photo being on the front page of the Glasgow *Evening Times*. The English had again taken it to the jocks and the days of Scots taking the piss were well and truly over.'

TURKEY 1987

'The Turks have a bit of a reputation but I found that, apart from stabbing you up the arse, they are very similar to the jocks in the fact that they just throw missiles and then 'do one' when you get within punching distance. I travelled over with Gary, who's a long-term mate and Forest through and through. We ended up staying in Bodrum and bumped into a few Southampton lads; one later got two months for ripping up a Turkish flag, which is a massive insult over there. There were a few mobs of English knocking around, notably Bristol City, Chelsea and Man City.

'On the day of the game, we caught a bus from Bodrum to Izmir. The journey was a nightmare and, from what I can remember, it took hours. Not much happened that we saw before the game and when we got in the stadium around 200 English lads were grouped up in the ground. This was the norm for a game like this – 200 hardcore.

'After the game, a boring-as-fuck 0–0 draw, the Turkish plod brought up two coaches to ferry us away. Trouble was, the transport couldn't get us all on. England fans crammed on the buses like sardines in a tin, hanging out of windows, faces pressed up against the glass, and it left around 35 of us to walk the two miles to Izmir town.

You've heard the saying 'run the gauntlet', well, we did all the way to town. It was total mayhem as Turks attacked by throwing the kitchen sink at us, then turning and running every time we charged. English lads were dropping like flies around you as hundreds of missiles rained through the air.

'If ever England needed to be tight it was this day, and lads covered in blood from head wounds were helped to their feet by their fellow countrymen. I'm proud to say this: a lad called Ian held England together that day. He is a Blade but doesn't really get involved with domestic football violence and has spent a lot of time living in London. He's relatively unknown with United's firm but that day, if it hadn't been for his leadership, we would have been done in, no doubt. Respect where respect is due. Time and again, the Turkish attacks were met by an England charge.

'When we got to the main bus station, the walking wounded English were battered but unbowed and, by now, a cocksure firm, so we went a bit daft with knocking windows through and so on. The army/OB put us in a bar; it was like *Emergency Ward 10* as lots of English were covered in blood from various injuries. The Turks were still patrolling the streets and kept passing the bar we were in. Then they came but surprisingly just stopped outside on the street chanting and making cut-throat gestures.

'We stood around the doors ready to repel any attack. That was it for the night as I caught a taxi and met back up with Gary, who was drinking with some Chelsea in a brothel. England had stood side-by-side; they all supported different clubs but, as it should be, we were as one that day, we had to be.'

6
DARNALL BLADES

Once in a while, you meet a group of lads who are game as fuck and, no matter what the odds, they stick together and stand and fight to a man. The Darnall boys have that mentality; they are a brotherhood and look after each other like one big family. Within their group they have some lads who like a drink, like a good time and, if trouble comes their way, then they like a fight. Growing up together in a mainly Asian area has taught them to keep it tight. Not that race is and ever was an issue within their group, as several black lads have been mainstays over the years. They are passionate Sheffield United and sometimes that passion leads them into trouble. If there could ever be a firm of 100 boys that had the trust, friendships and feeling for each other that this group have, then it would be invincible.

The group – who I will simply call Darnall – first started to travel together to matches in the mid-Eighties. Most had been schoolmates and the first time they really went as a mob to a match was when 25 travelled independently from the main firm via train to Barnsley in 1986. The day was also remembered as the time when the metal BBC badges I had made were confiscated off everyone and stamped on by the OB.

The Darnall firm had it with Barnsley outside a town centre pub. The plod arrived and split up the rival factions. Although Darnall had been well outnumbered, they had stood together and traded, and so started one of the gamest group of lads you could wish to meet. A late, great lad called Roy Zide steamed through police into Barnsley that day and Roy played a part in the attitude the Darnall lads adopt today.

To get their own story of their brotherhood, I went to meet up with the group one Friday evening. The drink had flowed and so did the stories.

SUNDERLAND 1989

Sunderland, if truth be known, is a tough old place to visit. Roker Park during the Eighties was a pit-helmet-and-boots affair for any travelling fans. I had personally been involved in bollocks up there and witnessed the hate the locals had for any invaders. That hate was double for non-whites and when ten lads in two cars travelled up for a game, the two non-whites were subjected to racist taunts.

The day was eventful and started with the drivers swapping cars, only to crash into each other, one car running straight up the arse of the other. You can just see it now – 'That's my car I've just crashed into... fuck!' After parking near the ground, a local gave them some sound advice: 'Don't go near the Fort.'

So what do they do? Go to a pub near the Fort, but only after the landlord was told to fuck off after trying to stop the two black Darnall lads from entering. Locals didn't like the intrusion and the tinderbox atmosphere was broken when two of the locals started flicking cigarette ends at the group. It kicked off in the pub Wild-West style. The 60 or so Sunderland in the pub threw the usual array of weaponry that can be used in pub fights; this caused Darnall to back out of the pub doors and make a stand outside. Sunderland were prevented from getting out as Darnall laid siege to the pub doors. The Mackems (Sunderland lads) couldn't get out, so smashed all the pub windows from the inside. The OB arrived and Darnall moved on to another pub, only to find it coming on top again.

As they left and it kicked off outside, the 40 Mackems couldn't budge Darnall at first, then the sheer volume of attackers had them backing off. It is at this point that it's usually game over for a group, as once you've backed off it's hard to get your shit back together, but Darnall are tight and they surged back in to a man. Sunderland traded blows but found themselves being forced back despite the numbers being overwhelmingly in their favour. The OB came again and advised the battled-hardened Blades that they should move towards the football ground or face arrest. The group moved off while police held locals at bay.

Just around the corner from the ground, Darnall walked straight into a group of Sunderland numbering around 25. Off it went again; this time Darnall ran the group straight away and one managed to pinch a hat off one of the slower-moving Mackems. He handed it over to another one of the group who put it proudly on his head. The OB came again and, by now, they had had enough trouble with this group of Yorkshiremen and got heavy-handed. Dogs were set on the group and a black lad called Reidy punched a dog as it savaged his arm; he was nicked along with another black lad, yet the whites were left alone.

Police shoved the Darnall lot in a van and made them wait 15 minutes before taking them to the ground. What greeted them when they got out of the van at Roker Park will live in their memories for ever. Una (one of Darnall's main men) said, 'I couldn't fuckin' believe it... As we got out of the van, loads of Sunderland boys started clapping us. They were shouting, "Game as fuck, lads." We smiled and waved back.' This didn't stop one of them pointing out his hat to police as it sat on an innocent Darnall head.

'Where did you get that hat from?' asked plod.

'Bought it last week.'

The police took the hat and, unluckily for the wearer, it had the original owner's name written in it. Another arrest.

In the ground, United were warning up and Boney M was shouting at a young Brian Deane who was doing his best to pretend he couldn't hear Boney. 'Deano, I want you...' Boney wouldn't let up. Deane then casually walked over thinking Boney wanted an autograph.

'Nar then, Deano... watch thee sen... here they are right racist cunts,' Boney advised him. Deano shook his hand, thanked him for the warning and walked off, no doubt (correctly!) thinking he was a nutter.

TOTTENHAM 1991

The BBC travelled in big numbers to this fixture. They ran the Spurs firm after the game and were also involved in pre-match skirmishes. As usual, the Darnall lot went their own way, preferring the trusted group they had rather than the large numbers that United's firm offered.

Around 12 travelled on a coach from Rotherham; the coach was full of 'norms' and 'shirters', so as soon as they got off they went on their way. At the side of the Corner Pin pub where a lot of Spurs boys drank, Morton went in the bookie's; he was soon back out with a shout of, 'Cam on then, you cant…' It went off in the street and, for two long minutes, Darnall went toe-to-toe with a group of around 20 Spurs lads. Neither side backed off an inch and punches were thrown at an alarming rate.

Just as both sides tired, the plod came and it was barely in time, as more Tottenham were running to join their ranks. Once again, they had stood side by side and the bond that had started was now fully entombed around the group. In short, they had no fear and cared little about the numbers that came their way. They trusted each other totally and knew if one was going to get it then they all were.

Over the years, the Darnall lads have had more than their fair share of bans with Mad-Dog receiving two three-year bans with only two weeks in between them. Cardiff's visit to the Lane saw MD cop another three years. In total, seven of them have received bans.

SHEFFIELD WEDNESDAY

For the away game in 2000, 20 Darnall had bought tickets for the seats in Wednesday's cantilever stand. Wednesday sussed the mob and came up the seats towards them. They paused just before, trading distance, and Darnall saw their chance and steamed in. A stunned Wednesday firm backed off over the seats, one falling over and pulling two more snorters backwards over the seating in panic. Boney M lost the plot and couldn't contain himself as he frenzied up in a battle against his most hated. Unsurprisingly, he was arrested, but this fact didn't stop him aiming kicks at mouthy Wednesday lads as he was taken out of the stadium.

Una had been sat on his own near the front and a few Wednesday saw him and started giving him the verbals. Una stood up and beckoned Wednesday on. He then improvised by pretending to pull a shotgun from under his coat, cock it and then fire two shots at the bemused Wednesday lads who were, by now, heading over the seats to him. He planted his back foot ready for war but the two Wednesday who were nearest him didn't fancy it until police came and dragged Una out.

In 2001, while 400 BBC had met up at the Punchbowl pub in the Crookes district of Sheffield, the Darnall lot did their usual by travelling to Hillsborough on their own. The 30 or so met at a pub up Halifax Road deep in the heart of Wendyland. They timed their arrival at Hillsborough so that it gave them maximum chance of a tear-up. Ten minutes before kick-off, they again infiltrated Wednesday's seats. Before they could group up inside, a few Darnall were sussed and realised Wednesday were moving in. The cavalry arrived and fronted up the Wednesday firm. Wednesday had undoubtedly the numbers but had they got the quality? Wednesday steamed in and two were dropped to the floor, causing the rest to hesitate.

'Wednesday... Wednesday...' the chant went up, but battles aren't won or lost on a chant. Darnall ran in causing Wednesday to back off and run. Two Darnall got lifted. Later that night, the mobiles were red-hot as rumour had it that Wednesday were going to hunt down Darnall to seek retribution. Over 150 BBC turned up in a fleet of taxis that night to help their fellow club-men out. Wednesday never showed; shame, really.

ROTTERDAM

With football banning orders only stating that lads were banned from football games in England and Wales, United's banned lads saw a chance to get to see the Blades and a bit of action if they were lucky. With probably 40 or so banned lads planning to travel, the OB moved the goalposts due to concerns over who was going to travel over for United pre-season friendlies at The Hague and Sparta Rotterdam. The police waited until two weeks before the actual games to send out a letter to each and every banned Blade, stating they could not travel and faced arrest if they did. The trouble was, a lot had booked their flights and accommodation, thus losing their money and chance to travel.

Twenty-two lads travelled from Darnall; of these lads, a few had their families in tow and not all were fighters. The night before the game, they had chosen to stay in Rotterdam while most Blades had chosen Amsterdam. It wasn't long before they were in trouble, as by their own admission they were acing up. The bouncers, who were massively oversized due to large intakes of Henri Lloyds (steroids), soon sorted out any potential trouble as they coolly brought a large cricket-bag style holder and unzipped it to show the visitors an array of baseball bats and clubs. Una then put his arms up as if to say, 'Fair do's... you win.' The group left but had been blackballed in all the pubs and clubs and couldn't get a drink anywhere. In the drunken haze, they got split up and Una later took a taxi on his own back to his digs.

As he stumbled about trying to pay the taxi driver, he noticed a figure watching him. He went into the bar that was under his digs, and the figure – a shifty-looking Moroccan – had followed him in. Another Darnall lad – Deano – was curled up asleep, the rest nowhere to be seen. Una leant his unsteady body on the bar. A voice at the side of him then said, 'You want lady?'

'No, fuck off.' Una then felt a hand touching the top of his pocket, or was the 'lady' feeling Una's arse? The pickpocket realised that although Una was very drunk, he had his wits about him. Una stood face-on to the thief and then felt another hand try to dip his pocket. Another Moroccan had tried it on so Una launched him with a punch that sent him sprawling to the canvas. He started fighting with the other one but the one on the floor got up and Una was in a bit of trouble. Deano then came to the rescue and they chased them out and up the street. One of the Moroccans picked up a bike and threw it at Una as he tried to grab hold of him. Una hurdled it but caught his foot in the spokes and crashed his face into the pavement. He copped a black eye and broken ribs for his trouble.

Una and the rest awoke to sore heads and brilliant sunshine. Una looked like an old man when he went down to breakfast; he was doubled over in pain from his ribs and everyone wanted to know how he'd got his shiner.

The day was pleasant as families of Blades mingled with lads; several bars were frequented without a hint of trouble. Despite quite a few of United's hooligan element travelling, there didn't seem the need to mob up and, with Sheffield OB monitoring United's lads along with their Dutch counterparts, trouble didn't seem very likely at all.

A mixed bunch of around 25 Blades were drinking outside a bar. They had seen nothing that resembled a lad although it later emerged that a cockney with an ICF tattoo on his arm had been quizzing some United lads. He left. He obviously had something to do with what happened next – what kind of Englishman sets up his fellow countrymen for a Dutch firm? Anyhow, around ten young Dutch boys waltzed up giving it the big 'un. They were laughed at and a bit of banter was exchanged. Looking back, the lads now know they were trying to get them to chase them and get them away from the pub. A few United got sick of them and chased them off. A minute later, they were back and this time they bounced about and a couple had bike chains hanging from their hands. It was becoming clear that this was a setup. The OB, including Sheffield's, watched on from a bridge as these events unfolded.

From behind United came an estimated 50 Dutch; they were Feyenoord, not Sparta. It kicked off big time. Glasses were used to keep the tooled-up Dutch at bay, their weapons ranging from chains, bats, knives, coshes and even a six foot fuckin' spear. In the mêlée, several United fans were injured, including one who was slashed across the hand as he tried to grab the attacker's knife. Another was hospitalised after being stabbed in the back of the head with either a knife or a broken bottle. All the time the battle went on the OB did nothing except film it. The few United lads who were there make no bones about getting backed off into the pub. Inside, it was like a Casualty ward, with several bleeding or suffering from blows caused by bats.

The OB took the fans to the match and the injured went to hospital; no one missed the game. The Feyenoord firm were given praise for their organisation, but slated for the use of tools. Their firm were a lot more organised than the OB over there, that's for sure.

After the game, which was witnessed by 700 travelling Blades, buses were brought to the ground. They travelled to different locations and only one bus went into Rotterdam where the Darnall lot wanted to be. They boarded with families of Blades, knowing that if it came on top it was them against the world. They were unceremoniously dumped at the train station in Rotterdam. As the ten Darnall and a few other Blades walked through the main bus station and came out at the other side, they noticed a group of 20 Dutch on the other side of the road, watching.

Iffil decided to take the bull by the horns, thinking another stitch-up would happen if action wasn't taken fast. Una told him semi-jokingly to take the big cunt out as his ribs were killing him from the previous night's bike trip. Iffil walked casually up, hoping to get a snide one in. It went off again, and again the Dutch pulled out weaponry. Toe-to-toe in the road, United stood firm. Iffil was twatted across the head with a bike chain. The Blades had them moving and, just before a tram came past, they ran them. The only trouble was Iffil's eagerness getting the better of him, and he ended up with the Dutch on one side of the tram while the others had to wait for it to pass before they could go and help their colleague. Reidy joined in the chase until they doubled back and went in a restaurant. The steak knives vanished up jumper arms or under tables as the United contingent sat waiting for another inevitable attack. The Dutch hooligans monitored the restaurant, then Sheffield OB showed up and taxis were ordered. The Dutch were even asking the taxi drivers where they were going to drop United off!

A mad weekend that could have ended up worse than it did. We English are no angels but at least we fight with fists. The Dutch firms of first Feyenoord and later Sparta had proved it's a different hooligan world over there. The OB are clueless and let known troublemakers roam the streets carrying weapons. There is no wonder that 200 Ajax and an equal number of Feyenoord met in a field in a prearranged fight that saw a person lose his life.

7
'THE TIDE IS TURNING'

That headline is a favourite saying from our blue-and-white rivals. Well, this tide never seems to come in. The United and Wednesday rivalry will go on and on with claim and counterclaim of who did what, who should have done this, there were only 50 of us and 52 of you. It never ends and, to be frank, it bores the arse off me nowadays. The Internet has seen a rise in cyber-warriors. You can get sucked into arguing the toss with complete pikelets on the net. After one of our top lads died, a Wednesday lad came on the United site saying the most insulting things he would never have dreamed of saying to the deceased lad's face.

When I used to go on the Internet, everyone knew who I was; I didn't hide behind an alias. So when I got into a heated argument with this pathetic cyber-Pig, I lost it. To cut it short, he said he knew me well and I was a wanker and that he would do me in. We came to an arrangement – I turned up and he didn't, so I mailed him with some abuse.

He then he sent me a private message apologising for his behaviour, so I posted it for all to see.

It's easy to tap on a keyboard. I don't bother with the net any more. Yes, we hate each other with a passion but for too many years now both Sheffield clubs have concentrated on each other rather than the opposition from other cities. In the early Eighties, United and Wednesday would drink side-by-side in the Blue Bell in town. Yes, it was strained and when the clubs met it was murder, but the week-in, week-out bollocks that goes off now has had the OB laughing little apples. I can't see the Sheffield rivals ever drinking together again.

United's firm have, and still hold, court in our great city. The tide will turn one day just as it did when we took over in the mid-Eighties. Wednesday treated our up-and-coming youngsters with complete disdain. They couldn't see this threat developing right under their noses and, like a cancer, we spread and grew stronger. Before Wednesday knew it, we had taken over. The danger is that United could adopt that same attitude. It's complacency but, to be honest, the United lads know that Wednesday need keeping in their place and what Wednesday don't realise is that a lot of their actions only serve to keep the BBC's hatred of them at fever pitch.

'Meet the Owls Crime Squad – the firm that became notorious for pulling off the most audacious invasions and legendary battles, no matter how the odds were stacked'. That's what the book's blurb says; whoever wrote that wants to start writing for Jack Dee, as it's funnier than any of his stand-up stuff.

Now I've nothing against Paul Allen, the lad who wrote

their book. I actually arranged to meet him a few years ago when he was back in this country for a few weeks, and I also gave him advice about how to write a book. I can fully understand the fact that the four years he was around the scene were probably the worst times for being a Wednesday lad. The middle-to-late Eighties had seen United's hooligan element totally take over the affairs in our fair city and the OCS were given a torrid time by the 'Blades Bully Crew' as he affectionately calls us. It's a cop-out to say United bullied them, but that subject keeps chipping away. The simple fact is United started to run Wednesday ragged and, like a dog with a bone, we chewed away until we were certain the job was done. It just makes me laugh at the suggestion that the Beeb were merely bullies; the plain fact of the matter was that our firm was too game and too strong for Wendy to deal with but, of course, it's hard to admit.

Well Paul, my friend, picture this – in 1980, a 16-year-old lad was in the Crazy Daisy nightclub on High Street one Friday night when one of Wednesday's older lads went up to him and said, 'Take that fuckin' badge off or I'll smash you all over.' The lad refused to take off his United pin badge and the Wednesday lad slumped off. Later, the young United fan was punched from the side while having a piss in the toilet. He was then volleyed into the piss trough by the Wednesday lad and his mates. That 16-year-old was me and the bully was a well-known knobhead called Granville who ran coaches for Wednesday's firm and was one of their main actors.

A year after the attack, I was in Steely's (later Roxy's) nightclub when I got talking to a lad called Kav who worked with me. Kav hung around with a lot of Wednesday and probably their main lad at the time was a big black fellow called Harry. He saw my United badge and spat lager on it. The young Blade went for him and I was bundled away by Kav. No doubt I would have been mullered, but it was my shirt and club that had been spat on. Kav later fucked Wednesday off and not only did he become a great friend of mine, he also became a top United lad, too.

I also remember Wednesday coming in the Red Lion at the bottom of West Street and basically the 50 or so of them battered the ten Blades in there. I was 17 and the little posse of Blades were all pups and Wednesday's main actors thought it funny to knock the fuck out of us. More recently, Wednesday thought it funny to smash one of our game lads all over with bottles when 100 of them went in a pub while we were at West Ham. No, that's not 'bullying' – that's fuckin' shite.

What I'm getting at is this: when I was a youngster, I was subjected to the bullying side but didn't go on and on about it in BBC. In fact, I never even mentioned it. It happened on both sides, as shit as it is. Paul seems to focus on United being nothing but bullies; it's bollocks and he knows it. OK, United had a couple of lads that overstepped the mark, but so did Wednesday.

During the same period that United were supposed to be big-time bullies, 50 of us walked into the Golden Ball in town and, in doing so, 15 Wednesday were trapped in the corner. Did they get battered? Did they get a slap? Did they fuck! In fact, a few arguments took place and I and a few of the townies stood firm against the out-of-town Blades who wanted to smash Wednesday there and then. (To check the truth of this, read Gary Armstrong's *Football Hooligans: Knowing the Score*.) One thing's for sure: if the boot was on the other foot, the boot would have been used.

There's so much in the book I could pull up but I suppose you have to look at how the hell they can try and justify being overrun for 22 years without bullshitting. Anyhow, I suppose there's a lot in my BBC (never been run, never been done!) book that he doesn't agree with, so it's horses for courses.

My last bit of trouble with Wednesday was over four years ago when 30 United were in town celebrating a lad's birthday (see update page XX). We later split up and I ended the evening in the Casbah with 15 others. Wednesday were around as we'd seen them through the club windows walking up and down having a sly look but not daring to venture inside. Near the end of the night, there were eight of us left, but a very high-calibre eight at that. To be honest, I was that shit-faced I'd forgotten about our foe until Drib came over and said, 'We'd better get together before we leave... Wednesday are still around outside.'

Sure enough, as we left the club around 15 young Wednesday lads bounced towards us, hoods up and caps pulled so low that they virtually covered their faces. We walked calmly into them but they shot off, leaving two captured lads screaming. United showed their class that night by just holding the Owls lads and tormenting them a bit. They never got touched except for a few flat-handed slaps but one was relieved of his P&S cap.

I was a bit embarrassed by the events as the lads I was

with were all touching 40 and some of the boys we were chasing were young enough to be our sons, but what do you do when they come for it? In truth, United's firm has dominated Wednesday off the pitch for over 22 years now and that looks like continuing for years to come. Sure, Wednesday have had the odd result but, by and large, it's been one-way traffic.

This fact was highlighted after Wednesday's home game against Leeds United at Hillsborough in 2006. Wednesday were out in numbers celebrating the stag night of one of their well-known lads. Also on Ecclesall Road, another celebration was taking place, as around 15 United lads were out celebrating the birth of Fozzy's first child. Unbeknown to the Blades firm, Wednesday were drinking just 100 yards from the pub they were in. Five United lads moved on to the next pub which made the rivals only 50 yards apart. It was then the alarm bells started to ring and a Blades lad rang a Wednesday boy to ask where he was. As usual, Wednesday denied where they were but exited the Nursery Tavern as they knew they had been rumbled, then headed down the road. Stood in their way were five of United's main lads. Despite being severely outnumbered, United's supporters stood solid and fronted the Wednesday firm. Wednesday couldn't budge the Blades lads and, apart from one boy copping a sneaky sidewinder, which resulted in a black eye, they were relatively unscathed. The OB came and a couple of United lads got lifted.

In short, it showed the gulf in class between the firms. If the boot had been on the other foot, Wednesday would have never stood their ground. During the next few days on the Internet, Wednesday tried to gloss over the events. They made lame excuses like they thought there were more Blades in the pub, but so what if there had been? Are they not into football for the purpose of having it away, or are they in it to chant 'Wednesday' and dance around like they did when the five Blades stood strong?

United first started to turn things around on the hooligan front in 1985; after a couple of years of even tussles, the Blades' new firm of young casuals had taken over from a shell-shocked Wednesday firm that had the upper hand in the late Seventies–early Eighties. Little did they know at the time that, over 20 years later, United would still be ruling the roost.

'The tide is turning' comment started to gather momentum after Wednesday had a bit of a result against the Beeb after a home game with Rotherham in 2005. United got it terribly wrong that night. Thirty United lads were drinking in the Mulberry Tavern when they got news through that Rotherham were holed up in the Brown Bear, which is only 200 yards away. Around 15 of the younger lads went for a nosey. The Rotherham firm was actually Wednesday and the 50 Owls attacked. United still had lads in the Mulberry but, by the time they had got their shit together, United were on the back foot.

Havo picks up the story:

'By the time we'd realised it was Wednesday, it was too late. No excuses like; we were just slow on the uptake. Our pups had put up a fight but, by the time we headed around the corner towards the Crucible Theatre, we were on the hop. Despite our shouts of 'STAND', Wednesday had got too much momentum. We split as we ran and around ten of us got chased by the main bulk of the

Wednesday firm right into the Banker's Draft, but this is where our fortunes changed... Or should I say we changed our fortunes. The ten of us picked up stools and glasses and defended the doors. Wednesday were in the street going shit-pot while they attacked the doors. We'd had enough and surged out into them. One was splattered as a wood-to-skull blow sent him reeling. This was enough for us to get them on the move. I couldn't really believe it but they just turned and ran.

'Like a fox after a rabbit, we followed and one grunter was caught and suffered a real mashing while his so-called mates didn't look back, despite us shouting for them to come and help him. He was sparked. There's a fat Wednesday lad who's supposed to be a main actor with them... Well, that cunt ran like fuck without a glance back.

'Wednesday regrouped near the Crucible but we had tasted blood and went through them again. The thing that night was they ran us, then we ran them, but to hear them go on over the next few days you'd have thought they'd won the Battle of Little Big Horn! But we knew that after the torment they had suffered over a long period of time then they would take any crumb of comfort. Wednesday started making big noises that the Beeb were finished and the tide had finally turned... I've seen John Hartson turn quicker than this tide!

'Another incident that proved that Wednesday were desperate to try to claim any result was when around 15 United older heads had to retreat into TP Woods after 50 Wednesday attacked them. Wednesday posted CCTV coverage of the brawl all over the Internet claiming the result. All it showed was the 15 United lads coming out to confront an equal number of Wednesday. The Wednesday lads backed off but, unbeknown to the Blades firm, another 30 or so Wednesday came running up behind United and they backed them into the pub – big deal. One Wednesday lad was rumoured to be dead after being sparked outside the pub. Later, Wednesday were full of it. The tide has turned!

'One fight proved that the Wednesday claims that the Beeb were on the back foot were as false as Jordan's tits. The so-called Wednesday upsurge coincided with the OB being intent on banning as many of United's lads as possible from football matches. The government had ploughed money into funding a new way of getting lads away   from football and the solution was civil bans.

'After Wednesday had returned from an away match at QPR in 2004, they plotted up 30-handed in the Yorkshire Grey. Not many United were out in town but, when a Wednesday lad rang his Blades mate, nine United lads left the town centre pub and headed towards Wednesday. The Owls firm knew they were coming but didn't know the numbers heading their way. CCTV followed the nine Blades; the crystal-clear pictures showed the events unfold. United walked across the car park giving the waiting Wednesday firm plenty of time to get out. Wednesday stayed put but grouped up around the doors. As United attacked, they just defended the entrance doors. One United lad put a few windows through with a telescopic cosh. Six of the nine were later arrested.

'The *Sheffield Star* ran the front-page story of how Wednesday hooligans had, according to witnesses in the pub, 'Stationed men around the doors... They were on their mobiles and shouting to each other that they were coming and to barricade the doors'. The six United lads escaped football banning orders because the judge reasoned that there was no evidence that it was connected to football, but they copped for large fines and curfews. No Wednesday were arrested; not surprising, really, as they had sat tight despite having far superior numbers. It was further proof if anyone needed it that United's firm were not only gamer but wanted it more than their Wednesday rivals.

'There was no disputing the result the Beeb had later that year when both mobs met head on. United, outnumbered two-to-one, sent a Wednesday firm scattering to the winds.'

AUNT SALLIES

The last league game of the season saw a few of us making a trip down to Vicarage Road. United were comfortably within the play-offs, and this was just a trip down for something to do, have a few beers and a laugh. About seven others and I were booked on a coach that runs from one of the boozers near Bramall Lane. The usual clientele were a mix of lads who weren't afraid to have a go when it came on top, some pissheads and a few shirters.

A lot of our lads were hanging back in Sheffield and drinking up Ecclesall Road. The Pigs were at home to Walsall and it's kind of traditional to try and meet up for one last tear-up before the season ends (although, in all honesty, there's scrapping all year round).

On the way back from Watford, we were checking up to see what had happened back in Sheffield. Not a lot, was the reply, but we were told we should try and get back as soon as we could. We landed back in Sheffield at about 4.30pm and met up with the rest of our lot on Ecclesall Road. There were about 50 or so lads out, largely made up of the youth with a few of the big-hitters as well. They had already seen some action as the 50 of them had shaken off the plod by going out of the back doors of the Pomona pub and taking a nature walk, during which they had tried to meet Wednesday near the top end of Ecclesall Road. The plod had managed to stop United's charge at Wednesday and a few Blades were nicked.

Later, back at the Pomona, a couple of young Pigs were spotted having a poke around and were soon sent packing. A few minutes later, riot vans turned up, with the rozzers decked out as though they were quelling a military coup. We sat in the boozer having a few more pints and a bit of the old marching powder.

A couple of hours passed and we hadn't moved, but we were getting calls from the Pigs saying they were making their way to town. The rozzers were still sat outside, and it looked like we wouldn't be able to shake them off. A few of our lads called it a day and buggered off home, and slowly we were getting down to about 30 lads, largely youth. Again, the Pigs were on the blower saying they were drinking 50-handed in a bar about a 10-minute walk away. Something had to be done, and some fucker came up with a plan so simple it was brilliant. We'd just go off in dribs and drabs, jumping in cabs in the rank outside the boozer, then we'd meet up in a pub closer to the Pigs. But we wouldn't tell them that.

Sure enough, it worked a treat. As our numbers

dwindled on Ecclesall Road, the rozzers began to scratch their heads, and they left what was left of us to our own devices. We made our way up to the boozer; by the time we got there, probably 30–35 of us had made it.

We sipped a pint, and the old adrenalin got going. One of our lads was scouting out on the road, looking for signs of movement from the Pigs who, according to their calls, thought we were still on Ecclesall Road.

The shout went up and we left the boozer and waited in the car park. The road along which the OCS were coming was about six feet higher up than the pub car park, but the boundary wall was a good seven feet tall on their side and about 15 feet on our side, so they couldn't see us. The boozer must've just had a refurb, because there was a skip outside, packed with handy-looking bits of wood. As far as we were concerned, we were outnumbered two-to-one, so getting tooled up was only fair. A few lads brought bottles and pint pots out of the pub. However, the best tool to come out was one of those pizza shovels they use to get pizzas out of the ovens – a big flat metal sheet with a wooden handle.

A little pep talk from one of the older lads called Tap and we were chomping at the bit. We waited for them to get within a decent range, and then we went for it. The look of total fucking surprise on some of their faces was worth it alone. With the barrage of glasses and bottles, the shout of 'BBC' went up and they shat it, turned and ran straight back to where they came from. We couldn't believe it. Some of their older lads stood, but got a good hammering and were left well battered. Whatever credibility the ITI/OCS had given themselves, we shattered it inside three minutes. The job had been done, but the rozzers were closing us down quickly, so we turned and did one back to the boozer.

Unsurprisingly, they weren't too happy that day. We'd made monkeys of them and let a few of ours have it when they were trying to get back in the pub. I went through the car park and met up with a few others, and we made our way quietly through a couple of estates and back to Ecclesall Road. We were buzzing our tits off, and well chuffed that we'd just completely destroyed the OCS while being so outnumbered. They had decent numbers but just 'did one', leaving a couple of their gamer lads to get shovelled in (literally).

One thing is certain, though – the war will continue. The 2008/09 derby at Hillsborough saw the BBC adopt a new tactic. They all got taxis to Hillsborough Corner and arranged it so that everyone would arrive bang on opening time.

Barry picks up the story:

'We'd got fed up of marching to Hillsborough surrounded by the Old Bill; it was the same every year and had got quite boring. The OB always made us late for the match so fuck 'em. In future, they aren't going to get an easy ride – fuck us around and we'll fuck you around. Every year we go to Hillsborough firmed up and there are never any takers. Wednesday always go on about us never going into Hillsborough Corner despite the fact that we've bounced through there on a couple of occasions. So this year we got it together and arranged to meet in Legends at 11.00am.

'I was in the first taxi to arrive. Already sat in the pub

were around ten Wednesday. They started to get twitchy as the four of us ordered drinks. Just as one stood up to come over to us, I looked outside and taxis kept arriving and pulling up. In walked one of our main men; he waltzed straight over to the Wednesday lads and said, 'Fuck off now... Today, my friends, this is a Blades pub.'

'The Wednesday lads got up and left unmolested as swarms more of our lot turned up. Within minutes, the pub was full of Beeb. We were sure Wednesday would show; after all, we were in their pub on their turf. No police had sussed us so we sat tight with a few of ours walking around Hillsborough to seek out our foe. After 15 minutes, the mugs had not shown up but the OB did – Section 60 time! So we turned up and, although they never came to dance, we'd showed that there is no safe haven for them.

'The Wednesday lads in the pub weren't touched; they were humiliated by the fact that we'd just made them leave their own boozer, but later in the same season, 15 Wednesday went in the Penny Black while we were at Barnsley and they had a home game with Doncaster. Inside were four of our youth and they tried to give it them, only for our youngsters to steam them out of the pub with stools. They then smashed the pub windows. There's no wonder they have a bad name and reputation all over the country with the antics they get up to, the mugs.

'By the way, the previous season I was banned and, as the 250 of our lot got rounded up in a pub near Hillsborough, me and around 20 other banned Blades lads were escorted to town. As we walked past a pub, a load of men came to the windows giving it the 'wankers' signs. It was Wednesday's banned lads, including their TV star. We went into town and, as soon as the OB left us, we got taxis back to the pub. Wednesday bounced out and threw glasses at us, some held on to stools as we ran towards them. They bottled it but, fair play to the TV star, he was one of the last to go, but he got decked and copped a bad beating while all his so-called mates had left him in the road. He was in intensive care for a week.

'The young United lads look like carrying on as top dogs. As for me, I don't hate Wednesday like I used to. I don't know whether it's because I'm getting old or the fact that I don't bother with the bollocks any more. I actually get on with quite a few of Wednesday's old school; to me, they are sound lads, although I didn't think that years ago when I was at it with them.

'My past caught up with me in 2008 when I found myself in the wrong place at the wrong time and was arrested for the eleventh time. At 43, I don't need that shit any more but, when it came along, it was like being transported back in time. Along with a few of our lot, I had arranged to have a charity do for one of our lads who'd developed cancer. I'd got all the tickets and posters printed and handed them out to our boys at the match. The lad who was ill was out and I decided to have a drink with him around town after the game. At bang on 11.00pm, seven of us were drinking in a bar when around twenty Wednesday turned up outside giving it the verbals. I walked outside.

'To cut it short, it kicked off. The seven of us backed Wednesday up the street and, despite Wednesday's far superior numbers, we kept them moving back. They were screaming "STAND"; we were also screaming "STAND" at them, adding that there were only a few of us. The lads

I was with were all game as fuck and I really believe that if just one of us hadn't got stuck in we would have struggled, we were so outnumbered. I copped a couple of punches but just kept moving forward.

'At the top of the road, I was rugby tackled by the OB who had run up behind me. Wednesday's lads hadn't even got the decency to let me know the police were around. I laid face down with the coppers on top of me. I was cuffed and frogmarched back to the van. The OB knew me and asked what I was doing getting involved in all this again. I just said, "Wrong time, wrong place," but added that I'd fuckin' enjoyed it, though. Not a lot had gone my way that year so I had a lot of pent-up aggression in me, and the fight was a good release.

'Wednesday typically put it around that I had been dropped in the battle, as they tried to get something out of another humiliation, but the only time I hit the deck was when the police tackled me. If I'd been dropped, I'd say so – I'm not Superman! I suppose they had to try to get something out of a fight that had left them humiliated once again.

'To be honest, I've got better things to do than run around town under the gaze of cameras, trying to win a war that was actually won over 22 years ago. I was in that group of young lads who turned things around and I've played my part in the history. I really don't know where, when, or even if, it will ever end, but I do think it will one day lead to a fatality, because the hatred between the two groups knows no bounds. Let's hope, for the sake of both sides, that doesn't happen, but the more the code of conduct is ignored, particularly by the younger element, then that scenario is a very distinct possibility.'

8
THE YOUTH
OF TODAY

The following pages are written by one of United's game youngsters. The growing youth element has increased throughout the country, as bored and sometimes angry young lads get into football. It's better than nicking and burning out cars (what's that all about, eh?). It's better than burgling some old dear then jacking your profit up grizzled veins, fuckin' your life up and everyone connected to you, including your family. It's better than standing on street corners in a TN hat supping cheap lager and smoking on a joint, then smashing a bus stop up on the way home.

That said, the young lads at football nowadays suffer worse than the aforementioned lowlifes when they hit the courts. A lad who fights with another lad at football…well, he gets two years' jail. A smack rat needs help? Yeah, someone *made* him inject misery into his veins. A burglar needs protection from householders because some high-ranking Lord says just because they have broken into someone's house doesn't mean they lose the rights they have as citizens.

BOLLOCKS!

If I catch someone in my gaff, then they are leaving in an ambulance – end of. The courts can do what they want but an Englishman's home is his castle.

The young lads at football now are persecuted; their rights are stripped from them and all because they like a bit of excitement on a Saturday afternoon. Civil laws should work both ways but, nowadays, the plod can give you a three-year ban from football just because you are seen talking to a 'prominent', as they like to put it. I feel sorry for the young 'uns involved today. They are on a hiding to nothing. United have just had the youngest banning order in the country with a 16-year-old banned for three years through the civil courts. Now this lad is as game as they come, but he has only been on the scene a year or so and he's copped a three-year ban! The OB would have taken five years to suss out a young lad who was involved when I was that age.

That same lad, along with another two youths, was recently arrested in breach of their banning orders. He was as game in court as he is on the street when he told the judge he had broken the banning order and would continue to do it, as he didn't agree with it. He and the others copped a £1,000 fine to be paid at £50 a week, no ifs or buts. Anybody making a name for themselves now at football is banned before you can say 'Come on then'. It's the way football has gone.

In June 2005, three Blades youth were given sentences of up to four months' imprisonment for chasing Wendy youth out of the Walkabout pub in town. Wednesday had been on the blower and called it on; nine Blades youth turned up and chased Wednesday, who didn't want to know, despite the fact that they had actually called it on and also picked the venue, which happened to be the most CCTV'd pub in town. None of the arrested lads, whose ages ranged between 16–18, had any previous offences, but the courts and police saw fit to remove them from society for a few months.

United must get back to the attitude of the old days – one big family. Youngsters were treated with respect and welcomed along with the main firm and we had trust and a bond together; we were, in short, second brothers. If one was in trouble, we all were.

There's full respect for the young lads at it today as I wouldn't like being a fledgling hooligan now. If our pups can take 25 Blades to Leeds and have a pop, then they certainly have some game lads.

Anyhow, here's a few pages written by one of United's game youth; these lads aren't scumbags but, to police and the courts, they are far worse than the deadbeats mentioned earlier who blight our society.

THE YOUNG PUPS

The following stories are told by a United youth lad called Penners:

'I moved from Madrid to Sheffield in 1996, partly to further my education, and largely to follow United. It wasn't until 2002 that I was first involved in scrapping for the good name of Sheffield United. Up until that point, I was probably best described as one of those fans that had some respect for the hoolies, but never really got an opportunity to further my interest.

'The only information I had on the activities of the BBC were from reports in the local rag, and the usual banter around the pubs and within the group of lads I went to games with. Back then, all of us were mad keen United fans; now we're mostly all mad keen United fans with an added interest in off-the-pitch goings-on. Our group stuck together, and had attended matches the length and breadth of the country; we knew each other and trusted one another to offer backing if needed. We'd had a few scuffles now and then but nothing to catch anyone's notice.

'A few of us knew some of the youth on the scene at that time, and often had a pint with them at away games, but we rarely looked for a scrap. That kind of changed when we started boozing in town after games, namely in the Mulberry Tavern. The Mulb was a boozer that the BBC used to booze in back in the days when you could get 100 or so lads in one pub without the rozzers noticing.

'A few of the old school still drank there – Herman, Big Codger, Speedy – and we used to have a bit of a shindig to the ska and speed garage they used to play in the place. The Mulberry still attracted the attention of the Sheffield 6 lot every now and again and, when the older lads got a call to meet up, we used to tag along. As is usual, after a while numbers were swapped and we were getting into the loop, getting to know where and when the lads were meeting up.

'And that was that really. It's been a fucking buzz so far, with scraps up and down the country, coming off worse sometimes, but usually escaping with nothing more than a thick ear or a bruise from a baton. At the start of the

2002/03 season, there seemed to be a shit-load of young 'un's up for a rumble, week-in, week-out. Good youth lads from Woodhouse, Chapeltown and Dinnington, along with the usual suspects of Arbourthorne, Manor, Heeley and Intake. On a good day, the youth alone could pull out up to, and, on occasion over, 70 game lads. By coincidence, or possibly because of this, the 2002/03 and the 2003/04 seasons are regarded as some of the more active that the BBC have seen in recent times.

'The youth, while more than capable of holding their own against many firms, have tended to knock about with the main lads of the established BBC, which seems to go against what I've heard and experienced about many firms all over the UK. Perhaps it's their ability to scrap with the best of them that sees them more readily accepted by the older lads. Those with axes to grind would say it's because the youth aren't capable of holding their own, which is bollocks.

'However, on the occasions where the youth have been let off the lead (so to speak), they've had some notable results, and some notable scrapes against both other youth mobs and the older lads. What follows is a roughly chronological account of some of the scrapes, rucks, rumbles and near riots the youth have played a major part in, or been wholly responsible for. These are my personal accounts of what happened from a youth perspective.'

WOLVES

'I'll start with a minor incident, which evolved into a major one, and has now led to a bit of a grudge. A small group of eight of us travelled to this fixture. The majority were not able to attend due to the funeral of one of the main faces, and the youth element were not really organised enough to sort something out themselves at the time.

'We arrived early doors, and went into the town looking for a boozer that would serve us. We were turned away from a couple of places because we weren't local, but on the advice of a doorman headed towards the pub nearest the train station, the Prince Albert. Once we got rid of the bout of sniggers over the name of the place, we settled down for a few pints. We should've really got an inkling of what to expect when, despite being the first in the pub that morning, the beer was served in plastic containers.

'It was an hour or so before the first sign of bother walked in. A Wolves "scout" came in, took a swift look and was on his blower before he walked out of the door. Within 15 minutes, there were a growing number of older lads standing across the room. In their eyes there was definitely the intent of doing us some damage. Another 15 minutes crept past and the pub was filling with their lads, probably about 50 or so. Their youth were knocking about round the pool table; their older lads were on the other side of the pub. One of the old SRA [Shoreham Republican Army] lot who travelled with us went up to explain that it wasn't really on, and got chatting to one of their old lads. Oddly enough they agreed, but we were told that their youth wouldn't listen. Sure enough, they started getting giddy.

'One of ours went to the bogs; the entrance was surrounded by Wolfies. He was sporting a decent baseball cap on his way there, but by the time he was back at our table it'd left his head and was now proudly worn by some Midlands gimp. Now our lad was probably one of the gamest in our little bunch (he's now banned after being bitten on the head by a police dog during a rumble with Derby), and wasn't standing for any shit. He grabbed an ashtray and one of the plastics, and turned around to front those laughing. The rest of us grabbed what tools we could (I had my hands on a fucking kitchen plate) and braced ourselves for a battering. It never actually materialised.

'Some quick talking and walking saw our SRA lads head off a certain kicking and we were bundled out of the pub with a couple of shoves and pushes. To their credit, the Wolves lads didn't follow us.

'Scott was fuming, though; he wanted a new cap and set about trying to relieve some poor sod of one. His determination saw him chasing a lad round a roundabout, twice, through the traffic, Keystone Cops-style. Funniest thing I'd seen in a while. He still didn't get the cap.

'The game went well, we won 3–1 and pissed on a very poor Wolves side. The bonus of the day was that the fans shared the same stand, separated by a row of spotty oiks and numpties, namely stewards and some netting. Needless to say, there was a fair bit of banter going back and forth, and also the odd cup of tea from our side.

'Now it obviously doesn't take much to rile the Subway Army. As we were leaving the ground, they charged the away end, straight into our scarfers, our little bunch and a few other piss-heads. In the to-ing and fro-ing that followed, a disabled lass got knocked flying and a few scarfers got slapped. Not particularly honourable but, again, to their credit I did see a Wolves lad pick the lass up and make sure she was OK. Wolves have a bit of a rep for shirt-bashing and I can see why.

'Beside that there was a lot of shouting and some pushing and shoving before the numbers got on top. Two police tried to hold back their lads and we tried to stand our ground. In the end, a couple from our group were the last to retreat to the relative safety of the away end, one nipping through just before the gates were shut on him. We were locked in for a good 40 minutes while the police tried to regain order outside. One of ours had got out of the ground and was on the blower, telling us that it was a full-scale riot outside.

'It later turned out that the game had been declared a 'low-risk' category game and therefore minimal police supervision was required; in effect, a police-free match, which goes some way to explaining why the Subway Army could get so close to our fans, and why they could riot for that long. A major cock-up for the local constabulary and a close scrape for the few lads that travelled.

'The return leg at Bramall Lane was heavily policed, and very little opportunity presented itself to have a pop at the Subway Army. After the game (a 3–3 cracker) a good 70–80 lads were mobbed up on a back street waiting for them. A few of our lads had it away with them more or less right on Bramall Lane, under the noses of the rozzers. Their lads fared poorly, and were quickly under the protection of South Yorkshire Police.

BRISTOL

'The play-off weekend in May 2003 was definitely one to be remembered for off-the-pitch antics, rather than what happened on the pitch. The idea was to go to Bristol the day before and have a bloody big knees-up and hopefully bump into either Wolves or some accommodating locals.

'Our lot got a transit van sorted and one of us came up trumps with some top-notch apartments just outside the city centre. We set off early doors and arrived in Bristol just after lunch. We got a call and met up with some more lads down on the quayside.

'After a while, I gave a Bristol Rovers lad a bell, and he came down and met up with us, along with two of the Gas Youth. This was a friendship forged when we'd played Rovers in a pre-season game the summer before. On their advice, a few of us split from our main lot and went up to the Walkabout to watch the Second Division play-off, and hopefully bump into some Wolves or City. No sooner had we been served, a call was received from our lads; they'd just had it off with some City lads bang on the quayside where we'd just been. Pints were put down and we legged it back to see what we'd missed. By all accounts, it'd been a right old ding-dong, which we came out of on top.

'We made a hasty retreat, along with most of our lads, as the rozzers turned up. The plan was to mob up later that evening and take it from there. After freshening up, we mobbed up in a boozer not too far from the quayside. There must've been a good 200 there and, despite what had gone off earlier, there were no police. The Gas lads were still out and were sure that City would still be around, looking for a bit of revenge. Me and Del went for a wander; Del knew the City lads and, despite being a Gashead, said he was safe with them and that I should shut up and let him do the talking.

'Sure enough, we found them, drinking in a bar on the

Waterfront. There seemed to be a good 40–50, all solid-looking lads. After a few minutes, two of the City boys agreed to take a walk with us and have a look at what we had out. Del told them we had a good 200 lads, and they said they weren't going to match that.

'It wasn't until we'd got a decent distance away from the bar that I opened my trap, and said that their numbers wouldn't be able to touch us. "No wonder you kept your mouth shut, kid," one of them said to me, referring to my accent.

'I walked up to our boozer with one of the City lads, but he wasn't too sure about coming in, so he did one. I went back to the boozer and reported back with what I'd seen, numbers etc. One of our older lads had a few words with the City lads that did come close. That was the cue for our lads to make a move. The boozer emptied sharpish and our numbers were more than I first thought; we were off towards the waterfront at a decent pace.

'We fronted them right on the quayside, a kebab van had its tables turned over and the top of one was subject to a bit of Frisbee-ing between the two sets of lads, a few chairs were lobbed and also some chilli sauce, which seemed to cover every fucker. There were now some coppers about, but they were so few in numbers we just went through them. We were backing them off down the waterfront; their 40–50 had dissolved into 20 or so, but they were all game as fuck and stood as long as they could. I laid one of theirs out right underneath the CCTV cameras (of which there were fucking millions), and kept going forward at a steady pace.

'The City lads were running by the time we got to the bridge back over the quay, and then the rozzers got their act together. The ankle-snappers turned up, and with no one fancying a shot of rabies we turned into town to find a boozer that'd take us.

'We ended up back in the original boozer for short while, everyone buzzing. We still outnumbered the coppers by a fair few so we made a move. We went more or less where we wanted but, finally, the coppers got their act together and managed to pen us into a street. They then escorted us out of town, to the Coliseum pub. In the argy-bargy on the way, one Gas lad got nicked, but was rescued by the lads and wrestled off the coppers.

'That was about it really for our little lot. We stopped in the Coliseum for a while then, once the coppers lost interest in us, headed back to the waterfront for a few bevvies. We got chatting to one or two City lads who said that what we'd done was fair game, and that we'd been the best mob they'd seen in Bristol for a long time.

'We woke up the next morning to see our pretty mugs all over BBC News 24, including some footage taken by what looked like a CCTV camera about six miles away. It showed the first scrap in the afternoon, and then some concerned locals moaning about "a good day out with the family ruined".

'We got well beat on the pitch next day but had made a big impression off it; if only the Blades side had as much fight in it as us.'

NORWICH

'August 2003 – Norwich at home. Not a fixture to get your adrenalin racing. Indeed, it was an uneventful day until after the game, which United won 1–0.

'We headed back into town, to one of our usual drinking holes, and decided to wait up in there until we got word of the Pigs arriving back from Peterborough. There was a good 50 of us out but mainly youth. After about an hour or so, we started getting calls through saying that the Pigs were coming into town (yawn...) and that they were up for it. It was their first season in the Second Division after being relegated the season before, and they were bragging about taking huge mobs everywhere to turn towns over. So we settled down and waited. We haven't anything to prove to them, so we would let them come to us.

'We had attracted the attention of the OB who were dressed in riot gear. It must've been about 7.00pm when we saw a few lads wandering up past the Crucible. No one recognised them, then we heard the chant of 'DLF... DLF... DLF... ' Fucking Derby had turned up about 20-handed, bang in the middle of our town centre. Naturally, we charged into them, and had them on their toes straight away; some of ours went round the back of the Crucible to cut them off to be greeted by a snarling, mightily pissed-off-looking Alsatian, attached to a copper. We ran round them and went for the two or three Derby lads that were at the back of their mob. After we put a couple down, the OB got their act together and managed to push us back up to the pub.

'They then turned their attention to getting these Derby lads to the train station, which kind of left us to our own devices. The OB rounded them up and escorted them back along Arundel Gate towards Howard Street. Only they didn't realise this would take them right past us again. We noticed the coppers' helmets bobbing up and down behind a wall, and realised that this was the escort. We legged it down to them and let them have a hail of bottles and glasses. The OB were taken by surprise, and didn't really know whether to confront us or keep the Derby lads in the escort. A few riot cops pushed us back, but still had their hands full. A minute or so later, another van turned up and more OB joined in. It was on top for us now, and we did one back to the pub. The police dogs came in, and one was let off its lead. It made a beeline for one of our lads and pulled him to the ground, then started biting his head. We were going barmy, and this kid was screaming. The OB had us penned in the pub and around the door while the kid was basically being eaten. They were struggling to keep us back, but we didn't get through.

'The kid was arrested and, after a lengthy court case, is now banned for three years from attending matches.

'All these events kind of put paid to our plans for the Pigs. The OB followed us round for the rest of the night, and the Pigs didn't show... Again! The incident made the local rag on Monday. The police stated that the lads from Derby had been on a birthday session when they were suddenly set upon by us. The lad who was attacked by the dog was arrested for 'threatening behaviour', and the rag played heavily on local theatre-goers being terrified by the brawl. In truth, when it does go off, most bystanders actually just stand and watch. I've never seen anyone ever run away screaming from a ruck with a look of terror on their faces.'

NOTTINGHAM FOREST

'For the match against Forest in September 2003, we met early at the train station. A few of us, including me, couldn't be bothered to hang around for the latecomers any longer and decided to jump on the train. We thought a few had got on in different carriages but it appeared that we were the only ones, seven of us.

'The plan was to get to Nottingham and hole up somewhere and wait for the rest arriving on a later train. The train we were on had a few shirters on and a few piss-heads and, by the time we got to Nottingham, the OB were on the platform herding all United fans into an escort to be put in a boozer safely and securely.

'We slipped the escort by nipping out of the station side entrance and set off walking into town. We got ourselves into the Walkabout, with a couple of other young 'uns that'd tagged along when we slipped the escort. We got on the phones to see where the others were. They were going to be about another half-hour or so, so we settled down with a couple of papers and a pint.

'About 20 minutes later, a mob of lads walked past the front of the boozer. We were sat bang next to the door, so they couldn't really miss us. They looked about 20-strong, and they were all in their late teens. One of them spotted us and piped up, "Hold on a minute, lads, I think we've got something here." They entered. The lad who spotted us first took a good long look at us. The rest shuffled in without throwing a glance our way. We sat there and took a good look at them.

'They got their pints and wandered over to a few tables and sat down. The gobby lad came over again and asked to borrow a paper. We duly obliged. He was giving it all the swagger he could muster. He wandered off for a short while. We got on the blowers to see what was happening to the rest of our lot. They had got into Nottingham but had been picked up by the OB at the station and were in a boozer. So it was us 9 Blades versus 20 Forest youth.

'We decided that if it came on top, we'd fucking give it them, launch everything we could and then do one before the rozzers turned up. The place was CCTV'd up to the bollocks, so anything we did would be caught on tape. We had to make sure it was them that brought it to us so that we could argue self-defence in any court appearances.

'Sure enough, that opportunity presented itself. Gobby came back over, saying, "You lads from Sheffield?"

'"Yeah, why? D'ya fucking want it?"

'That was the cue for us to go. We lobbed our pint pots into their mob and ran towards them. They shat it; the whole fucking mob was falling over each other to get out. We were clipping them as they ran away from us and a couple got a good hiding. A particularly fat lad got collared bang outside the door and was given a good seeing to. His Stoney badge was ripped from his jumper and he had his wallet cleaned out as well. Meanwhile a couple of us were still chasing the mob down the street. Even though there were only a couple of us they still didn't have a pop back. One of theirs was getting a hiding and they still didn't come back to help him, which is the worst thing to do in this game. Never leave your mates.

'The sirens were then heard above the racket and it was time for us to do one. We headed down a couple of side streets, found a small boozer and jumped in for a couple of pints and to piss ourselves laughing. We were buzzing and were straight on the blowers to the rest of our lads, letting them know what they'd missed out on.

'As there were only nine of us it was decided to jump in a couple of taxis up to the pub where the rest of ours were. As we neared it, four or five of the mob we had just done walked out of the shopping centre. Their faces were a picture as they realised who we were, and we were on them in a split-second. Again, a fat lad got collared along with another kid, both took a good hiding and again they were relieved of their Stoney badges. One lass stood nearby at a bus stop and asked us to leave them because they'd had enough and, as the OB were coming again, we did one.

'The game was shit; United lost 3–1.

'Towards the end of the game, we started to kick off a bit in the stand, and one of our lads – Dinno – ended up with a copper on him and being bundled out of the ground. We chased after the copper and managed to wrestle our mate from his grip. We then legged it into the car park following the lad, who thought he should make a quick exit. It was all a bit Keystone, swerving in and out of cars and round buses, but Dinno ran straight into a police horse which was round a blind corner. The rozzers got him again and there wasn't a lot we could do about it. About 20 of us were jumping up and down and causing a bit of grief in the car park, and then, for some reason, the OB just let us go. They let us wander into town with just two mounted police following us. I don't know why they did this; perhaps they thought the CCTV would pick us up, but it suited us just fine.

'After a couple of quick turns down some narrow alleys, we'd lost the horses and were on our own again. We had a couple of pints and then decided to head back to Sheffield. As we were walking back to the station, one of ours spotted a group of lads that looked vaguely familiar. It dawned on us that it was the round bloke and his mates who'd been giving it extra large throughout the game. We didn't need a second invite and were straight into them. They scattered all over, not one of them stood. The big lad got the most of it, but he was surprisingly light-footed and managed to avoid a good hiding by wobbling over a wall into the bus station.'

HILLSBOROUGH CORNERED

'You know when you have those really good ideas when you're pissed, and when they actually happen they're a bit shit and poorly thought through? Well, this is one of those. It was a spectacular failure.

'After a nondescript home game in the autumn of 2003, about 15–20 of us were out on the lash around town. We'd been getting the usual calls off the Pigs ("We're coming into town... we're 50-handed," etc.) all night and it was beginning to piss a few off. They hardly ever show in town when we're out in any kind of numbers and, when they do, they're always picking off a few Blades and claiming a result.

'It was getting on a bit and I was in a decent state of fucked-ness when a brilliantly simple plan struck me like a bolt of lightning. We'd go to them fuckers up on Hillsborough Corner and take it to them. A quick 'get-in, do-the-business, get-out type' thing. So simple – what could go wrong?

'I looked around and put the word round that we'd be going up once everyone had supped up. There were probably 10–15 who said they were up for it, and I was happy that would probably do. I rang a couple of the older lads; they were otherwise engaged and called me a mad fucker, but fair play.

'We boarded a tram and made our way up there. There were only about ten that made the trip; a few had cried off and said it was a suicide mission and that the Pigs would be on to us straight away and in large numbers.

'We got to the Deep End but the lad on the door wouldn't let us in, so we crossed over to Legends. The place was empty, so the 'straight-in, do-the-business, get-out' plan was going wrong already. We settled in for a couple of pints, and I got chatting to the bouncer, who recognised me from the Mulberry.

'"What the fuck are you lot doing here?" he asked.

'"Thought we'd come up and say hello."

'"Are you fucking stupid?"

'"Looks like it."

'It took a while but after about 20 minutes the first couple of Pigs came sniffing. One of our lads worked with them so went out to have a word. He was out there for about five minutes before another one of ours went out, walked up to them and twatted one. That was it then. The rest is a bit of a blur. We all piled out and waited for the rest of the Pigs to come. We ran the two lads after exchanging a couple of blows. They went into the Shakespeare pub and, about a minute later, a few more lads came out. They backed us off to the bridge; I took a few hits but stayed on my feet. Then the whole fucking pub emptied, along with what seemed like all the Blue Bell as well. We were fucked, no two ways about it.

'We stood there and gave them the big 'un; then I ran

into them. I can't really remember much else until I came round with four coppers round me and an ambulance siren blaring. My phone was ringing, but I was in no fit state to answer it. The swelling and bruising took a good month to go down. I know I was up against some railings at one point, trying not to go down, but the numbers were too much.

'By all accounts, there were about 50 Pigs that came out of the boozers, and I'd run straight into them shouting, "Come on then."

'Without being too biased, Wednesday's youth can't handle us. They are forever ringing us and arranging a meet but they never show. So we've started taking the Pig by the horns so to speak. A pre-season friendly at Huddersfield saw the Blades youth take a good 60 into Huddersfield town centre. Huddersfield knew we were around but couldn't muster enough to have a go. We were left frustrated so stopped off at Barnsley on the way home; again, no opposition showed and, after a while, the OB threw us out of town.

'When we got back to Sheffield, our numbers had halved. Wednesday were on the blower again; they were coming into town etc. We knew this was bullshit so, to a man, we thought, fuck it, we'll take it to them. We went to Hillsborough and plotted up in the Burgion pub; one of their old heads runs it so we expected a prompt response. Nothing was forthcoming so we rang them and told them we were on their patch and to come and have it. Around ten minutes later, they appeared with a lot of their old heads in tow. We ran out and steamed into them; despite their superior numbers they ran, so we chased them all the way to Hillsborough Corner. More Wednesday came and, with the numbers they had, it should have been on top but we just stood and traded. They seemed to prefer throwing glasses than actually engaging in combat.

One lad who was with them had actually gone to court and grassed up one of our lads a few months earlier; he got three months and Wednesday know he's a grassing twat but still have him in their firm. Still, I suppose they are desperate to have anyone tagging on with them, even grasses! Our youth had shown on their doorstep and had a result. Our main lads were as proud as punch.'

LEEDS 2004

'Leeds is always a big one. We'd played them twice the season before, in both Cup competitions, and done them on the pitch. Off the pitch, it had been a sea of luminous jackets, snarling dogs and fully suited-and-booted riot cops. We'd come close a couple of times but the coppers had been too numerous and had pushed us back each time. We tried to attack the Leeds escort from Sheffield station but the plod on horseback steamed into us.

'A lot of United's older lads don't like or rate Leeds. Their argument is that Leeds reckon they are the bollocks but don't prove it. I've started thinking along those lines as we had 100 waiting in Attercliffe for a pre-arranged battle with Leeds but, despite them being on the blower, they didn't show and then turned up outside a supporters' pub showing off, knowing full well we were down the Attercliffe (a district of Sheffield around four miles from Bramall Lane) patiently waiting for a firm that had no intention of showing.

'One of the Cup games was used on a TV documentary about policing in South Yorkshire, and it showed a fair reflection of what had happened in the Carling Cup game. Leeds had brought a mob, but largely by train. Coming by train to Sheffield (or indeed any town) is a sure-fire way of getting picked up by the rozzers. Unfortunately, it's still really the only way to get large numbers of lads into a town at the same time.

'We had a good mob out that day in August 2004; it must've filled London Road and, as we'd moved away to look for Leeds, I had a quick look behind and the whole fucking road seemed full of lads. I'd put our numbers at about 300–350. The rozzers earned their overtime that night, and managed to keep us largely apart.

'One moment that sticks in my mind – which I still piss myself about now – is when we were passing by a DIY store with some OB following us with force. A lad jumped in a skip and found a paint pot. He lobbed it and fucking covered a copper head to toe in white emulsion; now *that* stopped the fucker in his tracks. The paint splatters are still on the road to this day.

'The FA Cup game in the same season was an early kick-off – 12.00pm on Sunday. Several boozers had opened early and a few of us were nicely tucked up on London Road at about 9.00am. Word was that Leeds were coming in cars and vans; they must've learnt their lesson from last time. They didn't show before the game, or, if they did, they must've been really quiet, because we didn't pick up on them.

'After the game, the plan was to mob up on Shoreham Street, and have a pop at them as they came down St

Mary's Gate. The coppers had Bramall Lane sewn up and their lads were soon in an escort. Still, we had managed to avoid a large police presence and we loitered around a bit, waiting for their escort to come down the dual carriageway. Sure enough it came, and it was like a fucking walking prison. There was no way we would get anywhere near them.

'We decided to at least show our faces and took a walk across the front of the escort. The rozzers didn't quite know what to do, but just let us walk straight in front of the escort and head towards the train station. A few friendly gestures were swapped with the Leeds lads, but that was about it.

The next day, a post appeared on our Internet message board from a supposed Leeds lad who'd been in the escort that said our mob were Leeds as well and they didn't see any BBC all day.

'So, things were set for the league game. The coppers had deemed it necessary to make it an early kick-off, so it was half-twelve on a Sunday. There were all kinds of rumours and hearsay flying around; that the Donny Whites would be making a show, that the main Service Crew would be coming in early, or maybe even the night before.

'On the day, our lot got a bit split up. The majority ended up out of town, up near Meadowhall. A call had been made to Leeds and it was on for a meet, well away from the rozzers and away from the prying eye of CCTV. A few of us decided that nothing would happen before the game, and we got settled into a pub up near Woodseats. It'd opened up early doors and we were there for 9.00am.

'There were about 15 or 20 of us there by the time we

made a move towards the ground. Four or five jumped in a taxi while the rest were left to use shanks's pony. We got a call from the taxi lot saying the Donny Whites were acting up on Bramall Lane, and that they had been outside the Sportsman. That was a fucking waste of time; it was well known to Leeds that our lads would be out of town thanks to the pre-arranged meet and banning orders. They had been on the blower and said they'd be turning up in Attercliffe but, with our main firm laying in wait, Leeds chose to go straight to the ground. I think they did it just to say they had turned up, in full knowledge that they'd not come up against much opposition. Perhaps the 40 of them didn't fancy it. Well, we took 25 – mainly youth – up to Leeds, and that, my friends, is bottle.

'Anyhow, we picked up the pace to a brisk walk but, by the time we arrived on Bramall Lane, there was nothing to be seen. On the pitch, we did them 2–0, Ashley Ward getting a rare goal in between building houses for Wayne Rooney and the like, and Jon Harley making sure of it ten minutes later.

'The plan after the game was to get out of town and meet up with the rest of the lads. After a bit of running round and chasing shadows, we jumped in a cab and headed up to the boozer. As far as we were concerned, Leeds still knew where we were, and in principle should make the effort to come to us. Fair enough, it was our own turf, but with so many lads out on banning orders, getting to the town centre without some lads going down for breach of conditions wasn't a risk we were willing to take.

'We waited and waited. Nothing was happening, and it was becoming obvious that nothing was about to. A couple of panda cars came past and took a good look. About 20 minutes later, one of South Yorkshire Police's football spotters came into the pub, took a look around, had a word with the landlord and left. If something was going to happen, it needed to be soon because the OB would be on us before too long.

'It took a while to come, but finally someone made a decision. We would go to Leeds. Taxis were ordered and about 15 of us went to catch a train. A few others made their way up by taxi and car, and some of the up-and-coming youth tried to get a train from Sheffield, but the bloody idiots missed it. It seemed to take fucking ages to get there, probably because it did. We were buzzing, partly because we'd given the OB the slip, but largely because we were showing that if we want you, we'll come and get you.

'We arrived at Leeds station. A couple of bobbies were in the entrance hall and clocked us, but didn't pay too much attention. Maybe they thought we were Leeds lads returning. Whatever they thought, we were soon out of the station and heading towards a bar, to wait for the rest in cars to catch up and mob up. After a couple of bevvies, we moved down to a boozer closer to what was considered 'their' pub, only it turns out that the bar we were heading for was a bar with... umm... 'liberal attitudes'. We mobbed up in there; the few that were coming in cars found us and we had a couple of pints with the he-be-she-be's and the like. All in all, there were probably 30 of us tops, the large majority youth, plus around five older lads.

'One of the older lads knew Leeds quite well, as he worked up that way or something, and he knew the boozer we were going to hit was just around the corner. The OB hadn't picked us up and the Leeds lads didn't know we were there. It was a cracking chance at a surprise attack. After about 20 minutes or so, we were on the short jog to their boozer. We hadn't sent a scout up in case we blew our cover; we were going in blind and didn't really know who or what would be about. The adrenalin was going, and my heart was doing twenty to the dozen. We walked in the pub. "Who the fuck are these?" I heard one bloke say under his breath. There was no one of any note in there in the end; some scrotes who went very quiet, and a couple of older blokes who sat down and looked sheepish. We were a bit miffed, to be honest. The call went up to get out, get back to a pub out of the way and wait and see what happened. We filed out, and spread out across the road, making our way up the road towards some more bars.

'Out of fucking nowhere came a mob of lads out on a fortieth birthday 'bash' for one of their boys. They looked mighty fucked off. It took us a couple of seconds to realise what was going off, and they launched a few pint pots and bottles our way. We were spread out a bit and no one quite knew what to do. A few of us fronted them and started a bit of toe-to-toe. I had two blokes taking swings at me and more closing in. I managed to get a few punches out before they got me up against a car. I was doing me best just to defend their swipes, let alone try and get some in. I thought I was going to get a hiding, but then, by a stroke of luck, one of them tried to kick me and fell flat on his arse. I took my chance to get back to our lads, which meant going back through the Leeds mob. A few got some digs in at me but I made it back to our team, turned round and fronted them.

'It was only really then that I got a decent view of their

numbers; none of them were youths and more were starting to spill out from some other bars and add to their ranks. It was defo going to come on top. We held our ground for a while and then got backed off; a few punches landed, some more bottles came our way and a few of ours started to turn, back off and mob up further down the side street we were getting pushed down.

'Again, I found myself in amongst their lads trying to take out two of them, with our mob getting further away. I was sure I was going to get a good hiding as they had me up against a wall. I cracked off a couple of punches but none really connected. Then I swiped out and took one lad out. Again, realising that I was away from our mob, I had to get back through the enemy. Luckily, they were all facing our mob so I was able to get past a few without them realising who I was. But then one of them turned round and made eye contact with me; he ran towards me. I twatted him in the stomach with my knee and fucking kept going. He went down like a sack of shit and didn't get up for a while. I think I may have caught his bollocks or something.

'By this time, there was a solitary copper standing between us and them, baton drawn and shouting down his radio. Both mobs weren't really taking much notice of him, and a couple of the Leeds mob took him down, which I'd never seen before. We were still getting backed off down the street, towards a viaduct arch. That's when the bottle of some of ours went; we were on a hiding to nothing. It was almost a relief when a few vans of rozzers turned up; we would've got a fucking good going over.

'When they turned up I tried to make out all innocent

and walk quietly away into a side street, but they were having none of it. We were rounded up, searched and then frogmarched back to the train station. It was obvious a few of ours had managed to get away as there were only 15 left in the group. One lad had taken a beating; his eye was swollen up bad. Other than that we had just about got away with it. The coppers filmed us all, names, addresses etc., no doubt to be added to whatever files they keep on us. We were escorted all the way to Meadowhall train station and greeted on the Sheffield railway platform by a good few coppers.

'I managed a smug smile, knowing that we'd put one over them and gone some way in maintaining the reputation of the BBC. Yeah, we'd been backed off, but we hadn't been run ragged. We'd taken it to them, albeit unannounced, and given a good account. If we'd managed to get a few more up on the train, maybe the tables would've been turned, but that's just how it goes sometimes. We'd showed in Leeds after our game in Sheffield when they had conveniently avoided the meet. To me, it showed that our firm wasn't interested in the safety of keeping our reputation intact like Leeds was. We showed we wanted it more, and that's what it's all about, isn't it?

'To be fair to that little United firm that turned up in Leeds, they took it to Leeds and although they ended up on the back foot they went there and showed Leeds how it should be done, as they haven't got their shit together at Bramall Lane for a few years. The trespass into another city wasn't an original idea, as Barnsley did the same a few years ago.'

HULL

'I'd heard all the stories from the old school of battles with Hull's rated firm. According to our older lads, Hull away was guaranteed trouble. I hadn't had any dealings with them but their visit to ours in April 2006 promised a cracking day out. Prior to the match, much of the talk in the boozer had been the efforts of the up-and-coming Blades youth over the last few months. What was needed was a result, and a convincing one at that. It seemed that Hull could provide that opportunity to sort the real young 'uns out and bring them back into line.

'Not a great deal happened before the match. The rozzers in Sheffield have just about made it impossible for a pre-match dance nowadays, either through improved control over away fans or the banning of lads for the slightest, minor indiscretions. The best opportunity now is to get it sorted after the game when the plod's attention is focused on the match and Bramall Lane itself. This allows those who fancy it time to make a sly exit and get into town before anyone realises.

'We'd heard that before the match Hull had been marched 50-handed from the station by the OB. United won a cracking game 3–2, continuing our slightly faltering but ultimately successful march to the Palace of Glittering Delights known to all as the Premier League. During the game, word had been put out to meet at a pub not far from the Lane. With CCTV all over the gaff in Sheffield, we met at a pub with few or no cameras. We chose a route that away-fans would have to walk to get back to the station, upgrading our chance of a dance.

'At the pub, we managed to get around 30 lads together

with no OB in tow – result. The firm we had was mainly youth with a couple of older lads. I sent a couple of pups on a scouting mission to report back if any Hull had escaped the clutches of our plod. I was stood outside the pub with my pint when our two scouts came running around the corner.

'They'd sussed a mixed crew of around 20 old and young Hull lads. Hull were wandering up the street not far from us, so it was game on. We made our move to ambush them at a junction and, sure enough, as we got there, so did they. Everyone went forward as one, even our jumpy up-and-down youth. Hull stood, fair play, and a toe-to-toe kicked off. This went on for a couple of minutes and a couple of Hull got dropped and all our lot seemed really fired up for this, particularly our younger lads, who maybe had a point to prove.

'Hull eventually got legged up the road and we'd done the business, plus the added bonus of no one injured at all. Content with our work, we headed back to the pub, telling the tales of who'd done what and so on. Then one of the lads said Hull were on their way back into town. Fair play, they had some bollocks; these lads were like the Hull we'd heard about from our seniors.

'Sure enough, as we came back out of the pub for the second time, Hull were coming down the street and fanned out for battle. The shout went up and we were into them again. They stood their ground and we were belting into them left, right and centre. A couple of their lads got dropped and had to be dragged away by their mates. It didn't last as long this time, as Hull decided they'd had enough for one day. The soles of white trainers were visible again as Hull ran for the second time, leaving one of their comrades unconscious in the middle of the road. Two passers-by tried to help the lad wake up.

'Everyone was buzzing their tits off as we headed back to the pub. Just as people were beginning to question the youth and doubt their prowess, they came back with a cracking little result against a very game set of lads from Hull. Better still, the rozzers hadn't been anywhere to be seen so we'd pulled it off without arrests. One of the older lads gave the pups words of encouragement: "Perhaps you lads have been underestimated..." Words that had the young supporters grinning from ear to ear.

'Later that season, 20 Cardiff got done in at the back of a pub on London Road. They wore the gear, talked the talk, wanted a pop but, when they got done in, then suddenly they weren't lads. Cardiff are one of the most up-their-own-arse firms in England.

'Sorry, they are nothing to do with England – they are thankfully Welsh twats!'

LEEDS 2006

'The evening kick-off was played at night, when you did not want to be caught on the dark back streets that surround the Lane. This is precisely what happened to a small group of Leeds after the game while they were trying to find their way back to the train station. Laying in wait were a few of our youths holed up in a pub during the sell-out game.

'At full time, we made our way towards the ground in the hope of bumping into a few LSC. On walking around a corner, we bumped into a group of Leeds youth – game on. They bounced around and talked the talk. Without hesitation, our lot steamed into them; one of our team was carrying a large plank of wood and was on a mission as he swung it wildly. Unfortunately, Leeds didn't fancy it now and were quickly on their toes. One of our boys smashed a Leeds lad in the mouth and, in doing so, ripped open his knuckle.

'The long chase to the station began as 15 of our finest youth chased an equal number of Leeds. We gave up at the Howard as Leeds managed to get to the sanctuary of Sheffield train station which was heavily fortified with rozzers. It was the closest we have seen in recent years to a Leeds mob and they had quickly been put on their toes. This is what football violence has been reduced to: small pockets of boys having it away, while the police concentrate on prowling around the football ground. Where there's a will there's a way.

'The premiership has finally arrived after a 12-year absence and, with Middlesboro's visit to Bramall Lane, so did the violence. Fair fucks to 'Boro, they came in small groups and we had it all over the shop with them. The biggest group, around 20, copped it on London Road. There was plenty of trouble that day with United coming out on top, no doubt, but you've got to give 'Boro credit, they turned up, were game and well up for it. The shape of things to come is small groups of lads rather than big numbers that police simply wrap up.

'Regards and respect, the youth of today.'

9
THE YOUTH OF YESTERYEAR

What follows is the real story of what football violence at Sheffield United was like in the Sixties and explores how the scene actually started. It's written by Ronnie Sharpe, who is now in his fifties, and is dedicated to the late John Derbyshire.

'In the early Sixties, we always stood on the Shoreham End, usually right at the back directly behind the goal, where we climbed and wedged ourselves in between the steel girders that held up the corrugated iron-roofed Spion Kop. Sometimes, we'd venture to the front and lean over the white railings, close enough to smell the rubbing oils from the players' legs. The football was easy and slow. Five forwards attacked, five defenders defended. The half-back passed it to the inside-forward, who passed it on to the winger, the winger beat the full-back and crossed to the centre-forward who rose like a rocket, hung in the air for ten seconds before thundering an unstoppable header into the net. He then shook hands with his team-mates – no kissing, back-flips or hugging. The forwards were expected to score, the wingers were expected to run rings around the full-back... It was all about goals. Every player was greedy for the ball and not the money.

'United fielded the same 11 just about every week: Hodgkinson, Coldwell, Richardson, Joe Shaw, Summers, Allchurch, Russell, Kettleborough, Pace, Hodgson and Simpson.

'"Hodgy", the goalkeeper, was (according to the song) better than Yashin. He stood only 5ft 2in tall. A bit short for a 'keeper, you might think, but he was as agile as a young chimpanzee and could leap eight feet in the air and catch the ball with one hand.

'Only one keeper proved to be better than Hodgy in the whole land and that was Wednesday's Ron Spingett. He was the regular England goalkeeper. Ron's younger brother Peter also became a professional footballer and also played in goal for Wednesday. When he retired from the game, Peter became a copper and became a well-known face as the community bobby around Bramall Lane. He also became well known to the lads in the BBC as he spent some of the final days of his life chasing young Beeb lads around the back streets of the Lane.

'In those days, no players got injured, dropped or sent off. If a player broke his leg, the trainer ran on, rubbed a bit of best butter on the limb and the player then *walked* off the field. Managers were never sacked; the only way they lost their jobs was if they dropped dead. If a player was transferred, that was it, no speculation in the papers, no "shock moves". Why is every transfer a shock fucking move?

'Amidst old men in overcoats and flat caps, young boys looking like war evacuees dressed in short trousers, gabardine rain macs and school caps, I stood every week swinging my red-and-white rattle watching the drama unfold on the pitch.

'Sometimes we won, sometimes we lost; it was no big deal, no after-match analysis, I just looked forward to the next game. I watched footballers, not super-fit prima donna athletes, but they could and did wade their way through six inches of thick mud like it wasn't there and they could skim an orange ball over a foot of compacted snow with no bother.

'We usually took the bus to the night matches. The six-mile journey took us along the A61 road through Norton and then into Woodseats. As the bus turned the corner just past the quarry and ran down the hill towards Meersbrook, my heart skipped a beat as the floodlights came into view. I could see the Lane illuminated a mile or so away in the distance. Today's view sees the twin towers of the Lowfield mosque dominating the skyline!

'The night matches were special, magic even, close to a spiritual experience. The artificial glow seemed ten times brighter than daylight and made the Lane appear almost serene. On winter nights, the rain and the sleet could be seen 100 feet in the air, swirling sideways in the glare of the floodlights.

'When the game started, the dull lights under the Kop roof were turned off. Gazing out from the darkness, the ball flashed across the sacred turf. Directly opposite the corner flag, the Shoreham end curved around to the right. Sometimes, we stood on the bend behind the white wall.

From that vantage point, not only could we see the whole pitch but it also gave a sideways view of the crowded Kop. Every split-second, dozens of matches and cig lighters ignited, sparking up cigarettes, cigars and pipes. As the Blades attacked, the volume of noise slowly increased, reaching a crescendo as the ball hit the back of the net... then thousands of hands and rattles shot into the air. I loved those night games.

'Football violence really started to take off in 1965. Why 1965? I don't know. From the beginning of the decade, I'd been to many of United's home games and a few away games and, apart from the odd argument, I'd never seen any trouble at all. Liverpool and Everton fans had been smashing up trains since the late Fifties but trouble inside the grounds was rare.

'In 1964, I stood on the Kop at the Lane, by the side of a group of Manchester United supporters (20 or so); other similar-sized groups of Mancs (or wherever they were from) stood in other parts of the Kop happily chanting and cheering on their team. They didn't want to hit me or anybody else for that matter and, as far as I could see, nobody wanted to hit them or chase them out of the ground. How come that, about one year later, Man Utd and the Merseyside teams in particular would try to invade every football ground in the land and how come fans of the home team were ready to fight them? Who told them? Nobody (or very few) even had a house phone back then, let alone a mobile.

'Did it really happen so quickly? I think it did. Overnight, so to speak. Was it the scrapping of national service, where lads from all parts of the country bonded and got on so well together for two years out of their young lives? Was it the lack of wars? We hadn't had one for years. If we'd been born 30 years earlier, would we have been bouncing up the beach at Dunkirk? Yeah, of course we would. It was obviously territorial and it all began to happen in 1965.

'A group of lads had started to congregate behind the goal at the front of the Kop. We moved down from the back and, at first, stood just to the left of this new 'mob'. As we got a bit braver, we stood amongst them, joining in with the songs and the chants. Every set of fans was doing what was known as the "Brazil clap", first done by Brazilian fans during the 1962 World Cup. So for us it was, "Yoo-ni-ted..." clap-clap-clap, with the emphasis on the "Yoo". As the years went by, it gradually changed to "Yaa", which sounded more hard and aggressive. Their seaside battles put behind them, mods and rockers stood side by side on the Kop in the common cause that was Sheffield United FC.

'My regular companions at the games were Tiny and Ansh. Tiny had moved to Dronfield from Pittsmoor in Sheffield when he was about ten years old and we had been mates ever since. He lived in one of the posh houses on the next street. Both lads were a year older than me.

'Quite a few of the young lads in the mob (including myself) were now wearing green army combat jackets. These could be decorated with biro or felt-tipped pen, with the words "Blades" or "Sheffield United" written on the back. We were usually in the ground at around 2.00pm for the Saturday games.

'A group of older lads all dressed in smartly-tailored,

sharp Italian suits, white tab-collared shirts with gold cufflinks and slim, Windsor-knotted ties. They all appeared just after kick-off when the pubs had shut. These boys were all in their late teens/early twenties and were mostly from the Pittsmoor area where Tiny once lived.

'Suits had always been a sign of manhood, just as 21 years old was. If you were 21, it was time to wear a suit; you were a man and, in my inexperienced eyes, old and fucked. This all came before the arrival of the mod culture, and then things began to change; now, smart suits were hip, smart suits were cool.

'We were starting to get to know some of the lads in the mob, including the "suities", as we called them. Everyone looked up to Melvin Harrison, "The King of the Kop". Mel was a good-looking kid with an air of confidence about him. Tiny's first name was also Mel; the suities called him Tiny, so as not to confuse him with the "big" Mel.

'Willie Ward, a Heeley lad, vied with Mel Harrison for the title of King of the Kop. Willie would bellow out in a high-pitched voice, "Zigga-zagga-zigga-zagga…" and his minions would respond with, "U-NI-TED". Others in the little suit mob were Snowy (Mel's younger brother), Ted Devine, Lob, a big lad with a lazy eye from the Arbourthorne estate, Wailsey and a few others.

'Wailsey's claim to fame – so the story goes – is that after a game against Leeds at the Lane, he lay in wait for Jack Charlton outside the player's entrance. Old "Giraffe Neck" had riled him during the game. Wailsey sneaked up behind "Big Jack" and booted him up the arse. He then ran like a whippet up John Street with Charlton in hot pursuit, to the great amusement of the rest of the lads.

'Away fans were starting to appear at the Lane although not in large numbers; any that ventured on to the Kop and tried it on (so I was told) were dealt with by the suities and the older mods and rockers. I was surprised to see that the Leeds United fans wore white scarves with small blue-and-yellow bands on them. I imagined that their scarves would be all white, the same as their kit. Leeds brought a large following to the Lane but they all seemed to be old women who looked like my mother.'

EVERTON

'The first time I was involved in any sort of violence at the Lane came in September 1965. Liverpool were the visitors that night and some suited up "old blokes" who were at least 25 years old came to the front and started pushing us about. One of them kicked me up the arse and scared me half to death. I was relieved when they moved round to the Lane end for the second half.

'Later on in the season, Everton came to the Lane for a Saturday fixture. On arriving at the ground at the usual time, we found our spot taken over by a group of 100 or so Everton fans. A lot of them carried banners and flags and looked really impressive. As with their Merseyside brothers, they were a lot older than us and just as bad with their bullying tactics. They started pushing us around and threatening us, so we moved to the left-hand side to get out of the way. I couldn't help but keep staring at them; I hoped none of them would catch my eye and ask what I was looking at.

'A leather-jacket clad Blade standing near the Evertonians was pushed by a much older suitie. I was shocked to see him pull a knife from his back pocket and lunge at the Everton fan. He was overpowered in seconds as about six Everton piled into him; they took his knife away and then threw him to the floor. They rolled him over so he was face down, then one of them sat on top of him and slashed his coat open with his own knife.

'Nobody went to help; we stood transfixed to the spot. The lad got up and he slunk off towards the John Street side. He could easily have been stabbed to death. This was the cue for the Everton mob to start hitting any Blade in the vicinity. We ran and jumped in all directions and ended up at the back of the Kop, well out of the way. We eventually moved further down and stood on a raised bit just above the walkway that ran horizontally all the way across the Shoreham end. The Everton mob stood directly below us only a few yards away.

'The ground started to fill up and 15 minutes before kick-off more and more Blades gathered where we were stood. It was the nearest we could get to our own spot. We told all the newcomers about the knife incident. In between listening with fascination to the Everton songs and chants, I was picking up snippets of conversation from the lads around me. "Wait until Mel and Willie get in... they'll not be so fucking clever then." Right on cue and just after kick-off the suities arrived. What was going to happen? There must have been fights before because everybody talked about how good the suities were, but I'd never seen them in action.

'"What the fuck are you doing stood here?" Melvin shouted at us all. I was more scared of him than the Everton lot. He took off his jacket, as did three or four of the others, then they carefully folded them and passed them to lesser mortals. Sleeves were rolled up and neckties loosened. They were followed by a small group of rockers and marched into the invading Everton mob.

'Fucking hell, I thought, this is it. It didn't last long... The Blades waded in and the Everton ranks split. On seeing this, more Blades ran down. Some of the scousers leapt the fence behind the goal to escape the fighting, some tried to fight back but they were no match for the Blade boys. Half-a-dozen policemen came in to try and restore order. More and more Blades (who ten minutes earlier had been shitting themselves) joined the throng; it now looked quite safe, so the rest of us chabs [youngsters] swung under the crush barriers to reclaim our place. The Everton fans didn't run away, they just moved to one side and carried on singing and chanting as if nothing had happened. We were back in our own spot, though. I had never seen anything like it before; I was shaking with excitement.

'One thing I picked up on as I got to know more and more of the Sheffield lads was their dislike (and that's putting it mildly) of Sheffield Wednesday. Years and years of rivalry, going both ways, had turned into hatred and had been passed down through the generations from grandfathers to fathers and from fathers to sons. It wasn't as simple as that, though. Families could be split, with three brothers supporting the Blades and one the Owls. I've heard Blades say that all the rest of their family are "fuckin' Wednesdayites". Very strange indeed.

'"Fucking Wednesday bastards" could be heard when their scores were put up on the old cricket pavilion scoreboard, or "I hate them blue-and-white cunts". They called Hillsborough "The Shithouse". In Dronfield, it was probably an even split in the support of the two big city teams (although nearly all the lads at school were Blades). There was little if any animosity between the two groups but plenty of banter. It was a Sheffield thing at first but, as we got more and more involved in the new scene, the more we got to hate them.

'We had started meeting the Chesterfield lads – Sinny, Dave Parton, Podge, Dec Fields, Alan and Little Terry – at most of the home games and travelled back with them on the Chesterfield bus which stopped at Dronny on the way through. The way the Chezzy lads spoke made me smile; they called Chesterfield "Tairn", called each other "serry" and "mi duck" and the coppers "bobbies".'

LEICESTER

'Ansh and I arranged to thumb it to Leicester on Saturday, 19 March 1966. Parton, a couple of years older than me and quite a lad, said he would join us. One of the Chezzy lads told us (it just sort of just cropped up in conversation) that Parton had the biggest cock in Chesterfield and all the surrounding towns and hamlets. Whenever he was out and about, a posse of birds usually surrounded him. I don't know if the cock story is true, but he did go on to marry an American Country and Western singer with big blonde hair and giant bosoms.

'Parton gave us his address and we called at his house about 9.30 on the said morning. He invited us into his bedroom to show us his souvenirs and scalps; Blade pictures, banners and flags covered the walls. He had about

20 different scarves that he had nicked from fans up and down the land.

'"What shall I take today?" he mused, "Shall I take one of my banners? No, fuck it, I'll take my gun." What! I thought. He opened a drawer and took out a small revolver. Fucking hell, what's going on?

'"It's all right," he said, "it's only a starting pistol, but you want to hear the fucking noise it makes." He grabbed a handful of cartridges, slipped the gun in his pocket and we were off.

'We had trouble getting lifts but finally got one to Derby, arriving there around 1.00pm. Time was getting on so we decided to catch the train from Derby to Leicester, which wasn't too far away and only cost a few bob.

'We walked into the station and hung around the platform waiting for our train. A train rolled in and the roar and noise coming from it meant only one thing... a football special. Heads hung out of the windows, bottles flew through the air and smashed on to the platform. The doors opened and scores of Man City fans poured out. They walked past us singing and chanting. A group stopped in front of us, and one of them shouted, "Are you fucking United?"

'"Yeah," I replied.

'"Yeah, Sheffield United," Parton chirped in, "we're on our way to Leicester."

'"Oh, that's all right then," the City fan said, "I thought you were Man United."

'We arrived at Filbert Street about 2.30pm and joined a group of about 30 Blades stood outside Leicester's Kop. We entered the Kop at the left-hand corner and could see the

Leicester mob stood behind the goal. They saw us and walked over towards us. Parton moved to the front, pulled the pistol from his pocket and held it out at arm's length slightly above his head. Seeing this, the Leicester fans stopped dead in their tracks. We carried on walking towards them and, as we got closer, Parton fired a shot that echoed under the double-decker stand above us. The whole mob turned and scattered. The Blades with us were just as shocked. They had no idea they had a mad gunman in their ranks. We moved forward and occupied the spot behind the goal where the Leicester fans had stood.

'A couple of coppers that were stood pitch-side made no move to come into the crowd. They must have heard the shot – the whole ground must have heard it – but maybe they thought better of tackling some lunatic with a gun. More Blades arrived and joined us. The Leicester mob returned in dribs and drabs and took up a position just to our right. By kick-off, both mobs were stood side-by-side singing songs and chanting.

'I got talking to a Leicester fan called Greg. A good-looking, stocky lad with long blond hair, he wore a leather rocker jacket and a long blue-and-white scarf. We hit it off straight away and chattered about everything and anything but mostly about music and football. He stayed with us all the game and, when we left, we promised to look out for each other when our teams met. There was no trouble after the match. We hitched it back in good time and spent the night in Chesterfield with the Chezzy boys.

'What a bastard! Wednesday had made it to the FA Cup Final and I was jealous as fuck. The one thing I wanted more than anything else in the world was to see the Blades at Wembley. What could be better than marching along Wembley Way, up to the twin towers, singing "Abide with Me" and then watching the Blades skipper lift the trophy? FA Cup ties were always magic occasions, even the early rounds. The attendances rose by thousands. Cup replays, played under floodlights on dark winter nights had a special, breathtaking atmosphere that couldn't be beaten. The whole crowd sang the Yorkshire anthem "On Ilkley Moor Baht 'At" as the Blades ran out.

'"*Wheear 'as ta bin sin ah saw thee...*" we sang. The Cup Final was the only live game shown on TV so the entire football-watching nation tuned in to see it. Not only did it show the whole match, it also showed all the build-up and "How they got there..." with all the goals from the early rounds. I watched the game at home wearing my red-and-white scarf and Blades rosette.

'When Wednesday went two up, I nearly died but Everton came back with two goals from – I'll never forget his name – Mike Trebilcock, the man with three knobs. Then "Shovel-face" Gerry Young, the Wednesday left-half, let the ball slip under his foot for Derek Temple to run through and win the game for Everton 3–2. When the third goal went in, I danced out of the house, then up and down the street, whooping and screaming, waving my scarf round my head.

'A civic reception was laid on for the un-conquering Wednesday heroes. An estimated 100,000 Wednesdayites crawled out from under stones and emerged from forgotten dusty cupboards. They flooded the city centre and massed outside the town hall to welcome the team home. The Heeley Green mob also turned up carrying a large Blade banner. Slightly outnumbered, the Heeley lads had their banner pulled down, but not without giving a good account of themselves.

'The first home game of the 1966/67 season was against Nottingham Forest but all the talk centred on the Burnley egg-chuckers, who we had encountered the week before. Hats off to the bright spark that came up with that idea. Word spread around the Kop that, for the derby match against Wednesday at Hillsborough in a month's time, everybody would be taking a clutch of eggs. For the next few weeks, a new song rang around the Shoreham: "*Don't forget yer eggs... Don't forget yer eggs... Eee-ay-addio... Don't forget yer eggs.*"

'I was starting to meet and get friendly with more and more young lads at every game. It felt great to be on first-name terms with so many new mates, comrades even, all from the same or similar backgrounds. Our scarves and club colours identified us with our football team and with each other. The same thing must have been happening at every ground up and down the country as more and more boys gathered together to support their heroes, check out the latest terrace fashions and, just like the American street gangs, try to defend their "little bit of turf".

'Twenty, fifty, a hundred, two hundred, four hundred... The numbers didn't matter. Compressed together, we swayed, sung and chanted as one. When a goal went in, we surged forward, revelling in the noise, the colour and the chaos. Whether we ended up on the floor or squashed against a crush barrier, it didn't matter; euphoric, we hugged each other waving our scarves, whooping and screaming, "Yeeeeeessssss!"

'The main reason we were all there, though, was our love for the game. All the Dronny lads who attended the games were good footballers; same with the Heeley lads who came up to Dronfield a few times for a game in the park.

'At half-time during the Forest game, a gang of Parka-clad Blade mods led by a lad called Phil Connors (RIP) attacked the visiting fans by the old cricket pavilion as they walked round from the Lane end towards the Kop. The Forest fans were forced back. The mods returned to the Shoreham sporting red-and-white Forest scarves as trophies.'

STOKE

'Stoke-on-Trent has always been a terrible, grim and nasty place to visit. My first trip to the Victoria Ground came in September 1966. Throughout the years, Stoke – particularly at home – have always had, in my opinion, one of the worst (or best in hooligan terms) sets of lads in the country. We again travelled by train with maybe a couple of hundred fellow Blades. Many of the Blades now carried banners and flags, as was the trend. We marched out of the station looking pretty impressive with banners held aloft and our flags flapping in the wind.

'On reaching the stadium, we were approached by the police outside the Boothern end where we queued to get in. They told us that no banners and flags were allowed in the ground as the poles could be used as weapons. The banners were confiscated and the lads carrying them were told they could collect them after the match.

'We took our place on the Boothern end and stood to the

left of the Stoke mob. I was close enough to hear the accents of the Stoke fans; they sounded a bit like scousers, they looked hard and intimidating. I moved a bit further back. I wore a brand-new, sandy-coloured army surplus bush jacket (a new football trend) bought the day before from Yeoman's Army Stores, priced 7s 6d (about 37p). I hadn't had time to decorate it with the "SHEFFIELD UNITED, SHOREHAM STREET" slogans that most of the young Blades had felt-tipped on the backs of theirs.

'As kick-off approached, songs and chants filled the air. To the tune of the Beatles' "Yellow Submarine", we heard: "*We all live at the back of the Boothern end...*" ringing out from the Stoke ranks.

'"*We all shit at the back of the Boothern end...*" we retorted.

'Bottles and coins flew back and forth. I stood with Heeley Green lads and some young Stoke lads about our age came behind us; we stared at each other and a few "Fuck offs" were lobbed, but no punches were exchanged. The fighting (usually one-on-one) was done by the older lads.

'More Blades arrived from the coaches and gathered on the open end. We could have done with some reinforcements as we were well outnumbered by this time. The Stoke ranks swelled and banners and flags were raised from them. It seemed they were allowed to take them in the ground.

'The main Stoke man, the King of the Kop, looked to be in his twenties and, strange as it may seem, wore Father Christmas robes. He had pushed his way to the front alongside a big lad with deep-red, shoulder-length hair.

With their leaders at the front, the Stoke mob moved towards us. The cavalry arrived in the shape of the suities who pushed their way through to face Santa and his mate. Willie Ward let out a piercing, "Zigga-zagga-zigga-zagga..."

'"Yoo-ni-ted," we bellowed back.

'"Zigga-zagga-zigga-zagga..." Willie responded.

'"Stoke-ci-tee," echoed back from the Stoke troops.

'The coppers were now in the crowd trying to keep the two sets of fans apart. Lads from both sides were frogmarched down the terracing and thrown out of the ground. Again, I saw no trouble outside the stadium; the lads who had their banners confiscated had them returned, then we walked back to the station unopposed.

'As we waited on the platform, some Stoke fans arrived and a lad threw a Ben Shaw bottle at them. Ben Shaw pop bottles were the "daddies" of all bottles. Twice as big as a normal pop bottle with sixpence refund on them instead of the usual threepence, you hadn't been hit with a bottle unless it was a Ben Shaw.

'I had been to four away games already this season and there had been trouble at all of them; it seemed to be getting worse every week. This was the shape of things to come and, although I didn't know it, it was happening all over the country. Fucking marvellous – I didn't realise being scared could be so exciting and so much fun, just like a big dipper ride. Could it get much better? It certainly could – next Saturday would be the eagerly awaited "egg day" where we would march through the barren wastelands of Hillsborough, hopefully to do battle with our arch-enemies, Sheffield Wednesday.'

SHEFFIELD WEDNESDAY

'On the morning of Saturday, 24 September 1966, four fifteen-year-old Dronny Blades sneaked into Hopkinson's smallholding. Their mission: "a great egg blag". Johnny Hall – the mastermind behind the deadly plot – knew the layout well. He had worked there doing odd jobs at the weekends and during school holidays. Scores of hens and chickens roamed free around the sheds and the outbuildings laying eggs willy-nilly in makeshift nests, under bushes and in the corners of broken-down huts. The further away from the main house, the rottener the eggs were likely to be.

'After filling a carrier bag each, the lads were on their way to the bus stop to meet up with a couple of hundred or so fellow Blades who were gathering in Pond Street bus station at midday.

'Willie Marples, a classmate from school who was on his way to the match clad in his Wednesday gear, passed the lads on Dronny Bottom. Beetroot let fly an egg which splattered on Willie's back. Johnny Hall reckoned an old bloke walking past with his dog fainted from the stench and the dog dropped dead. Willie and Beetroot slugged it out, one-on-one for a few minutes. Beetroot ended the scrap by whipping off his belt and smacking Willie round the lughole with the buckle end. The ill feeling had started already. Beetroot (so called because the one and only time he ever got told off by a teacher he went as red as one) was a quiet, studious, intelligent lad who always did well at school. He always had a top pocket full of pens and would lend you one, no bother. Beetie, however, turned into a very naughty boy – a kind of Mr Hyde-type creature – whenever he went to a football game. I once saw him, after a testimonial game against Wednesday at the Lane, drag a Wednesdayite off a bus in Pond Street and beat him half to death with a walking stick and then laugh his head off when he'd finished.

'I had been in town since 11.00am armed with a carton of half-a-dozen eggs, obtained by leaving a note out for my mother's milkman. Many of the arriving Blades carried boxes of eggs. We set off on the two-mile trek with our banners, flags and eggs, picking up small groups of lads on the way as we walked through town. There wasn't a policeman in sight.

'We showed off our eggs to each other like they were some kind of new invention that nobody had ever seen before. Some with the little lion stamp, some large-'uns, some small-'uns, some free-range, some jumbo.

'"Look at them fuckers for eggs then..."

'As we reached the bottom of Penistone Road, about a dozen or so Pittsmoor lads carrying a large banner joined the mob. Any passing Wednesdayites we saw had the odd egg chucked at them.

'On reaching the ground at about 1.30pm, we queued outside the Penistone Road end (Wednesday's Kop). We paid the one shilling (or it might have been two shillings) admission at the boys' entrance. I emerged at the other side of the turnstiles to see a group of Blades telling the lads that the coppers were at the back of the open Kop searching everyone for eggs. The word must have got out. I hid my eggs in some bushes and walked past two coppers (yes, two) trying to pat down dozens of youths as they entered the Kop.

'"Got any eggs?" The copper asked me, patting my bush jacket; a couple of cartons lay at his feet.

'"No," I answered.

'"Go on then."

'At least ten lads had walked past as he did this. I waited a few minutes, walked back out and collected my eggs. Passing the same copper again, I said, "You've searched me once."

'"Yeah, go on," he said. The ground was all but deserted, except for us; we stood at the back of the Kop directly behind the goal waiting for the Wednesdayites to arrive. The plan was, at ten minutes to three, with our arms held aloft and to the chant of "Sheff United, hallelujah..." the mass throw would take place.

'By 2.00pm, 50 or so Wednesdayites had gathered at the front. This proved too tempting for some of the trigger-happy Blades and a few rounds of ammo were fired into their ranks. By 2.30pm, the ground started filling up; more Wednesdayites, more Blades and more eggs entered the stadium. At 2.50pm, with forty-odd thousand in the ground and the mass of Blades singing and swaying, hundreds of hands were raised into the air and the cry went up, "Sheff United Hallelujah... Hallelujah..."

'What a sight to behold, nowhere to run, nowhere to hide, it's raining eggs... Hallelujah! A huge roar greeted the teams as they took to the pitch. Raised blue-and-white Wednesday banners now had tinges of yellow slime running down them.

'"Scrambled eggs... Scrambled eggs..." we chanted. Our ammunition now used up, we turned to coins and other missiles. Stones were collected from the steep banking at the back of the Kop and thrown at the Wednesdayites. One of the young Dronny lads (who later went on have a distinguished career in the police force) was removed and thrown out of the ground by his future colleagues. The game ended in a 2–2 draw but the Blades had scored what we all thought was a late winning goal, only for it to be disallowed for offside. We left the ground en masse at the end of the game and marched back down Penistone Road towards town, chanting, "We were robbed..." but still laughing at any egg-stained Wednesday fans we saw.

'The following Monday's edition of the *Sheffield Morning Telegraph* reported the trouble. It told of the many ejections from the ground, of youths throwing sharpened steel washers and carrying flick-knives... but no mention of those vicious eggs!'

CHELSEA

'It was back to the capital and Chelsea in mid-November 1966, just six months after we had ventured on to The Shed. I was the youngest of eight Dronny and four Chesterfield lads who caught the midnight train from Sheffield Midland Station. Sinny, a scrawny, dark-haired Chezzy lad aged about 19 was the oldest of our little crew. Although roughly the same age as the suit boys, he was nothing like them. He dressed in the same way as us and knew, as we all did, that something was starting to happen – a new culture based around football that was fun, exciting and dangerous. He talked constantly about the gangs we were likely to encounter and what might happen if we did. He wanted to find out everything there was to know about this innovative scene; he relished every single second of it.

'No matter where we travelled, we had no idea what or who could be lurking around the next corner. We were stepping into the unknown but that was part of the fun and the buzz of it all. The bush jackets were left at home; not through fear, though. We were off for a weekend's fun in the big city and all wore our best togs for the occasion. Most of us wore red-and-white woolly scarves.

'Dave Parton brought along his old dented brass bugle which would nearly shatter an eardrum if he came up from behind and gave a blast from six inches; it also made a handy weapon. The thrill of rattling down south all through the night and the anticipation of the day to come was overwhelming.

'We got talking to a Man United fan on the train. He came from Halifax and was heading down to Southampton to watch his team. He bragged that Man United were the best-supported team in the land and fans travelled from all parts of England to watch them. Thousands, he said, went to every away game; everybody knew about Man United so I had no reason to doubt him. When told we were going to Chelsea, he spoke of all the trouble that had happened when they had last played there. Ten thousand United fans had invaded The Shed end, he told us, but they came in for a red-hot time. He looked amazed when we told him about the 100 or so Blades who had been there six months earlier. He clearly didn't believe us.

'"How many are you taking down today?" he asked.

'"Maybe a couple of hundred," we replied.

'"Fuck me!" he said, "You'll get fucking slaughtered!"

'We arrived at St Pancras at four or five in the morning and sat around the station chatting and messing about. A couple of us went for a walk and stole a crate of milk from outside a shop, which we brought back for the others to share. We found a café to pass a bit more time and, when the streets were aired and the Tube stations opened, we headed off to Buckingham Palace to visit the Queen. We walked up Pall Mall, singing, climbing on walls and swinging from trees. Nearing the palace, Parton let out a series of ear-splitting blasts from his bugle; it sounded like a dying elephant. Two policemen came strolling over to us; one of them beckoned Parton over and, pointing to a mansion across the street, calmly said, "Come here, son. D'you know who lives over there?"

'"No," Parton replied.

'The copper's voice grew gradually louder. "Well, I'll tell you who lives there, shall I? The Queen Mother... and she likes a lay-in on Saturday mornings, so if some scruffy bastard starts blowing a trumpet and wakes her up, it's me that gets the blame, so if you blow it one more time I'll ram it straight up your fucking arse. Understand?" By this time, the copper was bawling his head off.

'"Yes, sir... Sorry, officer," Parton replied, the rest of us doubled up with laughter.

'It was brilliant being in London, just walking around the streets, taking it all in. There was a certain air of magic and a promise of adventure about the place. I could smell London, taste it, I felt part of it... I loved it. Tremendous buildings with statues and monuments everywhere. Trafalgar Square seemed enormous; we climbed the lions, gazed up miles at Lord Nelson and scattered 10,000 pigeons. We spent the rest of the morning shouting at passers-by, ogling dolly birds in kinky boots and squeezing mini-skirted bums. We met and got chatting to a group of Newcastle fans.

'The Newcastle lads carried a black-and-white banner; felt-tipped in one corner were the words "CHARLIE HURLEY, CURLY BASTARD". I asked what it meant. Charlie Hurley, they told me, played for Sunderland; he had curly hair and they hated the bastard. Fair enough, it seemed hatred between local rivals was nationwide.

'We had a chat to some Norwich fans decked out in yellow-and-green and I swapped my Blade pin badge for one of theirs. All the different accents and club colours fascinated me. Fans from other clubs always got on; we were all in London having a good time so no one wanted to fight or hurt each other. Fans we met from the London clubs were always friendly, chatty and helpful. With the hooligan scene in its infancy, London was still a relatively safe place away from the football stadiums. Fans had not yet started to bear the grudges that, in the near future, would turn the capital into a battlefield when rival supporters crossed paths in the train stations or on the Underground.

'Reading the morning paper, we learnt that United had signed a "speedy left-winger" from Norwich City, a certain Billy Punton, as a replacement for the injured Gil Reece and he would be making his debut today.

'We arrived at Stamford Bridge about 2.30pm and went into the open corner bit of The Shed. A group of Blades stood camped under a weird-looking little stand on stilts. We walked under the main stand to join them. Only two coaches had made the trip plus about 20 or so who travelled on the morning train.

'As always, two lads carrying a huge silk banner were there. This banner was top class, the top half red, the bottom half white with "SHEFFIELD UNITED" in hand-stitched black letters emblazoned across it. There always been a few flags and banners dotted around the grounds but now more and more were starting to appear. I always counted how many we took to away games so I could brag to Wednesdayite mates, "We took 300 yesterday and we had ten banners..." If I missed an away game, the first questions I always asked the lads who had been were: "How many Unitedites went?" and "How many banners did we have?"

'The trouble with taking them to away games was that, unlike scarves, you couldn't hide six yards of cloth and two eight-foot poles up your jumper. Just like the wars of centuries past, one of the new trends at the games was the "taking of the colours", then ripping them to shreds in front of their owners. The lads came over and told us some Chelsea boys had been round earlier and tried to steal the banner. They said they'd be waiting after the match and were "having it". Parton told the Blade lads to stick with us and that he would carry the banner out at the end of the game.

'The teams came out and we couldn't believe it when we saw Punton. "Fuck me!" Tiny said, "He's 60 years old."

'"Who's that?" somebody else shouted.

'"Fuckin' Yul Brynner!"

'Bald Bill Punton turned out a good performance, though, setting up the equalising goal for Alan Birchenall in a 1–1 draw. We weren't to know it then but, a couple of months later, Punton would turn out to be a Blade legend, remembered for ever for one magic moment that would repay his £5,000 transfer fee ten times over.

'The game ended and 14 of us made our way out. Parton had handed his bugle to one of our lads and now carried the banner. As we hit the darkened streets, groups of Chelsea mods stood on both sides of the road. Another group headed straight towards us. I pushed my scarf under my jacket and could hear my heart thumping. Parton, who, bearing in mind was only 17 years old, didn't wait for them to reach us. He charged into them swinging the banner round his head. A tall, ginger-haired Chelsea lad wearing a Parka came from the side and landed a punch to Parton's head. He wobbled but managed to stay on his feet. Other Chelsea lads tried to grab the banner but he wouldn't let go. We pushed our way through, avoiding kicks and punches. Suddenly, we were through them... We didn't run and we weren't chased, it just stopped as quickly as it started.

'Parton's eye was already closing as we walked into Fulham Broadway Tube station; other groups of Chelsea fans stared at us but no one said anything. With a big smile on his face, Parton handed back the banner to the two lads. We caught the Tube and made our way up to the West End.

'Soho, the seedy red-light district of the capital was something else. A compact collection of sex shops, rip-off strip joints, flashing neon signs and sleazy peep shows. The roasted ducks displayed in the windows of the Chinatown restaurants, with their heads and long necks still attached, looked rather pissed off as they hung and waited their turn to be next on the menu. We walked through the narrow streets laughing and nudging each other – fucking paradise! I wished I could stay for ever.

'We called into a café for a cup of tea. I noticed a piece of string with a small lump of cardboard on the end hanging out of my cup. I went back to the counter and said to the girl who'd served me, "What the fuck's that?"

'"It's a tea bag," she replied. "Leave it in the cup to brew for a minute or two."

'I returned to our table, lifted the bag out and swatted it into the saucer in disgust. '"What about that!" I said. "It's a fucking tea bag; I've not seen one of them fuckers before." Everybody cracked up. Strange place, that London.

'We paid ten bob (50p) entrance fee into a strip club called The Red Mill. It was a small dingy hovel, dimly lit, with a raised stage at the front, about six rows of cinema-type seats and standing room at the rear. The place was packed and we squeezed in at the back. We whistled, booed, cheered and shouted obscenities as a succession of strippers emerged, one by one, from behind a filthy curtain. Some were OK; some were old dogs. As punters from the front left their seats, others moved from the back to take them. Parton, now sporting a beauty of a shiner, had somehow managed to get himself on the front row, bang in front of the stage. One of the strippers noticed Parton's eye and, pretending to pluck a hair from her fanny, leaned over to him and said, "That looks sore, darling... put this on it, it'll sooth it." Parton reached out, took the imaginary pube between his finger and thumb, held it up, then turned round and shouted, "I'm saving this fucker... 'as anybody got a matchbox?" The place erupted in laughter.

'On the midnight train back home, we swore revenge on the Chelsea bastards if they ever came to the Lane, little knowing we would be back there in less than four months.'

MANCHESTER UNITED

'Boxing Day 1966 and nearly 43,000, maybe half of them from Manchester, packed into the Lane for the visit of Manchester United. (The lad from Halifax was right then.) Entering the turnstiles near the cricket pavilion, it took a couple of mates and me a good 20 minutes to push and squeeze our way into the Kop.

'The Blade mob stood in their usual place at the front. The Manchester hordes stretched across the full length of the back of the Kop and on both sides of the Blades at the front. On reaching our spot, I wasn't sure I even wanted to be there.

'I gazed in awe into the Man United ranks. Scores of banners and flags made a magnificent sight; I had never seen anything like it. It hit me at that moment why any young impressionable lad could and indeed would be seduced by the phenomenon that was Manchester United. It was breathtaking; what must it be like to be part of a mob like that? And to have the added bonus of watching George Best every Saturday.

'So many marvellous new songs echoed round the Shoreham. I tried to store them in my head for future use. Man United were the team that everybody knew about. Before the 1958 Munich air disaster, when most of their young team died, they were just another team. The whole country seemed to sympathise and have a soft spot for "the

Busby Babes". I don't suppose anyone needed any credentials to be a Man United fan, no initiation ceremony, just turn up wearing red-and-white and learn a few of their songs and you were in, it was easy, too easy; anybody could be a Man United fan. Fuck 'em – I was still a Blade, just.

'The crowd swayed and surged forward. Young kids at the front leapt the fence behind the goal to avoid being crushed. Manchester fans pushed into us. A Blade with a small flag on the end of a four-foot long lump of timber smashed anyone who came near him. The police dragged one of the brawling Heeley lads with blood streaming from a head wound away from the mêlée. Another surge forward left me exposed a couple of yards away from some scruffy-looking young Mancs. One of them, who had a Beatles-style haircut, pointed at me and shouted to his mates, "Look at him, he's got longer hair than me... get the cunt." I felt quite proud when I shouted, "Fuck off!" at him, as another surge took me away from them.

'The coppers tried in vain to restore order. The game had kicked off but it was secondary to the action taking place on the Shoreham. Best, Law and Charlton may have been displaying their silky skills but I was on the lookout for flying bottles. The chaos continued as older, braver Blades fought to hold their places. I ended up on the floor with another lad on top of me; it went dark, then all I could see were legs and shoes scuffing my head. I looked around for my mates but they were gone. Panic set in as I scrambled to my feet only to be squashed again on to a crush barrier. Fuck this, I thought, I'm getting out of here. I made my way to the front and snaked along to the safety of the open bit of the Kop way past the corner flag. I felt a certain amount of shame in my retreat but also a sense of relief to be out of it.

'After the match, I walked down Shoreham Street to the bus station. All the roads leading into town were packed with Man United fans. Even though everybody wore red-and-white, I knew they were all Manchester; they looked different, and just like any other town, city or ground they visited, they had taken over.

'Some of my mates did make the return trip to Manchester, along with hundreds of other Blades. The lads had stayed in Manchester for a while after the game and were in the station just ready to board the train back home when a Man City fan (City had played at Hillsborough that day) who they described as a "walking mountain", wandered along the platform. One of the lads shouted, "Oi, ya big fat cunt," as he came wobbling towards them. Alan, one of the Chesterfield lads, ran up and booted him as hard as he could. The giant never flinched. The lads scrambled on to the train with the City fan in hot pursuit. They ran into a compartment and two of them, one on each side, held their feet against the sliding doors in an effort to keep him out. He simply ripped the doors open with his bare hands and proceeded to slap and throw the half-dozen lads around the carriage. Ansh said he'd never been so scared in all his life.

'A couple of years later, we were talking to some Man City fans in some train station somewhere or other and we told them the story. "Yeah," one of them said, "that's so-and-so... I used to know him, he's dead now, he got hit by a bus in the centre of Manchester."

'"Thank fuck for that," one of our lads replied. "I bet the bus was a fucking write-off!"

'The front-page headline in the following day's *Sheffield Star* screamed out at me: "VANDALS RUN RIOT ON BLADES TRAIN". It showed a photo of a guard in one of the smashed-up carriages and went on to give a detailed description of all the damage done on the train carrying hundreds of United fans back from Manchester. All the breakages were listed – 50 light bulbs, 10 light shades, 3 toilet seats, 6 door frames etc. A £25 reward was offered for information leading to arrests.

'Oh, how I would have loved to have been on that train, loved to have smashed some fixtures and fittings. The trains British Rail laid on were falling to pieces anyway. Fusty-smelling seats covered in dust and toilets that looked like they'd been smashed up already. But it was only just starting; there would be plenty more "soccer specials" to smash up. The football hooligans were starting to make the headlines. The newspapers called us "yobs" and "louts". I liked being called a lout; it had a nice ring to it.

SHEFFIELD WEDNESDAY

'Sheffield Wednesday, the old enemy, were due at the Lane for the third home game of the season on 2 September 1967. A meet was arranged for midday at the Howard Hotel near the train station in town. Fifty or so Blades stood outside the pub with more holed up inside. Half-a-dozen Dronny lads joined the throng. The Sheffield lads were buzzing, confident and cocky. "We're gonna fuckin' kill the bastards today..."

'Word was out that Wednesday were meeting at the same time in Fitzalan Square, only a few hundred yards away in the centre of town. Some more lads turned up saying there were loads of Wednesdayites up at the Square. It never crossed any of our minds to go up to the Square to confront them; in those days, the fighting would be done inside the ground.

'Half-an-hour or so later, we moved off towards Bramall Lane. An assortment of weapons, bricks, lumps of wood and iron bars were collected from behind buildings and back yards as we made our way up Shoreham Street towards the ground.

'On arriving, we found more Blades, 30 or so, sat outside the turnstiles on the corner of John Street. Yet more Blades arrived in ones and twos, boosting our numbers to around 150. None of the turnstiles were open so all we could do was wait. Word came in that a big mob of Wednesdayites had been seen marching down the Moor.

'A mass of blue-and-white filling the road appeared at the far end of John Street and walked down towards us, their numbers roughly the same as ours. Blades leapt to their feet and, as one, sprinted towards them. Both mobs reached the player's entrance halfway down. At this point, the Wednesday mob turned and scampered back down the road. Nobody followed or chased them, nobody said, "Let's do this…" or "Let's do that…" There were no leaders, and no one was in charge. None of the older suities or rockers were with us; I don't think anyone was over the age of 18. The hatred everyone felt towards Wednesday had fired us all up.

'It was the first time we had done it on our own; we were coming of age. We turned, walked back and sat down again. It was a natural instinct to do what we did; we were there to defend our Kop, a bunch of young kids playing war games. It never even entered my head that I might get hurt.

'The Wednesday lads didn't run far; they congregated outside the Lane end turnstiles, still on John Street and still in our view. A few minutes later, they tried it again, this time they didn't even reach the halfway line before turning and running again.

'The turnstiles opened at about half-past one. We piled into the Kop but instead of going to our usual place at the front behind the goal, we lined up along the back. Whether this was planned or not I don't know, but nobody dished out orders. Again, I think instinct took us to the high ground.

'I didn't have a clue what was going through the heads of the Wednesday fans, whether they had leaders or what, but having been run twice in the space of a few minutes, back they came and began queuing outside the Kop.

'From the top of the steps we could see out into the street. Everyone expected them to try and walk up the back steps to enter the Shoreham and that's where we all congregated. The first 20 or so through the turnstiles came in for a barrage of rocks and lumps of timber. They retreated behind a wall to the right, then underneath some steps leading to another entrance. This led to the bottom corner where the fenced-off kids' pen was later built.

'More and more Wednesday fans entered the stadium but they were fucked. No matter which way they tried to get into the Kop, we had the higher ground and showered them with stones and other missiles. So where were the coppers while all this was going off, you may ask? The simple answer is, well... nowhere. There were one or two dotted round the ground but that was it. They obviously didn't fancy the prospect of tackling a few hundred, armed-to-the-teeth, rampant, red-and-white teenagers.

'Four, five, six times the Wednesdayites tried to reach the back of the Kop and each time they were forced back to the bottom corner. Somebody, somewhere, must have been in charge of the police operation that day and, after half-an-hour or so of chaos, a squad of coppers finally arrived. Around 20 or so police surrounded the Wednesday fans and the combined mob of Owls and police walked up the steps towards us. We charged down, throwing everything we had. The coppers were just as bad as their new mates – they turned and ran. More police arrived and tried a new tactic, pushing us back, mingling in with us and nicking those they saw throwing missiles. This allowed the rest of the police to bring the Wednesday mob up the Kop and deposit them at the back to the right-hand side of us.

'I could just imagine *Sergeant Plod to PC John Law*: "What do you reckon, John? We've got 200 U-bleedin'-nitedites throwing bricks and going mad and a couple of hundred Wednesdayites cowering in this corner..."

'"Well, Sarge, why not put the Wednesday fans on the terrace or even take them round to the Lane end. That should stop the trouble."

'"Nay, lad... The Wednesdayites have every right to stand where they like. We'll take them up to the back, two yards from the Blade mob, form a line in between and try to protect them."

'Policing at its best, eh? The ground started to fill up with more lads from both sides joining their respective mobs only a few feet away from each other. I'll say one thing for the Wednesdayites – they were quick on the uptake. The missiles that had been raining down on them for the best part of an hour were now being returned into the Blade ranks.

'Mcduff was the second eldest of the six Cordell brothers (three were Blades, three were Owls). At 14 years old he already stood head and shoulders above me. Mac got his nickname from the tall, thin, comic-book character Lofty Mcduff. Mac wore a white pith helmet (the type African white hunters wear) borrowed from me. My mother had bought it from a jumble sale and I had painted the letters "BLADES" in red paint on to the six segments of the hat. Mac staggered backwards as a half house-brick smashed into the cork helmet, leaving a large dent in the side. Injured fans from both sides were led away to be treated by the St John's ambulance brigade stationed at pitch-side.

'There weren't too many black lads around at the games back then. One of the Heeley Green mob and the only Wednesdayite in their crew was a black kid called Mick Grudge. Mick, at the forefront of the Wednesday mob, laid into any Blade who came near him. Seeing this, Herman, Scanno, Mouse and the rest of the Heeley lads, even though he was their mate, steamed in, forcing him back into the crowd. There was only one black lad in the Blade mob that I can remember, a lad named Black Arthur; he wasn't really black, though, just mucky-looking.

'In our ignorance, we were terrible racists at that time. There were no black people at all in Dronfield. The only black men we had ever seen were on the Tarzan films, at the Bug Hut and the Abbeydale school cricket team. We were even scared to death as kids when told, "If you don't behave, a black man will get ya…" or "Weer's me mam?" "She's run off with a black man." It was quite acceptable for Alf Garnett on Saturday prime-time telly to call them "darkies, wogs and coons". Attercliffe, with a large immigrant population, was supposed to be the place where all the black men lived.

'"*I'm gonna tell ya where the black men live… they all live down Attercliffe…*" We sang awful songs about the Ku Klux Klan nailing niggers to the door and Pakis eating Kitty-Kat and Kennomeat. A variation of the "Zigga-Zagga" chant – "Nigger-nogga, nigger-nogga… wog-wog-wog" – was often chanted at the matches.

'In 1968, Enoch Powell's *Rivers of Blood* speech stirred up even more racial hatred. "Enoch, Enoch, send the wogs home…" could be heard at most football grounds. Well into the Seventies, the ethnic minorities still copped for it. In *The Comedians* TV programme, everyone from black people, to "thick Irishmen" and wheelchair-bound spastics were fair game. I'm not quite sure if Charlie Williams, the black Barnsley comic, inflamed or made the situation more acceptable by taking the piss out of his own race.

'We really didn't know any better and just went along with it. No one amongst us thought it was wrong, anyway, and none of us had the balls to do anything about it even if we had wanted to. It wasn't until the early Seventies that we started to meet and get to know black lads at the games and in the pubs and clubs around town. The shouts of "Black bastard" were then reserved for coppers and referees.

'Anyway, at the Lane, kick-off approached and, with 36,000 fans in the ground, the fighting continued. Both managers made loudspeaker appeals for calm. Like anybody gave a fuck! We were having a good time. Every now and again, lads from both sides would recognise a friend, workmate, neighbour or relative and shout out a greeting, "Nar-then, Steve, how tha' going? See ya t'neet," before piling back in again.

'The Wednesday mob, lucky to be on the Kop in the first place, didn't try to make any inroads and stayed over to the right. With the game now under way, things calmed down slightly but missiles continued to fly back and forth. Lads were arrested or thrown out of the ground, some of the injured fans were treated on the spot, with the more serious cases whipped off to hospital. Even before "Iron lung, legs of plastic" John Ritchie scored a late winner for Wednesday, their fans started drifting off. We left the ground and did the usual march up the Moor into town, trying to find the Wednesdayites. We were pissed off, obviously, about the result but pleased that a bunch of young lads had successfully defended the Shoreham end.

The front-page headline of the Saturday evening sports paper, the *Green 'Un*, read: "SIX HOSPITAL CASES MAR RITCHIE'S DERBY WINNER" It went on to give a detailed account of the all the trouble. The paper got to know about the meeting place of both mobs by interviewing young lads. Their names, ages and their home districts were printed in the paper. It told of the Blade mob gathering stones from outside the Howard and the Midland Station, "the scrap" on John Street before the game (which wasn't really a scrap, just a chase) and how the Shoreham Street end had been turned into a battlefield.

'It also said, "By 2.15, five teenagers had been taken to

hospital and at least another dozen had been treated on the spot for head injuries. Amongst the weapons seized were a large piece of lead, which had struck a boy in the face, jagged tins and house-bricks. One fan said his friend had been struck on the head by half a house-brick."

'The quote of the day, however, came from the United chairman, who dismissed the violence as just "unfortunate pre-match excitement". The Monday morning nationals picked up on the story, and Sheffield United topped the league table of arrests and shame. Fucking great stuff, I thought, top of the league at last.

'The day after the game, I was walking along Stonelow Road with a couple of mates when Paddy O'Brien's father – also called Paddy – came staggering home from the Sunday dinner session. Paddy, a staunch Wednesdayite shouted, "What about that then, Sharpy, ya little cunt? Up the Owls... What have you got to say about it? Ya not so fuckin' clever today are ya? Up the fuckin Owls." Now this wasn't a bit of friendly banter; he was drunk, granted, but from the way he spoke I knew he was after some trouble.

'"Fuck off, ya drunken old cunt," I shouted back. Paddy slipped off his coat, took out his false teeth and put them on a garden wall, which was about two feet high. He held up his fists in the Queensbury Rules style. "Come on then, Sharpy, I'll fuckin' kill ya, you little fuckin bastard."

'Well, Paddy was a bloke in his forties; men were old in their thirties back then, and at forty they were fucking ancient. I was only 16 and a little bit scared but he had called me a bastard and I didn't like being called a bastard and, besides, he could hardly stand up. I walked over and with one punch knocked him over the wall. My fist sunk well into his face; it was like punching a sponge pudding. He lay sparked out in the front garden. We all walked away laughing. Ten minutes later, we went back for a look; he was still out cold, maybe more from the beer than from the punch, but Paddy never bothered me again.

'I loved playing football just as much as I loved watching it and, even though it would be a wrench to miss the Blade games, I signed up (along with some of my old school mates) for the Dronfield youth club Under-20s team. We played on Saturdays in the Sheffield Junior League, so the only time I could get to see the Blades would be at the night matches. We trained twice a week in the gym at Gosforth School and on youth club nights played five-a-side games on the floodlit asphalt tennis court at the side of the youth club. After a couple of months of training and playing, I felt as fit as a violin.

'Saturday, 3 October 1970... I don't think we had a game but, if we did, I must have feigned injury to be at the Lane for the derby against Wednesday, nothing in the world would have kept me away from this game. It's about 15 minutes before kick-off when I enter the ground with Sinny (his head freshly shaven for the big occasion) and a few more Chesterfield and Dronny lads. We walk up the back steps and Sinny says, "Right lads, get fuckin' ready... It's our skins against their grease and their grease against our skins today."

'Now, I don't quite know why; could it possibly have been that this 19-year-old who'd been playing football for a few weeks had learnt a bit of discipline and grown up a little bit? I'm thinking; fuckin' hell, what's he saying? He's 23 years old and he's talking like a little kid. This unexpected mature moment vanished as I heard that special, amazing, war-like roar that can only be heard at a Sheffield derby. It's not a chant; it's more like a growling, neck-vein-bulging scream that starts in the pit of the stomach and extends from the bottom of your heart: "Ya-ni-ted..." all three syllables delivered with equal venom, "Wens-dee..." "Ya-ni-ted..."

'"Wens-dee..." "Ya-ni-ted..." "Wens-dee..." echoes around the stadium as Blade and Owl try to out-shout each other. It's not for the team, there're not even on the pitch, it's for us, the mob, the Blade mob, we've got to be louder than our greatest rivals. We screech, we yell and we bawl, we're the fuckin' loudest and we're the fuckin' hardest.

'Thousands of Wednesdayites occupy the right-hand half of the Shoreham, screeching, yelling and bawling just as loud as we are. Where the fuck has this lot come from? How long have they been in? How did they get in? Three years ago, they were stuck in the corner, heading house-bricks, surrounded by police, but today they're here in force. Crombie-clad skinheads and hard-mods dressed in checked Sherman's stand on the front line, fierce fuckers, confident, gesticulating, screaming threats, standing firm, more than ready to fight and because the Wednesdayites are so up for it. We've got to match them, got to be a little bit braver, got to defend the Shoreham end at all costs.

'The two mobs stand only a yard from each other. The front-row boys from both sides throw punches past a line of police trying to separate them. The new buzz word on the terraces is "Aggro... aggression... aggravation..." "Ay – Gee – Gee – Ar – Oh... AGGRO!"

'The odd missile flies back and forth but that's not good

enough, everyone wants to get in close, feel a face at the
end of their fist and a bollock on the tip of their boot. The
mood is pure hatred, they're invading our end but this is as
far as they're going, this is our bit, this is where we stand,
directly behind the goal. We're not shifting, the buck stops
here. 40,000 voices roar out the teams and both sets of fans
take their eyes off each other for a few seconds to welcome
them. They sway and surge forward, waving scarves and
banners, celebrating like a goal has gone in. The Blade
ranks swell as latecomers from the boozers join the throng
and the force of 50 new bodies collapses the police line;
yes, the fuckin' nutters are here.

'Wednesday win the toss and opt to kick towards the
Lane end. This means the Blades attack the Kop in the first
half, a slight disadvantage as tradition dictates that the
Blades kick toward the Shoreham end in the second half.

'"It's worth a goal start, isn't it?" The crowd settles
down slightly to focus on the game but every few seconds
Blade eyes glance to the right, Owl eyes to the left,
watching and listening for the roar of confrontation.
United are well on top, Colquhoun and Deardon put the
Blades 2–0 up. This sends us crazy and sparks off more
vicious fighting. Into the second half and Wednesday pull a
goal back, then the bastards somehow manage to draw
level and the brawling kicks off again. The game is finely
poised, the atmosphere electric.

'So here we are "*feeling sad, feeling blue, United 2,
Wednesday 2...*" then on to the pitch comes John Tudor
– yeeeees! Substitute John (King) Tudor's through on his
own, one-on-one with the goalie, he's got loads of time
and loads of space, there's not a Wednesday defender in

sight. The Wednesday 'keeper runs out narrowing the angle, Tudor's got to score, got to dribble round him and put the ball into an empty net... but no; what's he fuckin' doing? He shoots, low and hard, straight at the goalie. Shit! But the ball goes through the goalie's legs... and into the net. "Yeeeeeeeessssssssssssssss!" Three fuckin' two, get in there.

'Incredible noise and celebrations greet the goal that turns out to be the winner. "Hallelujah... King Tudor... King Tudor..." The Shoreham boys are having a fit, we hug, kiss, dance, surge forwards, sway sideways, fall down, get back up, it's sheer chaos, it's sheer delight, it's fuckin' party time. Wednesday fans look dejected, crestfallen, the goal's knocked the stuffing out of them but it gives us an adrenalin boost that takes us punching and booting through the police lines. For a few brief seconds, the Wednesday fans back off but order is soon restored. Then it's all over, the final whistle blows.

'There's no need for feet as the momentum of the crowd carries me down the steps on to John Street. We march on to Shoreham Street 300 strong, singing, laughing and jigging. The Wednesday fans have split and melted, they walk alone or in small groups, staring at the pavement. A derby day defeat destroys the soul, their desire to fight has disappeared. We don't want to fight either, we're too happy, we've beaten the old enemy, we've beaten the Wednesday bastards, let's get into the boozers to sing and drink the night away.

'We walk through Pond Street bus station and the chant of "Ya-ni-ted" nearly lifts the roof off the main terminal. Blades congregate around the Threepenny Bit kiosk, congratulating each other. The boozers'll be open in ten minutes. "Let's get fuckin' bladdered."

'The day's events got me thinking, did I really want to give all this up to play football? But it wasn't like this every week; the exceptional buzz of a derby match only happens twice a season. The other thing that made me think were the huge numbers and, more importantly, the actions of the Wednesdayites. We'd more or less had it our own way since the mid-Sixties. Could this be the same set of lads who'd been humiliated inside their own ground on "Egg Day" four years ago? Only six months earlier, we'd swanned around Hillsborough like we owned it but, today, they'd matched us for fervour, hostility and aggression. A bit of a shock, really; I didn't like to admit it but it looked like things were starting to even out on the Sheffield hooligan scene.

LEEDS

'Moose had just finished his latest spell in jail and was now a free man for a while and back among the fold. September 1974 and it's Leeds United at Elland Road. We all knew what to expect at Leeds; a few months earlier, 10,000 of the bastards massed on the Shoreham two hours before kick-off and had basically taken the piss. Like a poor man's Man Utd, Leeds were starting to attract the 'glory hunters'. They now boasted a huge following, boosted by lads from most of the towns in the Yorkshire region and from towns and cities all over the country.

'A couple of hundred Blades, stuck in the right-hand top corner, held on for a while but overwhelming numbers eventually shifted us. We were there just long enough to welcome the Blades as they took to the pitch. We gave out the usual chant of "Tony... Tony... Currie" to TC. Currie looked up at us and waved his arms, beckoning us over to behind the goal where we usually stood. Yeah, I thought, it's all right for you, fuckin' Currie, you're stood on the safety of the pitch.

'Moose, Dick Dung, Wafe, his brother Alex, Sam Shirt and me caught an early-morning service bus from Pond Street that arrived in Leeds at 11 bells – opening time. Some of the other lads were supposedly catching the train around dinner time. I knew for certain that we were in for a rough ride but we were out to do our own thing and if the other lads were coming (which I doubted very much) we expected to bump into them somewhere or other in Leeds.

'None of us wore colours, we didn't really need to. Moose would let anyone who wanted to know who we were. We did a couple of virtually empty pubs in the city centre for an hour or so and, by the time we were back on the streets, there's plenty of scarved-up (all the lads wore scarves at the time) Leeds fans knocking about.

'I'd purposely sunk as many pints as I could to get a bit of the Old Dutch before the inevitable happened. Moose was at it straight away, barging into passing Leeds fans.

'"What the fuck are you looking at, cunt? Yeah, we're from Sheffield, what the fuck are you gonna do about it?" The rest of us are trying to look and act as hard as we possibly can. A small group of Leeds lads who were sat on a wall looked us over as we passed through a shopping precinct. One of them, a big fat cunt festooned in scarves and sew-on badges covering his denim jacket, jumped up and walked towards us. "Where are you from?" he asked, arrogant as fuck, in a broad cockney accent.

'"We're from Sheffield, ya fat bastard," Moose answered. "Do ya fancy it, me and you, one on one?"

'The fat cockney's face dropped.

'"Come on, fat cunt, ya fuckin' big enough, aren't ya? Go and fetch your fuckin' mates as well," Moose said.

'"I don't want any trouble," Fat Bastard said.

'"Well, fuck off then, before I rip ya fuckin' head off," Moose said.

'By about two o'clock we're still in the city centre and there's Leeds fans, fuckin' hundreds of 'em, everywhere. I had a word with Moose, who was still at it, saying, "We're gonna have to calm down a bit, Mulligan, there's too many of the fuckers, we're gonna get fuckin' killed here."

'"Fuck 'em," Moose said. "They're all a bunch of fuckin' wankers."

'Moose reluctantly calmed down a bit and we made our way up to the ground, reaching Elland Road just before kick-off. Wafe, Alex and Sam said they were going in the Peacock boozer for the last 'un; Moose, Dick and me decided to go in the ground. We went in the standing bit of the South Stand; the seating part was under construction at the time. We'd only been inside for a matter of minutes before hundreds of eyes were focused on us. Moose had clipped at least half-a-dozen Leeds fans round the head as we pushed our way in, shouting, "Get out of the fuckin' way, ya Leeds bastards."

'I noticed a small patch of red-and-white on the Lowfields terrace. "Come on," I said, "There's some Blades over there." We moved off, followed by at least 50, mostly young, 16–17- year-old Leeds lads. Moose kept stopping and challenging the ones nearest to us, but none of them would take him up on it. This was the front to end all fronts; it can't last much fuckin' longer, I thought.

'We reached the group of Blades on the Lowfields to find they were old blokes, women and a few young kids. There were now a good hundred Leeds fans on our trail. The group of Blades melted when they realised what was happening.

'The Leeds fans massed behind us and normals moved out of the way, leaving us stood in an empty circle. Just three of us, and a good hundred Leeds, with more arriving all the time. We stood facing them, smiling, arms outstretched and hearts pounding. This is what it's all about; this is the fuckin' buzz. If you're not scared in situations like this, what's the point of doing it?

'"Come on," we shouted, "there's only fuckin three of us..." So what did they do? They started singing at us, no shit, they started singing and pointing at us: "*In their Sheffield slums... In their Sheffield slums... They look in the dustbin for something to eat... They find a dead rat and they think it's a treat... In their Sheffield slums...*"

'Moose's face turned to thunder; I don't think I've ever seen anybody look so mad. "Fuckin' slums?" he shouted. "You saying I live in a fuckin' slum? I'll fuckin' kill ya' bastards!"

'Moose ran in, kicking and punching, causing the Leeds fans to domino over. Dung and me followed, booting and stomping on fallen bodies. That was the end for us; we were attacked from all sides. Hundreds of fists and boots rained into us; we were hammered down to the fence at the front and dragged over pitch-side by the coppers. It always amazes me how we came out of incidents like that with so few injuries. We gave the Leeds fans a smile and the rods to show them we didn't give a fuck, as the coppers grabbed our collars and marched us around the perimeter towards the Gelderd End. The Gelderd Enders let rip a deafening chorus of "*Hey rock 'n' roll... Cloughy's on the dole!*" (Brian Clough's 44-day reign as the Leeds manager had just come to an end). I thought we were nicked but the coppers just took us to an exit gate and chucked us out.

'I looked down at my brand-new pair of brogues, bought the day before for six quid from Rotherham market; they were completely ruined. We were ragged to fuck but nowt serious; we laughed about the whole incident and I started singing "*In our Dronfield slums...*" which made Moose smile.

'We caught a bus back to the city centre and decided to catch the train home. It was only about four o'clock when we reached the station. On the forecourt, we saw a group of a hundred or so Blades, mostly singers, normals and young-'uns stood against a wall flanked by three or four coppers and a couple of cop dog-handlers. A few of the lads were there, shouting to us. The lads told us about 20 of them had come on the special that had arrived in Leeds at 2.00pm. As soon as they came out of the station, they were attacked by hundreds of Leeds fans and chased back in. They said the coppers had done fuck all to protect them, saying they shouldn't have come; they'd been stood outside the station for two hours.

'The coppers realised we were from Sheffield and tried to push us in with the group. I thought, I'm not standing here for another couple of hours.

'"Look," I said to this copper, "we came on the bus this morning, we're going back on the train so we need to get tickets, and we're going in the station to get them."

'"You're not going anywhere," the copper said. "Stand here, you're going back on the special with this lot."

'"Are you fuckin' thick or what?" I said to the copper. "I've just told you we haven't got tickets."

'The next thing, an Alsatian's got my hand in its gob. I booted the dog, it yelped and let go, my hand was covered in slaver and blood. I went crazy, screaming at the copper. "I'm fuckin' reporting you, ya bastard... I've got your number, eight fuckin' three one... You're in deep shit... I've done fuck all wrong... I've just told you we don't have tickets and you set the fuckin' dog on me. I've got all these as witnesses."

'Everybody was shouting, "Yeah, we saw what happened..." I really was fuming and my hand hurt like fuck.

'The copper looked a bit worried. "Go on then and get your tickets, but I want you back here," he said.

'"Fuck off!" I shouted, "And don't think I'm not reporting you, 'cos I fuckin' am."

'We went and bought tickets and caught the service train back. My hand was throbbing and bleeding, my clothes were ragged and my shoes were scuffed and scratched to fuck. Ah well, I thought, just another day in the life of following the mighty Blades.'

MILLWALL

In recent times, a lot as been said about the unwritten rules of football hooligan combat – fight firm-on-firm, don't pick on shirters and don't use weapons. The BBC fell in with this. This story tells a different tale, though. In the early days, weapons were very much in evidence.

Ronnie continues:

'Many years ago in 1980, I ran two Blades coaches to Millwall. The cost, if I remember rightly, was £350 for both coaches. I took 120 names and we were all up for it; we were going onto Millwall's manor to have a go at them. I started taking deposits weeks before the game; some of the lads paid the full whack, and I had pockets full of dough and started to spend some of it, thinking the extra 20 names I had would pay for my little dips. Anyway, come the day of the game, we are all assembled in Pond Street at eight bells waiting for the buses to arrive. Trouble was, only 80 lads turned up.

'We piled on the buses and just about every lad had some kind of weapon on him. Most of the Pitsmoor lads had cutthroats; there were iron bars, screwdrivers and coshes, fucking all sorts of shit.

'Time to pay the driver and I'm £30 short, so it's hat round the lads for an extra 50p or a quid. Most of them paid up but some were saying, "Tha's spent the fucking money, you cunt." The drivers were paid and we set off. I didn't have a penny left in my pocket.

'Anyway, we called in at Leicester Forest services on the M1 and came across about 15 young Blades whose van had broken down. I'd seen one or two of them before and they were invited on to our coach. These young fuckers had the bottle to travel to Millwall on their own so they were more than welcome to come with us. They got on the bus and off we went. I went over to talk to them and said, "Sorry, lads, but I'll have to charge you a quid each… you know how it is." They all gave me a quid. A couple of years later, these young pups had taken over and were some of the main faces in the BBC.

'The same day we travelled, Villa were playing at West Ham in the Cup and, as we neared London, we got in a traffic jam with about ten Villa coaches. They were giving us the expected two fingers and threats as you do; next thing, hatchets, hammers, carving knives, spanners and numerous other weaponry appeared at our windows. The Villa fans declined our offer to get off for a chat.

'The coach company, Richardson's, said they were going to drop us off a couple of miles from the ground. We thus had to make our own way back into London, where we were to be picked up at midnight at St Pancras. We stopped at a boozer on the Old Kent Road and 95 lads piled off the buses. Herman kept insisting we were on the wrong end of the thoroughfare and we should make our way to where the Millwall boozers were; someone else said we were on their patch and it was their job to come and find us. After much arguing and debating, it was agreed we should all stick together and stay where we were.

'After a while, the coppers turned up and parked their vans outside the pub. After a good session, we left the hostelry and set off to the ground. The coppers surrounded us; there were small groups of Millwall all over, but no major firm as such. As we got closer to the ground, a mob of about 30 came from behind some flats and tried to steam in, but the coppers held both sets back. We got to the ground and, during the game, all sorts of shit, including a large plank, was being thrown backwards and forwards. The Millwall firm were going crazy, 60-year-old men were trying to scale the fence to get at us; great stuff.

'At the end of the game, our mob and about 20–30 others who had come on the train were held in the ground for about half-an-hour. We were then escorted to New Cross station. Again, there were small groups of Millwall all over, but nothing went off. We were put on the train back into London, then suddenly a few Millwall appeared at the train doors trying to pull them open. The doors opened and one of the Pitsmoor lads jumped out and slashed a Millwall fan. The coppers came back on the train and arrested a Rotherham lad for the slashing. He was released later without charge; good job, really, as he hadn't done it.

'In the summer of that same year, I went over to Amsterdam to visit six of the lads who were on that coach, who had gone to live out there. We got talking to some Spurs fans in a bar who told us it was all over London that Sheff United were one of the few firms that had turned up at Millwall mob-handed.

'It was during the Eighties that the BBC became a force within the hooligan realm at Bramall Lane. The SRA were still in existence; in fact, the BBC were quite secretive at first, they had been running together as a firm for a while before they got christened. Actually, we didn't even know it had been started until the now famous song was heard, to the tune of *Lord of the Dance*:

> *"Fight, fight, wherever you may be*
> *We are the firm from the steel city*
> *And we'll fight you all wherever you may be*
> *We are the famous BBC..."*

'United's young hooligan element had emerged; their numbers seemed to grow and grow by the week and, not long after, a new hooligan firm had emerged – the BBC.'

10
FULL TIME

Violence at football has been happening now since the 1960s. Some five decades later, it's still here. The hardened football hooligan from the late Seventies/early Eighties is now forty plus. He's married, has a few kids, a decent job, he's a few stone heavier than when he was in his prime and his hairline has disappeared like Wednesday in a set-to. Well, that describes me, anyhow.

These are the lads who have seen and been involved in the violence at its height. Many now have their own businesses and have plenty of money, but they all have one thing in common: they miss the buzz of two rival mobs going toe-to-toe. The adrenalin rush you get from combat is second to none. That rush has gone for most lads now, but the memories will never fade.

Do I miss the violence at football? Certainly I do. I miss the buzz with the lads and the feeling I had when battle commenced. I don't, however, miss the hangers-on, lads who have no intention of getting stuck in but think being in a mob is sound. In every firm, you have people just there for the ride. When it kicks off, they're the ones dancing around at the back but doing very little, if any, fighting. Whether a mob is good or bad depends on the front 20; you can have a firm of 100 lads, but it's the front 20 that really are the firm. The rest can dance and prance but it's the lads at the front that hold things together.

My memories will never fade; even when I'm asleep, I'm often reminded about my past through vivid dreams of terrace warfare. My missus often asks me if I was fighting in my sleep, saying, 'You were throwing yourself about and mumbling away to yourself.'

Funny, really. Although I've packed it in, I still manage to get stuck in at football through my dreams, albeit subconsciously. Football has, and always will be, a release for lads; it's like releasing a pressure valve on top of your head. When you've had a good rumble, you feel cleansed. Trouble will ebb and flow; some seasons, it looks like the trouble has all but gone away but then it comes back with a vengeance. Cup games always throw up a chance of teams meeting their rivals and it's these games that kick off more often than not.

The Old Bill has powers now to tackle football violence. In fact, they have more powers at football than they do with foreigners who practise and preach hatred.

Football is now back on track; crowds are at record highs. Families have come back to the game; stadiums have improved facilities. The police have what is left of the firms under wraps, most of the time. Nowadays, you get banned for anything. The BBC has been hit severely with the banning orders. At the last count, we have 97 lads on banning orders (most are up now) and more will follow. The civil courts have been used by police and lads are getting bans left, right and centre.

Some of the evidence used in these cases has been laughable, as police try to hit the targets set for them as a way of justifying all the money that the government ploughed in to support the police in their battle against the football hooligan. A paedophile has more rights than a football lad – fact. Imagine this: a scum paedo who's sexually abused a three-year-old girl gets two years' imprisonment; he needs help and counselling! Bollocks! He needs a bullet in the head.

One of our lads was dawn-raided after a fight with Barnsley in Sheffield. There was a TV news channel to film him coming out of his own house. The United lad didn't even get charged with anything, it seemed like a PR stunt.

The two Chelsea lads caught on camera by investigative journalist Donal McIntyre in his BBC documentary were simply talking about what they may or may not do at football and got seven years. A couple of lads caught up in the trouble at the infamous Sportsman incident after the derby a few years ago got 26 months *for a first offence*!

'Take him away…' This is what is happening in our courtrooms across the country. Think of a paedo or a lad who runs with a firm. Which one would you prefer living next door to you?

Lord fuckwit judge, who has not got the foggiest idea about what is happening in our once great country, passes his arsehole verdict. You can get in a car pissed as a cunt and mow down and kill a little boy, then drive away from the scene without stopping. What do the courts give the offender? Fuckin' 200 hours' community service!

The OB know who the football lads are but the authorities don't even know who's here or who's not here. I'm not trying to excuse football lads; we know that what we've done is against the law, but a person who fights a like-minded individual or someone ruining a child's life or blowing up some unsuspecting innocent family sat on a Tube... Which one would you want stopping?

Some of the evidence used in the civil cases has no substance whatsoever. Talking to someone who is a so-called 'prominent' hooligan or talking on a mobile outside a pub is about as incriminating as drinking a bottle of Tizer, but this is the evidence that the police are using against lads to great effect. The OB know that to defend yourself in a civil court is going to cost you anything up to £4,000. Then you're relying on an old fuddy-duddy judge to sympathise with you and quash the police's evidence as circumstantial.

It does my box in that these laws can be used on football lads but nothing is getting done about the hundreds of thousands of illegal immigrants and asylum seekers that are flooding this country, and a lot of them are contributing to the resulting crime wave.

Football lads have had to get smarter, to think ahead. When the BBC took a coach full of old school to Hull in 2007, the police captured the coach and took it to a pub on the waterfront. The BBC got restless after hearing 50 of United's youngsters were already in Hull town centre. So, one by one, they climbed and dropped over a ten-foot wall and disappeared into town, as 60 police sat outside guarding an empty pub! To me, football lads are just geezers who like to let off steam with like-minded individuals. We're not totally innocent upstanding gentlemen and know we risk arrest for our actions, but let's put it into perspective: if we get nicked at football for fighting and get jailed or banned, let's have the same punishment across the board. What's the difference between a lad dressed up in designer gear having a fight, and a town centre tear-up between two rival groups of asylum seekers? Simple, the asylum seekers will get let off and the lads that follow football will get the book thrown at them.

My days of terrace warfare are over and, looking back, it's brought me so much grief in my life that I doubt it's all been worth it. Then again, I think about the beano on London Road with Birmingham; the running battle with Leeds; the result at Forest; the fact that when we were youngsters, we overpowered a few years of Wednesday rule; the fashion culture that we football lads created; and the camaraderie and togetherness that we had.

Yes, great days indeed.

For more information from and about the author and the
Blades, visit: <u>www.stevecowens.co.uk</u>